CW00569475

INTERNATIONAL PERSPECTIVES IN CURRICULUM HISTORY

International Perspectives in Curriculum History

EDITED BY
IVOR GOODSON

CROOM HELM
London • Sydney • Wolfeboro, New Hampshire

Croom Helm Ltd, Provident House, Burrell Row,
Beckenham, Kent, BR3 1AT

Croom Helm Australia, 44-50 Waterloo Road,
North Ryde, 2113, New South Wales

British Library Cataloguing in Publication Data

International perspectives in curriculum
history.
1. Curriculum planning — history
I. Goodson, Ivor F.
375′.001′0903 LB1570

ISBN 0-7099-3826-8

Croom Helm, 27 South Main Street,
Wolfeboro, New Hampshire 03894-2069, USA

Library of Congress Cataloging-in-Publication Data

International perspectives in curriculum history

1. Education, secondary — Curricula — History.
2. Curriculum change — History. 3. Curriculum planning —
History. I. Goodson, Ivor.
LB1628.158 1987 375′.001 86-24015
ISBN 0-7099-3826-8

Printed and bound in Great Britain by
Biddles Ltd, Guildford and King's Lynn

CONTENTS

1. INTRODUCTION

Ivor Goodson

This collection developed from two beliefs. Firstly a highly personal belief that we need to develop further our 'sense of history' about curriculum so as to develop and deepen our understandings of the curriculum endeavour specifically and schooling in general. Secondly a growing conviction that curriculum histories are now being undertaken by an increasing and impressive body of scholars from varied disciplinary bases and with differing political orientations.

As the papers in this collection show the range of methods and style is considerable, so too are the number of countries and locales in which this work is being undertaken. So varied in fact are the range of methods, styles and locations that the book provides a diverse 'shop window' of the variety on offer. No attempt has been made to qualify multifariousness or to present some spurious unity whether this be in format, referencing or content. To do so would be to impose a pattern or paradigm at a stage which is quite clearly pre-paradigmatic.

The range of studies hint of course at a whole list of reasons why curriculum history might be expanding at this point in time. Since I cited personal belief as one rationale in this particular collection, it may be worth briefly explaining the root of my own conviction. Partly, no doubt, this grew out of my initial doctoral work at the London School of Economics. This was a fairly conventional piece of historical research in economic and social history - looking at the social and educational assimilation of Irish immigrants in Victorian England. In the event the work seemed mundane and lifeless compared with the excitement of being at the LSE in 1968. (This was of course the year of the 'sit-in', of 'occupations', of the 'Grosvenor Square riot'.) I resolved that action might be more fruitful (and life enhancing!) than scholarship.

As a result, I left my research for more 'active' arenas. In the newly emerging comprehensive schools it appeared there was a fascinating arena where action would be directed towards the alleviation of inequality and the pursuit of social justice. This at least was the rhetoric and given the momentum of 1968 I was inclined to believe it (it is instructive to try and reconstruct one's consciousness at a particular time, or more ambitiously the collective consciousness of a period: certainly they seem to me, looking back and talking to others, to have been 'heady times').

Hence, in 1970, I found myself leaving the working class community in which I had lived for most of my life to go and work in a radical comprehensive in Leicestershire. Here was a school trying to give a full education to <u>all</u> students: in particular this meant seeking to extend modes of learning and instruction, once reserved for the middle and upper classes, to a predominantly working class community very similar to the one I had just moved from. For myself, university-educated its true, but still strongly connected to my home community's views and beliefs, the confrontation was at the same time both stimulating and utterly disconcerting. It was disconcerting I think primarily because remaining so close to my class roots, and still being young, I saw the school more through the eyes of the pupils than I did through the eyes of the teachers. What I saw over a period of years made a deep and unforgettable impression.

For a State school the environment was quite amazingly liberal: there were no punishments and no compulsion, no uniforms, Christian names for teachers, no bells, no regimentation, no collective assemblies, no school teams. The staff were as gifted and as dedicated as one would ever assemble (certainly more intellectually gifted and alert than some of the university Schools of Education I subsequently became acquainted with). Hence, most of the normal 'stumbling blocks' or 'coercive and repressive devices' which we hold culpable in our accounts of schooling were absent. The relationships with our working class clients were quite simply wonderful (this is not idealized retrospection, there is much supportive evidence). Yet the educational endeavour still proved highly problematic. One feature assaulted me with its intractability of form and irrelevance of content: the curriculum, especially the curriculum for examination.

I remember sitting one night after a day of utter frustration saying to myself again and again 'where the hell, where on earth, did this thing come from?' (i.e. the curriculum). I think it was on that evening in February 1971 that I first resolved to try and find out.

As the years went by in the school, the intractable nature of the examination curriculum continued to occupy the 'high ground'. No amount of pedagogic re-orientation or schools-based re-organization could do much to erode this. If there was a heart to the problem: this was it. In the internal structure and the formal categories of the examination curricula it seemed were 'deep structures' of curriculum differentiation, institutionalized and unchallengeable and clearly with long histories. The forces of social justice and school innovation ran rapidly into the structures and legacies of curriculum history.

Yet in looking for information and guidance on curriculum history, we school innovators found ourselves in uncharted territory. Plainly if school innovation was ever to be a serious contest (or indeed if the failures of innovation were to be understood) maps to the uncharted territories would need to be provided.

Of course, experiencing the salience of the academic examination curriculum and arguing for studies of its history is not a new insight or exhortation. For instance, David Layton is quoted in this collection as asserting 'the overriding importance of cultural contexts and the relative unimportance of classroom factors in determining the outcome of attempts at curriculum innovation'. Yet although such insights are scattered through the literature on schooling over a long period, they appear to have led on to precious little in the way of work on the origins and ongoing construction of the school curriculum. This is a profound and damaging omission and seriously hampers our studies of schooling.

Yet if the foregoing rationale for curriculum history is too English and too personal, in fact too ethnocentric and too egocentric, there are a range of studies which do highlight the pervasiveness of the problem. R.W. Connell's recent pioneering work in Australia, for instance, focuses in part on just this problem (as in Making The Difference: Schools, Families and Social Division and Teachers' Work). In the latter book (1985), Connell focuses on the consequences of curriculum construction for teachers for 'as well as being a definition of the pupils' learning, 'the curriculum' is also a definition of the teacher's work. The way it is organized and the social practices that surround it, have profound consequences for teachers'. Connell found that in all the schools studied 'a particular way of organizing knowledge and learning was hegemonic'.

> "I will call this the 'competitive academic curriculum'. To say it is hegemonic is not to say it is the only curriculum in those schools. It is to say that this pattern has pride of place in those schools; it dominates most people's ideas of what real learning is about - its logic has the most powerful influence on the organization of the school, and of the education system generally; and it is able to marginalize or subordinate the other curricula that are present." (Connell 1985, p.87)

In Making the Difference it is clearly shown how the competitive academic curriculum alienates and eventually excludes the majority of children. This poses a harsh dilemma for the teachers: a dedicated group who do not willingly wish to fail the majority year in and year out. But, says Connell, 'the competitive academic curriculum makes the sorting, and the hardening of hearts a central reality of contemporary school life'. This stiffens the dilemma for teachers, for most of them do not need researchers to tell them that the testing and streaming system has ill-effects on school life'.

As a result, the persistent failing of the majority through the academic curriculum leads to recurrent calls for reform: particularly attempts at unstreaming. Connell describes one such initiative where a new social science curriculum was introduced to unstreamed classes. Far too many problems arose however for the experiment to be sustained. A range of 'behaviour problems' arose, particularly problematic was that the top ability children needed 'more reward'. The teachers concluded that since children are not 'equal' you cannot teach them as if they were. So, says Connell, runs the argument but he judges that it misses two vital ingredients.

> "One is the politics of the situation where unstreamed classes have been tried ... generally introduced in the face of scepticism and resistance lacking support staff and relevant training, short on appropriate and varied materials."
>
> The second
>
> "more subtle but perhaps more basic, is the question of where these conceptual categories of ability and pace, this unit of teaching, and this conception of learning, actually come from. They do not fall from the sky.... I would argue that they arise from particular educational practices; specifically that they are generated by, or at least strongly shaped by, the competitive academic curriculum. It is the kids ease and skill with this particular organization of learning that is constantly at issue in the 'streaming' debates. To the extent that the school defines its offer of teaching in terms of this curriculum, 'mixed ability' becomes a problem and steaming a resolution of it. The connections are so close that steaming can virtually be regarded as the institutionalized form of the competitive academic curriculum. It is very difficult to run that sort of curriculum without a streamed school." (Connell 1985, p.92)

What Connell is arguing is the case in Australia in the 1980s which is remarkably similar to the argument I pursued in School Subjects and Curriculum Change (1983) when commenting on innovations in English comprehensives in the 1970s. In this book I concluded that

> "the deep structures of curriculum differentiation are historically linked to different educational sectors, to different social class

> clienteles and occupational destinations, to different status hierarchies. Differentiated curricula and the (existing) social structure are matched on very firm foundations: by building on these foundations comprehensive reorganization has had to accept the antecedent structures which contradict its stated ideal."

Yet this concern with the fate of innovations in comprehensive schools is only a particular historical instance of the importance of curriculum history. For as Randolph has reminded us, the curriculum 'is the place where we tell ourselves who we are'. Any social history aspiring to insight and understanding must therefore involve a history of curriculum. The current paucity of knowledge is plainly an omission of the most fundamental sort. The curriculum is, in short, an important social artefact and a vital documentary source for any social history. Over a quarter of a century ago, Williams reminded us of the interlinked nature of curriculum, culture and society. Writing then before comprehensive schools were organized, but with an eye to their inception, he prophetically warned that 'the crucial question, in any such programme, is that of curriculum and teaching method'. For

> "it is not only that the way in which education is organized can be seen to express, consciously and unconsciously, the wider organization of a culture and a society, so that what has been thought of as simple distribution is in fact an active shaping to particular social ends. It is also that the content of education, which is subject to great historical variation, again expresses, again both consciously and unconsciously, certain basic elements in the culture, what is thought of as 'an education' being in fact a particular selection, a particular set of emphases and omissions. Further, when this selection of content is examined more closely, it will be seen to be one of the decisive factors affecting its distribution: the cultural choices involved in the selection of content have an organic relation to the social choices involved in the practical organization." (Williams 1961, pp.145-6)

Case Studies in Curriculum History

The case studies in this collection provide a range of insights and understandings with regard to curriculum history. The comparative element - comparing different national systems and locales - also provides evidence to test the sort of contention summarized in the foregoing quote from Raymond Williams.

In the first study, Bjørg Gundem provides an analysis of the emergence of English as a subject in Norwegian secondary schools. She reminds us that the unbroken seven year common school for pupils up to fourteen years of age was a unique phenomenon in Europe up until the 1950s. She believes that "the idea of equality and justice through the postponement of choice and differentiation has been a non-controversial issue in Norwegian school politics". However, "the elitist element represented by 'English' was ... a sore thumb spoiling a much desired image". To cure this sore thumb became a pressing concern by the 1950s. For the "political unrest was caused by the fact that a selection was taking place and by the way this selection was carried out, functioning to 'reproduce' the class society and undermining what was seen as the true function of education: to further the democratization of Norwegian society". In the case of English teaching therefore, "what was needed, was a democratization of the teaching of English in the common school".

What is interesting in comparing this study with Stephen Ball's study of English in England, is the apparent relationship between political will (and rhetoric) and subsequent action (and rhetoric). It is almost as if in curriculum we have a visible and well-documented litmus test of the political process in a country. In Norway, the birth of the common school led to a clear political commitment to democratization of curriculum form and content. This (notwithstanding the problematic relationship between rhetoric and reality) seems a long way from the experience of many western countries.

Hence in Norway, after the common school was founded, the form and content of the written curriculum in English were changed (in the new version of the aptly named Government Mønsterplan). Gundem notes 'it was good-bye and farewell to the mastery of formal grammar and the knowledge of literacy texts as ingredients of the teaching and learning of English in compulsory schooling ...'. Optimistically she writes 'Everybody would receive the same teaching ... all pupils would learn the same, if not by the same means at the same time. The teaching of English was in this connection crucial, changing from being an elitist subject to a subject to be mastered and enjoyed by everybody.' Truly a case of 'English for everybody'.

Not however a curriculum change entirely divorced from pragmatic consideration or from the economy. Elsewhere in the article we learn 'it is however, worth noting that the main official legitimation for English for everybody was not "the democratization of the Norwegian society in a social democratic direction" but the necessity for practical language schools'. This, of course, opens up an explanation where political 'social democratic' intent is allied with questions of labour skills and the needs of the economy. We are some way, but not totally, back towards something far more 'normal'.

Ball's study reminds us of these more 'normal' configurations. Here we see English as a subject at the intersection between school knowledge and society. As a result we have a subject liable to powerful 'moral panics' about its content and its capacity to interfere with 'normal' patterns of differentiation: I am much reminded of Feinberg's statement that a key indicator of educational equality is the extent to which the secondary educational values are distributed among different groups within an educational system and then between systems themselves.

Some English teachers developed a critical consciousness which came through in their teaching. For 'by the nature of their subject (they) were in close contact with the experiences of working class children; it offered them a microcosmic view of the contradictions of schooling in a capitalist society'.

> "Such teachers were doing no more than focusing on a range of social injustices endemic in our society and asking questions about the value and relevance of a pedagogy and content which did not acknowledge these facts. They felt the need to incorporate an extra dimension in their practice (which) ... tried to inject into the English curriculum the kinds of knowledge and

> experience which would give working class pupils an understanding of inequality and its cause; the emphasis would be on solidarity rather than upward mobility."
> (Simon and Raleigh: Ball in this volume)

This radical 'social realist' view of English was seen as threatening both reproduction and differentiation. As a result, the political order in England showed clear signs of concern. They both brought about and responded to a moral panic about "standards" in English. "Standards" in this case can clearly be seen as a rallying cry to reassert the values of "traditional" English (i.e. the original 'political setlement'). The Bullock Report was then 'a specific reassertion of the economic and political role of English teaching in relation to capitalist society. The emphasis given to "basic skills" and "language across the curriculum" underlined the role of English in preparing pupils for work and the need for a literate labour force.' In significant addition "the repositioning of literature, that is the literature of the great tradition, as having a central role in English, underlined the role of English in the moral education of youth, the civilizing process".

The Norwegian and English experience juxtaposed then point to very different 'political settlements' in English as a subject. In one "the civilizing process" leads in the teeth of comprehensive re-organization and "rhetoric of equal opportunity to a moral panic over undifferentiated, radical English and a defiant re-assertion of traditional English". We may be witness to the curriculum subversion of the comprehensive ideal. In Norway, the converse happens. The common school does lead on to the democratization of English and it was indeed "good-bye and farewell to the mastery of formal grammar and the knowledge of literary texts".

I have commented on these two papers in some length because they powerfully illustrate some of the challenges to a "taken-for-granted" objectivistic view of school knowledge which curriculum histories provide. Nobody, in comparing the two studies, would again assume that "traditional" English was in some sense "given" rather than in an important sense a social construction which in England all too clearly seeks to achieve "an active shaping to particular social ends".

Rowell and Gaskell's study of school physics in British Colombia highlights some of the points made by R.W. Connell (quote earlier) about the salience of the teacher's work process. This sometimes led to a divergence in university and school teacher perspectives. Hence we learn that 'the university viewed the upgrading of teacher qualifications as an important strategy for improving the quality of instruction, whereas the teachers of university bound students considered the time and facilities available for instruction to be key factors in improving the level of achievement. These teachers advocated streaming of university bound students so that the pacing of the course would not be hindered by "average" students.' Here we are back with Connell's 'hegemonic' academic model being institutionalized through streaming.

Likewise with "new" physics the teacher's work process sat at the centre of the judgements over implementation and take-up. Speaking of the summer schools for teachers on "new" physics, we learn that

> "their enthusiasm was contagious, not least because implementation of the program called for new equipment and laboratories. Instead of teaching a single year of disciplinary physics, teachers would now teach two, and in large urban schools this meant a reduction in the number of general science classes taught by the specialist oriented teachers."

At the heart of the hegemonic academic tradition Rowell and Gaskell locate 'an educational constituency supporting school physics as a subject preparatory for university physics'. Both school and university physics teachers defined the 'purity' of the category but also the purity of the clientele. Hence 'university physicists impose severe restrictions on the entrance to honors programs, and high school counsellors directed only the most able students towards school physics. University physicists and physics teachers share a belief that physics is the fundamental science.'

Crucially in the committees that made curricula this university/school academic alliance held power. Rowell and Gaskell contend

> "the alliance of this unrepresentative group of teachers and physicists, backed by a government

anxious to invest in human capital, made possible the introduction of an ahistorical, decontextual course of studies which emphasised the structure of the discipline."

The focal importance of academic examinations in sustaining this alliance and constituency is clearly defined.

"... the annual gathering of teachers and physicists for marking of examinations also contributed to the sustenance of the constituency. But even though it had become apparent to many that the mandated version of school physics was inappropriate for all but a very select clientele, the constituency was not openly challenged until after the removal of government examinations."

The challenge to the academic alliance was mounted and sustained by the growing teacher organizations.

"The organizational and intellectual resources of the teacher organizations ensured that however well qualified, such an unrepresentative revision committee as that of the sixties would not be appointed. The absence of university physicists in the initial appointments to the 1979 revision committee was an indication of the apparent decline in the ability of the constituency for university physics to define the purpose of school physics."

Smith points to other notions of constituency as important at the more local school board level in the USA. He examines curriculum change in the (fictionalized) town of Alte over a century. He believes that

"any kind of change in curriculum and teaching will produce positive and negative reactions in individual parents and teachers. Those reactions, as they aggregate, become direct political forces in school board elections and indirect forces in the day-to-day workings of the schools."

The studies of Rowell and Gaskell and of Smith point up the importance of understanding the role of what Meyer has called 'publics' or 'constituencies' in curriculum history.

> "These interested publics which pay for and support education hand over its work to the professional (i.e. the teachers) in only a limited and unexpected sense. For while it may appear that the professionals have power to determine what is taught (at school, district or national level, depending on the country in question), their scope is limited by the fact that only those forms and activities which have significance for external publics, can in the long run survive." (W.A. Reid in I. Goodson and S. Ball (eds) Defining the Curriculum 1984, p.68)

The role of constituencies has been articulated in both Defining the Curriculum: Histories and Ethnographies and in The Making of Curriculum: Essays in the Social History of Education, so it is unnecessary here to develop the point at length. But both these studies point to the significance of the concept in accounts of curriculum history.

In Hodson's study, there are some of the concerns about the political and social order that occur powerfully in Gundem's study but are present in most of the studies in this collection. He argues that it is important to test the assertion that 'political and social control of the masses could be, and should be, established through the school curriculum'. Where the curriculum proposals are unexplicit or silent about their political or social intentions, he believes 'the refined concept of social control motivation is a useful analytical tool, providing the researcher with a means of penetrating the rhetoric surrounding the proposal'. In this case, 'the proposals' are the 'Science of Common Things' movement in Victorian schools in England.

In fact, the study points to a substantial degree of complexity with regard to the groups behind the curriculum movement and their intentions. Hodson argues that whichever line of argument individuals supported, whether 'conservative' or 'liberal', "one assumption was always made: that the lower orders were only to possess an inferior kind of knowledge". In fact, however, the Science of Common Things appeared to lead in precisely the opposite direction towards a superior knowledge for the lower orders. The contradiction was plain and potent. Such 'contradictory gaps' seldom last long; and the Science of Common Things was no exception. It does however point to the potential for unpredictability in the short run terrain of curriculum history, even if the long run configurations are all too clear. Thus Hodson sees the culminating pattern of school science in this way:

> "it is socially constructed, being the product of particular sets of choices made by particular groups of people, at particular times in furtherance of their own interests. Thus, it represents the triumph of a particular interest group."

He quotes Marx's works:

> "the ideas of the ruling class are in every epoch the ruling ideas".

The culmination Hodson describes may confirm this but we should be warned against the notion that any settlement in curriculum (or indeed elsewhere) is final or at any point in time predictable. The Science of Common Things movement warns us of the continuing contestation over curriculum and of the possibility that at particular points in time, contradictory gaps do open up: in these gaps consciousness may be changed. We should remember the 'poor boy who hobbled forth ... (and) gave forthwith so lucid and intelligent a reply' to the scientific question asked. Reproduction is not inevitable and given, it is a continually worked for and achieved situation.

Colin Marsh moves us away from the scientific curriculum to look at the forces impinging on Senior School Geography. His approach shows that a range of methods can be deployed in seeking to understand the development of a school subject. Marsh is here concerned to postulate, develop and test 'a model of curriculum decision-making'. He locates this attempt within the clearly defined parameters of the Western Australian educational system.

Stanic is concerned to provide an historical perspective on the justifications provided for the teaching of mathematics. He makes use of Kliebard's (1981) classification of curriculum interest groups: the humanists, the developmentalists, the social efficiency educators and the social meliorists (an extension of Williams division into the public educators, industrial trainers and old humanists). He illustrates that 'different justifications for teaching mathematics arise from different assumptions about what mathematics is, who should be encouraged or recognized to take how much mathematics, and what it means to be an educated human being; and they have different implications for the mathematics curriculum'. Hopefully he adds that invoking a particular justification for teaching mathematics should mean that such assumptions and implications are recognized and accepted. Certainly his developed historical perspective aids such recognition.

Moon is also concerned with mathematics - new mathematics - in the period 1960-1980. Again, there is a focus on the interest groups involved in curriculum negotiation. Hence he argues, 'the outcome of educational change reflects a much more complex interaction between interest groups than the unified concepts of control of the curriculum would imply'. Thus the general features of a system of education offer limited guidance to our understanding of how the curriculum is made at any particular point in time. Moon argues that:

> "Whilst over time traditions and linked procedures become established within educational systems, it does not always follow that they will be adhered to. The context of curriculum change involves the integration of a range of very disparate groups which might 'loosely' be seen as institutionalized within the curriculum arena, but which have markedly different power bases which change over time according to other conditions prevailing. Whilst the strategies of such groups may be categorized, and whilst the relationship of such groups to traditional structures may be explored, there is nothing predetermined about the outcome of any particular period."

Lundgren is concerned with the history of an educational theme as opposed to a curriculum area. This is a vital terrain for curriculum history. The history of school subjects alone builds in its own myopia. Lundgren shows the link between progressivism, modernization and urban-industrial development. Franklin, likewise, in assessing Ralph Tyler's contribution to curriculum history, picks out the crucial nature of responses to urban-industrialization.

> "Tyler ... was a product of the rural small town who found his career in an America that was becoming increasingly urban and industrial. And like other intellectuals of his day, he sought throughout his career to find a way to preserve those qualities of small town life he thought necessary for the furtherance of democracy, its harmony and intimacy, in urban, industrial America. It was this desire, I have suggested, that led him to propose a more functional curriculum, one that was dedicated to instilling youth with the value of co-operation."

These two last papers adopt very different approaches - thematic and biographical/life history - to the study of curriculum history. Such approaches are important if curriculum history is to escape from its current predeliction for studies of secondary school 'subjects'.

In a fascinating epilogue, McCulloch speculates on what curriculum history might emerge in New Zealand. The speculation leads him to question certain predelictions in the English 'school' of curriculum history 'the emphasis on secondary education and the tendency to "stress" complexity, failure and disappointment.' In this he certainly is correct as he is in suggesting new focuses on the primary school curricula, on the history of curriculum topics of various levels of the education system and on aspects of informal education.

Bibliography

Connell, R.W. (1985)
Teachers Work
N. Sydney, George Allen and Unwin.

Goodson, I.F. (1987)
The Making of Curriculum: Essays in the Social History of Schooling
Barcombe, Falmer Press.

Goodson, I.F. and S. Ball (eds) (1984)
Defining the Curriculum: Histories and Ethnographies
Barcombe, Falmer Press.

Williams, R. (1961)
The Long Revolution
London, Penguin.

2. RELATIONS, STRUCTURES AND CONDITIONS IN CURRICULUM CHANGE: A POLITICAL HISTORY OF ENGLISH TEACHING 1970-85 (1)

Stephen J. Ball

'History is not retrievable as human project: but neither is it comprehensible except as the outcome of human project'.
Foucault.

This paper is the latest in a series in which I have explored the curricular history of English as a subject in English schools (2). My interest in English as a subject is twofold. First, substantively, English has come to be regarded, primarily through its association with the skills of reading and writing, as a crucial and essential component of the schooling of all students right up to the legal school leaving age. And yet, since it first appeared as an identifiable single subject in schools, English has been riven with disputes over what it should correctly and appropriately consist of. The subject has been the focus of major internal conflict between competing coalitions and interest groups. Second, English provides a living case study from which it has been possible to develop a general schema for the analysis of conflict and change in school subjects. In this paper, I intend to pursue both interests further. I shall present an account of the developments and pressures acting through and upon English teaching during the 1970s and 1980s. I will also use this account as the basis for the further exploration and development of my analytical schema.

The schema is a simple one; it contains three elements, as follows:

1. Relations of Change - the power struggles between social groups, coalitions, and segments within the subject community, each with

their own 'sense of mission' and differing and competing vested interests, resources and influence.

2. Structures of Change - the institutions, organizations, procedures, roles and persons that constitute the formal channels of educational policy-making and administration through which or in relation to which change must be accomplished, mediated, fought for and negotiated. These would include the Department of Education and Science, Her Majesty's Inspectorate, the Schools Council (perhaps now the Schools Curriculum Development Committee), the Examination Boards and other examining agencies (RSA, BTEC, CGLI), the Further Education Unit and the Manpower Services Commission, also committees of enquiry (as in this instance the Bullock Committee.) These structures lay outside of the subject community but may be influenced or captured by community members or the structure may, at times, impinge directly upon the constitution of subjects by influence, authority or legislation.

3. Conditions of Change - the political and economic context, the ebb and flow of public opinion and consciousness, the 'limits of tolerance' within which the subject community works. These conditions provide both a material frame and social climate for conservation and change. These conditions play a significant role, at times, in the constitution of the discourse within which subjects are formed and changed, as Foucault argues 'Discourse is not about objects: rather, discourse constitutes them' (Sheridan 1980). As conditions change, the degrees of freedom available for the subject community to construct its own discourses also change.

The schema is intended as a framework for analysis, for the examination of the construction, conservation and change in subjects over time. In previous papers on English teaching I have concentrated in particular on the relations of change, the internal micro-politics of subject communities. Here the emphasis is more upon the structures and conditions, the external influences and determinations which impinged upon English teaching in the period 1970 to 1985.

The History and the Politics of English 1970-85

The dominant voices in the work of school English teaching in 1970 were undoubtedly those which emanated from the University of London, Institute of Education and from NATE (the National Association for the Teaching of English). In both cases the work of James Britton, Harold Rosen and Douglas Barnes, and their followers and collaborators, was the major point of reference. This version of English, which I shall call 'the London School' had developed through the work of LATE (the London Association for the Teaching of English) during the 1950s and 1960s, in part at least as a challenge to the version of English proselatized by F.R. Leavis and his students, which I shall call 'the Cambridge School'. While the Cambridge School saw English as firmly and inevitably resting on the British heritage of 'great literature', the London School argued for the centrality of the language, written and spoken, of school students. As John Dixon (a key figure in the London School) explained, 'In the heritage model the stress was on culture as a given. There was a constant temptation to ignore culture as the pupil knows it .... (1975 p.3). In contrast, Frank Whitehead (a key figure in the Cambridge School) pointed out that, the 'English as language' advocates had 'done a disservice to teachers by assimilating pupils' stories and poems (the literature of the classroom) into the mature products of real authors' (1976 P.13 My emphasis).

The beginning of the assertion of the London, 'English as language' paradigm and its swift ascendency in the field of school English, is most clearly marked by the report of the 1966 Dartmouth seminar (a joint meeting of British and American English educators) written by John Dixon under the title Growth Through English. Accounts of the actual work of the seminar differ and Dixon's account has frequently been criticized for its partiality (See Allen 1980 chap. 2). Allen points out that in the activities of the seminar 'some voices were discouraged; others were lauded ... Dixon, Barnes and Britton seem to have gained an audience Whitehead, Thompson and Holbrook did not'.

Clearly, at one level such segmental disputes can be viewed as highly materialistic, control over the subject through teacher-training, publishing and examining is at stake (See Ball 1982). But at the heart of the dispute between the two schools there is not simply two views of a subject but more profoundly two conceptions of the 'good society' and of the nature of civilization. In crude terms, the schools rest upon commitment to two opposed knowledge bases, one elite knowledge and the other the knowledge of the masses. Furthermore, these alternative bases are articulated in terms of moral principles. The vision of the subject presented by the Cambridge school is frequently linked to an imagery of missionary endeavour and struggle against the forces of evil.

> "As teachers of English we may sometimes be led to question the assumption that, in this field, children's welfare can safely be left to the free play of the profit motive. We find ourselves compelled to expend much of our energy in a ceaseless struggle against the mainstream of contemporary 'mass-civilization', and we may be forgiven if we are sometimes a little discouraged."
> (Whitehead 1966 P.57-7)

English teachers and the great literary heritage with which they are entrusted are to stand against the deprivations of the machine age, industrial society, and the accompanying outpour of comics, cheap novels, newspapers, advertising and worst of all, television. The Cambridge School harks back to a better time before the coming of the urban society, when social order and morality were invested in and maintained by the village community.

> ".... literary education, we must not forget, is to a great extent a substitute. What we have lost is the organic community with the living culture it embodied. Folk songs, folk dances, Cotswold cottages and handicraft products are signs and expressions of something more: an art of life .... growing out of immemorial experience, of the natural environment and the rhythm of the year."
> (Leavis and Thompson 1933)

In contrast, the London School celebrates the immediate life, culture and language of the school student. And for the majority of London teachers, that meant primarily the lives, culture and language of the working class. Below the level of opposed knowledge bases there are also opposed ideologies and political commitments. During the 1970s this matter of political commitment was to become an increasingly important aspect of the reaction against the dominant modes of English teaching and the English teachers themselves, as we shall see. The London School presented within its view of the subject a significant challenge to traditional pedagogies and authority relations.

> "The fact is that in sharing experience with others man (sic) is using language to make that experience real to himself. The selection and shaping that language involves, the choices between alternative expressions so that language shall fit the experience and bring it to life 'as it really was' - these activities imply imaginative work."
> (Dixon 1975 p.6)

Here the role of literature is subordinate to the pupils' own experiences and to their own talk and writing, 'only in a classroom where talk explores experience is literature drawn into dialogue - otherwise it has no place' (Dixon p.60). The teaching of literary criticism and interpretation as separate skills, as ends in themselves, were seen to turn literature into a 'dead hand'. Reading and writing, which are the primary pedagogical strategies in the cultural heritage classroom are to be subordinated to talk and drama: 'a sense of the social system of writing has so inhibited and over awed many teachers that they have never given a pupil the feeling that what he (sic) writes is his own (Dixon P.44).

Alongside the abstract arguments about the role of literature and the status of the pupil-writer, the London School also identified its concerns about English teaching with the introduction of comprehensive education. And extending this the 'dominant voices' in the Dartmouth seminar also set themselves against the practice of 'streaming' pupils. 'When language is used for interaction in talk or drama, it is essential for a class to have a wide range of experience and background' (Dixon p.101). And also it was recognized that in the heterogeneous class teaching methods would have to change. 'Without a good deal of individual study, work in small groups, assignments and project work, as well as work for part of the time with the whole class, no pupils will attain that individual growth in language which is basic to his (sic) progress in other subjects and his capacity to live fully and actively in society' (Dixon P.103).

The major progammatic statement of the London School is probably Britton's Language and Learning, published in 1970. It became a key point of reference for a whole range of project work which took up the 'English as Language' position in the early 1970s. Drawing in particular on the work of American psychologist George Kelly, Britton argues that language provides the child with a representational system through which predictions about the world may be constituted and tested out. In other words, language is the basis of experience and experience serves to differentiate for persons their unique 'world representation'. The implications drawn for teachers were that 'talking and doing must be given major stress' and that 'language must continue to grow roots from first hand experience' (p.137).

Following the Dartmouth seminar, the London School quickly gained the ascendancy in the public arenas in which definitions of English were debated and forged, in particular in the recently formed Schools Council. Certainly, as measured in terms of support from public funding, the London School made a considerable impact in the period 1965-75:

The Written Language of 11-18 Year Olds 1966-71
James Britton and Nancy Martin £33,517

Writing Across the Secondary Curriculum 1971-74
Nancy Martin £31,000

Language Development in the Primary School 1969-71
Connie Rosen £50,000

English in the Middle Years of Schooling 1970-72
Bernard Newsome £18,000

Oracy 1967-72
Andrew Wilkinson £15,750

English 16-19 1975-79
John Dixon £77,000

It would be a mistake to portray the rise of the London School simply as a 'revolution of ideas'. These changes did not occur in a vacuum. Important social, economic and political changes in the context of education also had an important part to play in challenging established positions. Not the least was the gradual spread of comprehensive schooling and the new demands that this was making upon teachers, especially those who had previously worked in selective grammar schools. As indicated above, English teachers were frequently in the forefront of moves to introduce mixed-ability teaching (see Ball 1981 chap.6) which itself brought increased pressure for new teaching methods and a more 'relevant' content. In the late 1960s this quiet revolution in the classroom was given a more radical flavour and dramatic impetus by events elsewhere in the worldwide 'crisis in education'. Students riots and sit-ins and the work of writers like Friere and Illich presented a vocal challenge to the authoritarian relationships upon which traditional teaching methods were based. Additionally, in Britain, in 1971, the school leaving age was raised to 16, and pupils who had little interest in or reason for staying on at school were now there to be taught. New courses, new examinations and new teaching relationships were being sought by the teachers who had to cope. Anything seemed possible. Education had re-entered a sort of golden age. In the background was a widely held belief that change in education was necessary and healthy, the so-called 'progressive consensus'. This was a consensus based upon industrial growth, economic surplus and apparently free expansion in government spending of public services.

This then is how English teaching stood in Britain in the first years of the 1970s (always assuming that is, that the public versions of the subject bear some relation to what was going on in classrooms up and down the country).

Politics, Standards and Panic

In a sense the beginning of the end of the 'progressive consensus' is marked, in 1969, by the publication of the first of the Black Papers (a series of right wing, popularist-conservative critiques of progressive education and the comprehensive system).

The Black Papers initiated a public critique of 'progressive' education, in all its forms, that was quickly taken up by sections of the media. What ensued was a 'moral panic' about the condition of education in Britain. As the economy began to crumble and public disorder increased, scapegoats and a basis for moral reconstruction were sought.

> "Societies appear to be subject every now and then, to periods of moral panic. A condition, episode, person or group of persons emerges to become defined as a threat to societal values and interests; its nature is presented in a stylized and stereotypical fashion by the mass media; the moral barricades are manned by editors, bishops, politicians and other right-thinking people; socially accredited experts pronounce their diagnoses and solutions; ways of coping are evolved or (more often) resorted to; the condition then disappears, submerges or deteriorates and becomes more visible."
> (Cohen 1972 p.28)

This scenario captures quite potently the situation in which teachers generally, and English teachers in particular, found themselves in by the mid-1970s. The media, together with influential pressure groups, had created a public image for the English teacher as a dangerous and subversive social deviant. The 'progressive teacher' and 'left wing teacher' were 'named' by press and politicians as responsible for major social (and economic) problems in British society. They quickly assumed the status of 'folk-devils' in public discourse about education. At a time of national anxiety stemming from industrial unrest, rising crime, the oil crisis, and economic recession, the 'progressive teacher' was a ready target for scapegoating - the 'demon myth of deviant teachers' (Cohen 1980 p.xxiii). Reports which seemed to indicate a decline in national literacy, employers complaints about school leavers who could not do simple sums, a spate of student sit-ins and violent street demonstations, an apparent epidemic of vandalism and mugging by youthful criminals (Hall et al 1978) all pointed to things having gone wrong in the schools. Teachers, it appears, could be blamed for virtually all of the social, economic and political ills of society. And this perception of teachers once established in the public imagination was both further exploited and fuelled by the later Black Papers. (Each of the Papers consisted of a series of essays by writers, politicians, journalists, teachers and academics, many, but not all, with direct links to the Conservative Party. Certainly there was a clear basis of access to the mass media, legal and scientific bodies and political authorities among the contributors (Cohen 1980 p.112). The Papers presented two main lines of argument; one, a critique of progressive education in all its forms, the other, a defence of traditional educational values which were seen to be under threat from progressivism. The appeal was to normative consensus, it was for the preservation of all that was 'good and right' in English education. This formed the basis for a powerful and effective 'symbolic crusade', a 'moral enterprise' where 'someone takes the initiative on the basis of interest and uses publicity techniques to gain the support of the organizations that count' (Cohen 1980 p.112). In this respect the Black Paper writers possessed the legitimating values, the enterprise and the power, which Cohen suggests are the necessary basis for successful moral entrepreneurship.

On two counts English teaching was an obvious and important focus for attention and critique in the Black Papers. First, in being responsible for language learning - reading and writing - it was possible to posit a direct link between the English classroom and the economy. Declining literacy was identified with economic stagnation, the deleterious effects of an ill-prepared workforce. Second, and in contrast, having taken on a concern for literature, English teachers were seen, in Leavisite terms, as carriers and transmitters of the great traditiion, the British cultural heritage. What was at stake, as far as the Black Paper writers were concerened, was not simply the preservation of literary worth but also the fostering of values and moral judgement. By neglecting, even deprecating the works of 'great' literature, English teachers were threatening national identity, normative consensus and social order. Thus, the Black Paper writers saw it as their responsibility to 'blow the whistle'; they were engaged in 'the creation of a new fragment of the moral constitution of society' (Cohen 1980 p.145). English teachers' attempts to achieve 'relevance' in the classroom by drawing upon social issues affecting the lives of their pupils was regarded with utmost suspicion. Robert Conquest writes in the first Black Paper (Cox and Dyson 1969):

> "This 'sociological' attitude has penetrated the teaching of literature too. To be 'relevant' it is necessary to concentrate largely on the modern. Yet 90 per cent of what any educated man would read for its sheer quality will not be the product of the past half-century. And since without this no-one would be able to judge even the literature of our own times, this means that the student's mind is being effectively sabotaged or blocked. Moreover, since modern literature has not yet found, even roughly, its true valuation, he is having inflicted on him a peculiar and almost certainly wrong-headed selection even of that. My wife found that the teaching of English in her secondary school had suffered this sort of perversion. Instead of teaching literature, teachers presumed to be teaching 'life'. Thus, fiction about barrow boys on the Old Kent Road was regarded as the right thing to teach the boys of the area. There are obvious objections, even leaving aside the basic lunacy of the whole idea: first there is no literature of even barely tolerable quality about this theme, so bad literature had to be taught in preference to good. Second, the boys had no desire whatever to read the subject, preferring Treasure Island. Another typical evil is the idea - and the practice - of poetry in schools. Children are encouraged to write down, regardless of rhythm, any reasonably emotional or intense set of phrases, provided this is divided into the appearance of lines. Of course, the product is usually both silly and bad, and such is bound to be the case whatever children write.

In the fourth Black Paper (Cox and Boyson 1975) these concerns were taken up by G.H. Bantock.

> "As an example, let us see how 'relevance' works in relation to the teaching of a specific subject at secondary level - English.
> The traditional emphasis stressed, among other factors, the centrality of literature; it was

not always well taught, but it constituted an attempt to grapple with the language of its finest point of excellence. Recently the centrality of literature has been under attack. Drama has become spontaneous, 'active' drama revealing too often little other than the linguistic and histrionic impoverishment of the children creating it. Such literature as has survived has become mainly contemporary and often radical, necessitating in many cases the study of inferior texts which an earlier age would have, at best, prescribed for private reading. The progressive emphasis on either endogenous creativity (undisciplined by any inwardness with the language of greatness) or social relevance (applying the human reductiveness characteristic of much of the contemporary) has replaced an earlier concern for quality. Where language is concerned, middle-class speech structures are being attacked in favour N2 ACQC043ay' speech. 'A new respect for everyday language is needed', writes Miss Nancy Martin in one of a series of articles published in *The Times Educational Supplement* (17 March 1974), the net effect of which (despite occasional disclaimers) is to deprecate the structures of educated speech in favour of the putative superior 'expressiveness' of the everyday. One does not need to be wedded to the turgidity of *some* school writing not to see the dangers of *this* - with its implied cult of an unregenerate and surface expressiveness. It is the same attitude that defends the introduction of 'pop' into the schools."

If we look now in more detail at the Black Paper critique, three constantly repeated themes are evident.

i) Perhaps the most important of all as far as English was concerned, that standards in schools were in decline as a result of the use of progressive methods. The argument was that teachers had renaged on their responsibility to 'teach' and pupils were left to 'choose' their own activities and set their own standards. As far as English was concerned, progressive teaching methods were identified with a supposed decline in standards of reading and writing and a general increase in levels of illiteracy.

ii) That changes in the teacher-pupil relationships and the teachers' abdication from their traditional role 'in authority', the 'permissive revolution', was resulting in a massive growth of violence and indiscipline in schools. In some accounts schools were being blamed for an increasing crime rate and student violence in street demonstrations. As time went on other 'evils' were added to the indictment. Permissive teachers were blamed for the growth in the use of drugs, the spread of pornography, teenage sex and the general corruption of the young.

iii) That teachers with 'left-wing' sympathies or affiliations were both indoctrinating pupils with their views and manipulating schools so as to produce 'socialist societies in miniature'. The very fabric of British society and traditional values were, it was argued, being undermined by these politically motivated teachers.

i) Standards

'Progressive' or 'informal' teaching methods in English were being specifically linked to declining reading standards in primary schools and an increase in illiteracy among leavers from secondary schools. As early as 1968 Dolores Moore was writing in The Daily Mail (A right-wing popularist newspaper with a strong anti-comprehensive, anti-progressive, 'school-bashing' editorial policy).

> "Read the numbers, published now and then, of illiterate school leavers each year. Notice at an open day, just how few seven-year-olds, and even eleven-year-olds, can actually write and spell correctly. Look at the standard of reading books. It is generally low. Sometimes very low. Yet more money is spent each year on educating our children."

This last point is an interesting one and was to come more to the fore in the late 1970s as these sorts of criticisms became re-articulated through the framework of monetarism and Thatcherism. The argument is that no relationship exists between levels of expenditure and standards of performance; it is standards of teaching, school ethos and classroom regime that counted, not expenditure. This was to provide a powerful vehicle for an education policy which at one and the same time argued for the need to raise standards and cut spending on education. A policy which hit schools in inner-city areas most directly.

The moral panic was given further impetus in 1972 by the publication of an NFER report (Start, K.B. and Wells, B.K. The Trend of Reading Standards which suggested a measurable decline in reading standards in the late 1960s among 'certain groups of children'. Here then was 'proof', it was all true, literacy was in decline. English teaching was in chaos. The very future of the nation was at stake. Something had to be done.

In response to this 'climate of public concern', Mrs Margaret Thatcher, the then Secretary of State for Education, was moved to set up an inquiry under Sir Alan Bullock, 'to consider in relation to schools, all aspects of teaching the Use of English, including reading, writing and speech'. The tide was about to turn. The report A Language for Life, published in 1975, attempts to review the state of English teaching from the earliest development of pre-school language skills through to the teaching of English literature to 16-19 year-olds studying for A-levels. But as the title indicates, the emphasis of the report is on the development of language skills. 'The time has come', the report concludes, 'to raise language as a high priority in the complex life of the secondary school.' However, in response to the critics of 'progressivism' the committee's detailed research provides no evidence that formal work in English was decaying 'in a climate of unchecked creativity'. The report is critical of 'the notion of English in the secondary school as almost exlcusively a source of material for personal response to social issues' (p.7) which was regarded as often lacking in direction and tending to produce cliches in pupils' work. This approach was seen by the Committee to be diminishing the pupils' experience of English work. Alongside this, literature is strongly defended against the inroads of 'thematic' work.

(Perhaps it is John Dixon's 'social realist' view of English that is most clearly under attack here). The undue emphasis on 'creativity' in the primary classroom, was also seen as worrying when other types of work were 'neglected'.

> "We have equal lack of sympathy with the notion that the forms of language can be left to look after themselves. On the contrary, we believe that the teacher should intervene, should constantly be looking to improve the quality of the utterance." (p.8)

Strong encouragement was given for the need for teacher intervention in pupil's work. (Here then the traditional teacher role is reinforced over and against attempts to develop less hierarchical forms of classroom relationship.) In many respects the report attempts to steer a middle course and to establish a 'coherent' basis for English teaching which draws together some of the diverse and competing versions of school English that had been in contest during the period 1960 to 1975. Thus alongside the criticisms of 'unchecked creativity', the teaching of 'grammar' as an isolated topic is roundly condemned; 'Competence in language comes above all through its purposeful use, not through the working of exercises divorced from context.' (p.528)

And while 'social realism' and 'grammar' are given little support in the report both 'English as language' and 'English as literature' receive positive reinforcement. And the paradigm of literature teaching which is clearly underwritten in the report is that sponsored and developed through the work of F.R. Leavis and the Cambridge School of English, the tradition of literature teaching 'which aims at personal and moral growth' and stresses 'the 'civilizing' power of literature.' (p.125)

> "Literature brings the child into an encounter with language in its most complex and varied forms and is a valuable source of imaginative insight. It should be recognized as a powerful force in English teaching at all levels." (p.525)

The ideas in the report about 'English as Language' clearly draw on the work of Britton and 'the London School', which is specifically mentioned in the report. Considerable attention is given to <u>oracy</u>, the report argues that 'a priority objective for all schools is a commitment to the speech needs of their pupils and a serious study of the role of oral language in learning'. Also, support is given to the role of linguistics in English teaching and teachers are encouraged to acquire 'an explicit understanding of the operation of language'. Two central themes - language and learning, and teaching - lie at the heart of the report. A continuing programme, aimed at the development of pupils' language from pre-school to school leaving is the main recommendation, with the 'reading curriculum' seen as an integral part of the total 'language curriculum'. Two keywords widely taken up from the report into educational discourse reflect these primary concerns. First, the notion of 'basic skills', which in the report refer not simply to the starting point of language development but to a concern with language competence throughout the pupils' school career. Second is the concept of 'languge across the curriculum'. The need that is for schools to have a language policy which addresses the problem of language development across all the subjects of the curriculum.

> ".... we must convince the teacher of history or of science, for example, that he (sic) has to understand the process by which his pupils take possession of the historical or scientific information that is offered them; and that such an understanding involves his paying particular attention to the part that language plays in learning." (p.188)

Both of these keywords sparked off a considerable barrage of 'noise' in schools, local education authorities and the media. Following the publication of the report, hundreds of schools, both primary and secondary, established working parties to examine and devise a policy for 'language across the curriculum'. Equally, in many schools, teachers were given posts of responsibility for 'language across the curriculum' and numerous in-service education courses were soon being offered under this title. However, one cannot take for granted that this public 'noise' and activity was translated into widespread changes in the classroom practices of teachers. More generally the symbolic and political functions of the Bullock Report are probably in the long run of greater significance than its specific findings. In one sense it demonstrated the power of 'public opinion' and the mass media to stimulate government action to intervene in teachers' classroom decision-making.

I shall return to the Bullock Report below.

ii) Politically Motivated Teachers

Since the time when the London School had begun to gain ground in English teaching, the adherents of the Cambridge School were critical of attempts to link English teaching with social studies and the 'use' of English, as they saw it, to examine social issues. In particular, they wanted to defend literature against the inroads of thematic teaching, which became popular in the late 1960s in the new comprehensive schools, especially where English was taught as a part of an integrated studies course. Whitehead wrote in 1975, in the Cambridge School journal Use of English:

> "Increasingly literature has been 'used' - 'used' to propagate a social or political message ...; 'used' as a launching pad to get children talking or writing ...; 'used' to illustrate a predetermined theme ... "

It was the work being done on 'projects' based on themes like war, poverty, old age and pollution that was under attack. But it was not only what was going on inside the classroom that attracted the label 'political' to teachers of English, it was also their stance in more general aspects of school policy: for example, in advocating mixed-ability, mode 3 examinations, the abandonment of corporal punishment, and staff democracy. In various ways it seemed that attitudes and commitments embedded within their teaching and their view of their subject, the political vision noted above, were being translated into general concerns about education and schooling. English teachers were thus frequently in the forefront of progressive change in schools.

The English Magazine, published by the Inner London Education Authority, English Centre, reviewing the development of English teaching captures this period in the following terms and gives a sense of the relationship between the conception of the subject in the classroom and broader social issues and concerns.

> "The growing sense of confidence among English teachers which NATE both drew on and inspired, was to deliver an addition to the three main strands of English teaching: English for critical consciousness and change. The events of 1968 in Paris, California and, more modestly, in Britain, had a powerful effect on the thinking of many teachers. One half of the counter-culture veered off into drugs, mysticism and utopian life styles; the other half developed a more political perspective. It was not an illogical progression. While the counter-culture was not subversive in itself, it did have built-in oppositional ingredients: 'The cult of being true to your own feelings becomes dangerous when those feelings are not the ones that society would like you to feel'. (Juliet Mitchell) That disjunction was especially pertinent for English teachers, who by the nature of their subject, were in close contact with the experiences of working class children; it offered them a microcosmic view of the contradictions of schooling in a capitalist society. Such teachers were doing no more than focusing on a range of social injustices endemic in our society and asking questions about the value and relevance of a pedagogy and content which did not acknowledge these facts. They felt the need to incorporate an extra dimension in their practice which faced the conflicts at the heart of a model of personal development which the rest of the school and society at large had no time for, except in the case of a very small minority of pupils. It went beyond the Reflections-style interest in social issues; it tried to inject into the English curriculum the kinds of knowledge and experience which would give working class pupils an understanding of inequality and its causes; the emphasis would be on solidarity rather than upward mobility." (Simons and Raleigh 1982 p.28)

What was being attempted here by English teachers may be seen as a positive and radical response to the establishment of comprehensive education. The construction of a working class curriculum. A version of English which took seriously both the lives and culture, and alienation and lack of opportunity of working class pupils. This amounts to what Aronowitz and Giroux (1985) call 'critical literacy'.

> "Critical literacy responds to the cultural capital of a specific group or class and looks at the way in which it can be confirmed, and also at the ways in which the dominant society disconfirms students by either ignoring or denigrating the knowledge and experiences that characterize their everyday lives. The unit of analysis here is social, and the key concern is not individual interest but with individual and collective empowerment." (p.133)

Such a form of practice is certainly romantic in its conception of working class culture but it is also deeply subversive and threatening to the representatives of the dominant society. It challenges both the established curriculum and the cultural selection that that embodies and the patterns of advantage and privilege which that selection gives rise to and perpetuates. It represents an attempt to profoundly radicalize the practical ideology of schooling, 'what to be taught entails', by the 'teaching' of and empowerment of a counter-hegemony. Reaction was inevitable. And in real terms, the gap, the moment within which these radical versions of English were able to flourish was short-lived. Thus while these attempts at radical practice demonstrate again the cruciality of English as a medium of liberation, they also highlight the 'necessities' of control.

The image of 'radical' and politically motivated English teachers clearly has its basis in concerns and commitments such as these. And as already noted, there is a powerful interplay between accusations of radicalism, or political bias, and criticisms of decline in standards of literacy. The 'radical', and social realist versions of English undoubtedly existed, the difficult questions to answer are how widespread they were and whether the range of sorts of practices labelled by critics as 'politically motivated' merited the sort of reaction that emerged through the 1970s. In a sense though both questions are ultimately irrelevant in this analysis, the threat posed by the 'new wave' of 'radical' English teachers lay in <u>their critique of the traditional English curriculum.</u>

Their analysis of the social class bases of 'correct' language and 'great' literature and their linking (in some cases) of critical knowledge with social action were basic transgressions of the dominant view of education as an apolitical source of cultural harmony and social differentiation and reproduction. This represented a response to comprehensive education which went far beyond the simple re-organization of school buildings championed by the Labour Party. The attempt at the construction of a working class curriculum by a few, young, inner-city teachers was to 'stand for' English teaching as a whole. A small number of examples of radical practice were used to vilify and condemn all English teachers. Thornbury (1978) identifies the 'radical' version of English in particular with the work of Harold Rosen and as being fairly specific to the inner-city comprehensive school. And he suggests that the teachers employing this approach were 'largely graduate, invariably secondary teachers, members of the 'new English movement' through their organization the National Association of the Teachers of English (NATE), shared the black romanticism of the anthropologists in admiring working class culture, especially the seedier side of life'. (p.136)

He goes on:

> "These young teachers created an English teaching revolution in the classroom. They set great store by personal, creative writing arising from children's own experience. Fluent discussion and writing, and relatively little attention to accurate spelling, formal grammar, or systematic teaching of reading skills was their classroom emphasis. Young English teachers in the 1960s revived the romatic nineteenth century notion of 'enthusiasm', encouraging the working class child to remain a literary primitive .... Many of the new English teachers indoctrinated themselves and their classes in attitudes critical of the police, local government bureaucracy, industry and employers. They did not hesitate to encourage this ideology in the children's writing, or classroom discussion.... The new wave of English teachers was committed to the comprehensive school, to unstreaming, subject integration and team teaching. They were enthusiastic curriculum imperialists. They wished to

> see policies for 'language across the curriculum' which involved their collaboration with other subject departments." (p.136-7)

In some senses, the English teachers were seen as a threat to their colleagues, as well as to social order. Their partisan commitment to the interests of the working class student was regarded by defenders of the educational status quo as educational luddism. Boyson, then a comprehensive school headmaster, later to be a conservative junior minister of education, writing in the Black Paper of 1975, takes this view:

> ".... it was reported in 1974 that at Tulse Hill School .... the efforts of the caring staff were 'being ruined because some members of the staff are telling the boys that their chances of success in society as it exists today are nil'. It is significant that most of the 'group of extremist teachers, a dozen or twenty', at that school, came from the English Department." (p.138)

But Grace (1978 p.205) in his survey of urban teachers conducted in the 1970s, found few examples of clearcut progressive extremism. He presents a much more mixed and moderate picture.

> "Although English departments had been cast by conservative defenders of the traditional curriculum as centres for the subversion of standards, there was little in the discourse of the eighteen teachers of English involved in this study to give support to this view..... English teachers represented a complete spectrum of ideological positions in education, from the Arnoldian to the Marxist stance. If they differed significantly from other groups of teachers, it was not in respect of a thorough-going radicalism designed to subvert the conventions of English usage .... but as a group they contained more teachers who exhibited 'radical doubt' and critical reflection about the curriculum, than was the case with many of their colleagues."

Grace's interpretation is very much to the point, the logic of the 'English as language' paradigm did lead to a questioning of traditional practice, to pressure for change, but only occassionally to classroom revolution. Nonetheless, the development of 'English as language' in schools and in particular its 'social realist' wing was clearly and firmly interrupted by the Bullock Report.

The significance of the Bullock Report is twofold. Firstly, in a fairly arcane fashion, it is one form of official response to the 'moral panic' about English teaching. It is an attempt at social control. A curriculum policing action aimed at sanctioning the unacceptable aspects of 'progressive' teaching, and redefining the boundaries of acceptable practice. The role of monitoring the response of English teachers was to be taken on by the APU (Assessment of Performance Unit), set up in 1976 with a brief to devise reading and language tests. At first sight this appeared to be a step towards the establishment of and testing for national standards of literacy and was received by the teaching profession with some scepticism. Indeed, it seemed like one further attack on their already fast-fading classroom autonomy. And writing in 1980, Lawton saw the development of the APU as both anachronistic and dangerous and the establishment of testing on a national basis as likely to have massive and untoward 'backwash effects' in the classroom.

> ".... having moved away from the Scylla of laissez-faire the DES show no signs of possessing an adequate theoretical base for curriculum change and is in danger of getting too close to the Charybdis of behaviouristic, mechanistic approaches to curriculum and evaluation."

In fact, the Bullock Report and the role given to the APU were to be the first in a steady stream of increasingly direct interventions into the school curriculum.

The second significant aspect of the Bullock Report is that it articulated a specific reassertion of the economic and political role of English teaching in relation to capitalist society. The emphasis given to 'basic skills' and 'language across the curriculum' underlined the role of English in preparing pupils for work and the need for a literate labour force. The repositioning of literature, that is the literature of the great tradition, as having a central role in English teaching, underlined the role of English in the moral education of youth, the civilizing process. National efficiency and social order were at stake. As we have seen, declining 'standards' and the 'politicization' of English were seen by critics as being linked to, if not posited as causes of, the failings of the British economy and increases in crime and social disorder. In microcosm we have a representation of the classic relationship between education and the economy, the reproductive functions of the technical preparation of the workforce and the maintenance of social control.

Leaving aside for the moment the dangers of 'raiding history', it is tempting to point to the parallels between this 'panic' and those of the mid-nineteenth century (Johnson 1970), when state education was seen by many as a solution to the threat to social order posed by the 'barbarous habits' of the urban working class. Culture, through schooling was set against the potential for anarchy, and culture was seen as a potent basis for social harmony (Arnold 1869). In this context, as Grace suggests:

> "The ideology of the special mission of the English teacher had elements of romanticism, anti-urbanism and social control, compounded together with genuine concern for notions of 'quality' in aesthetic experience." (Grace 1978 p.21)

In the 1970s a similar role was being re-created in the face of increasing political and social disorder, crime and violence, and permissiveness. The English teacher was once again to be a 'preacher of culture' but in this case not the culture of the literary heritage, but the culture of industry, the culture of technological change. Thus there is an alternative, or perhaps complimentary, point of analysis to be drawn from the Bullock Report. The emphasis given to skills in the report marked a significant shift in the discourse of English teaching, excised of its 'social realism' and political criticism 'English as language' emerged as a 'form without content'. This vacuum was quickly filled. Reading and writing as bare skills, as tasks, were to be increasingly oriented towards 'the world of work'. Under the influence of models drawn from the technical colleges and further education teaching, areas of English are being colonized and reconceptualized as 'communication'. Courses like TVEI (the Technical and Vocational Education Initiative) and CPVE (the Certificate of Pre-vocational Education) are attempting to link literacy 'skills' directly to the needs and demands of employment. Literacy is reduced to form-filling and letter writing, oracy to answering the telephone. Vocational realism has replaced social realism. The world of work, or rather employment, is the dominant reference point. 'This represents little more than a particular form of mass vocational literacy that shifts the responsibility for the reproduction of workers back onto themselves'. (Gleeson 1986 p.57)

Those students who are guided into these educational careers are beginning to experience versions of English very different from their high status, O-level taking colleagues, whose work is now once again firmly set within the Cambridge tradition.

What I am suggesting here is that the Bullock Report served as a vehicle for restructuring English. Its role was symbolic in giving public censure to significant aspects of the 'new wave' English and in creating space for the insertion of alternative concepts of the role and purpose, and form and content of English teaching. It gave credibility to those voices which said 'things have gone too far'. And the new emphasis on 'skills' continues, as has been the case in previous periods of crisis, the notions of standards and functional English (functional for industry, for the economy) have become linked to grammar, 'correct' English. The 1984 HMI consultative document English from 5 to 16 urges that grammar, spelling and punctuation should be brought back to the forefront in English teaching and attempts for the first time (since the Revised Codes of the nineteenth century) to set specific objectives for English teaching. The Times (3rd October 1984) commented:

> "The paper puts parental concern about literacy, and ability to communicate intelligently and accurately, back in the forefront of educational aims. The proposals are certain, however, to lead to criticism by some teachers, who will view its emphasis on learning grammer (sic) as a reversion to traditional teaching methods."

Here crucially and typically, the interests of parents are counterposed to those of teachers. The image of the subversive teacher is sustained.

But it would be crude indeed to suggest that the Bullock Report was simply a mouthpiece for the voices of reaction. Certainly Bullock had little that was positive to say about the teaching of grammar. It is clear that the educationalists of the 'new right' found the Report unsatisfactory. The Daily Mail (that model of objective reporting on educational issues) summed up its view of the report in the following ironic headline:

> "WHITEWASH spells whitewash. Sir Alan Bullock's report on the teaching of English shrouds the reality in trendy pieties." (19th February 1975)

Clearly, from the Mail's point of view the report had failed to come to grips with the 'realities' (to which the Mail itself had privileged access). And a great deal of the press attention centred not on the main findings of the report itself - which included a refutation of the suggestion that reading scores were declining - but on the minority report of the one dissenting member, Stuart Frome, a Black Paper contributor, who argued for a return to traditional forms of teaching English in the primary school. This is where the re-emphasis upon grammatical skills emerges.

> "My own observation in a number of schools leads me to the belief that in the zeal for 'creativity' by teachers today, there is not the rigorous critical marking of spelling, punctuation and grammatical errors which there used to be, while the traditional systematic 'doing of corrections' is fast disappearing. This has lead, in my view, to the wretched solecisms exhibited in students' written work, and I believe that the Committee should have made even more of the unfortunate side effects that the policy of free, uninhibited creativity has engendered.
> And I believe the Committee is in error in putting undue emphasis upon talking as a means of learning language. It has its place, but in my view, one of the causes of the decline in English standards today is the recent drift in schools away from the written to the spoken

word." (p.526)

Furthermore, James Britton sat as a member of the Committee and clearly made his views felt in the writing of the report. Although, cryptically, Thornbury (1978 p.137) suggests that this might have been no assurance that the 'social realist' version would have gained a hearing.

> "Many of the original revolutionaries were by now establishment figures playing for higher political stakes. Those few who stayed in teaching jobs, like Michael Marland, had throughout pursued a more moderate stance - and sometimes been lampooned for it. Their influence, together with the best of the new tradition, was evident in the recommendations of the important Bullock Report."

What Thornbury is suggesting, probably quite accurately, is that the Report itself was a compromise. What is significant is that ultimately it is Frome's version of English, and not that of Britton, which found its way into the HMI document English 5 to 16.

What Bullock and the Black Papers provided for was a reconstitution of the purposes of English teaching in schools, in particular its relationship to the world of work was fundamentally altered. Furthermore, the locus of control had shifted away from groups and interests within the organic community to external agencies and influences. The form of the discourse and the control of the discourse within which English was set had been politically reconstructed. As Foucault suggests '.... discourse is the power which is to be seized'.

The 'critical literacy' (Aronowitz and Giroux 1985) attempted by the 'new wave' English teachers had been substantially routed and displaced. The dominant discourse was now instrumental and technicist, oriented not to a critical examination of work, but to the preparation for employment.

Footnotes

(1) I am indebted to Ivor Goodson for his constant encouragement over a number of years to pursue my interest in English teaching and for his critical comments on the development of the analytical schema employed in this paper.

(2) Ball and Lacey (1980), Ball (1982), (1984), (1985).

Bibliography

Allen, D. (1980)
English Teaching since 1965: How Much Growth?
London, Heinemann.
Arnold, M. (1869)
Culture and Anarchy
Aronowitz, S. and Giroux, H. (1985)
Education Under Siege: The Conservative, Liberal and Radical Debate over Schooling
Mass., Bergin and Garvey
Ball, S.J. and Lacey, C. (1980)
Subject Disciplines as the Opportunity for Group Action: A Measured Critique of Subject Sub-cultures' in Woods, P.E. (Ed) Teacher Strategies,
London, Croom Helm.
Ball, S.J. (1981) Beachside Comprehensive
Cambridge, Cambridge University Press.
Ball, S.J. (1982)
'Competition and Conflict in the Teaching of English: A Socio-historical Analysis'
Journal of Curriculum Studies Vol.13, No. 4
Ball, S.J. (1984)
'Conflict, Panic and Inertia: Mother-tongue Teaching in England 1970-83', in Herrlitz, W. et al (Eds) Mother Tongue Education in Europe, Studies in Mother Tongue Education 1, International Mother Tongue Education Network, National Institute for Curriculum Development, Enschede, Netherlands.
Ball, S.J. (1985)
'The Making of a School Subject: English for the English 1906-82', in Goodson I.F. (Ed) Social Histories of the Secondary Curriculum: Subjects for Study,
Lewes, Falmer Press.

Britton, J. (1970)
Language and Learning,
Harmonsworth, Penguin.
Bullock Report, The (1975)
A Language for Life
London, HMSO.
Cohen, S. (1980)(2nd Ed)
Folk Devils and Moral Panics,
Oxford, Martin Robertson.
Cox, C.B. and Dyson, A.E. (1969)
Fight for Education: A Black Paper
The Critical Quarterly Society
Cox, C.B. and Boyson R. (1975)
The Fight for Education: Black Paper 1975
London, Dent.
Dixon, J. (1975)(3rd Ed)
Growth Through English
Oxford, Oxford University Press.
Foucault M. (1981)
'The Order of Discourse', in Young, R. (Ed)
Untying the Text
London, Routledge and Kegan Paul.
Grace, G. (1978)
Teachers, Ideology and Control
London, Routledge and Kegan Paul.
G.B. Department of Education and Science,
Her Majesty's Inspectorate,
English 5 to 16,
London, HMSO
Gleeson, D. (1986)
'Further Education Free Enterprise and the Curriculum' in Walker, S. and Barton L. (Eds),
Youth, Unemployment and Schooling
Milton Keynes, Open University Press.
Hall, S. et al. (1978) Policing the Crisis: Mugging, the State and Law and Order, London, Macmillan.
Johnson, R. (1970)
'Educational Policy and Social Control in Early Victorian England',
Past and Present, Vol.49,
Lawton, D. (1980)
The Politics of the School Curriculum
London, Routledge and Kegan Paul.
Leavis, F.R. and Thompson, D. (1933)
Culture and Environment,
London, Chatto and Windus.
Sheridan, A. (1980)
Michel Foucault: The Will to Truth,
London, Tavistock.

Simons, M. and Raleigh, M. (1982)
'Where We've Been' The English Magazine No. 1, pp.23-28.
Thornbury, R. (1978)
The Changing Urban School, London, Methuen.
Whitehead, F. (1966)
The Disappearing Dias, London, Chatto and Windus.
Whitehead, F. (1975)
'Stunting the Growth', Use of English Vol. 28, No. 1.

3. THE EMERGENCE AND REDEFINING OF ENGLISH FOR THE COMMON SCHOOL 1889-1984

Bjørg Brandtzaeg Gundem

INTRODUCTION

The State of the Art: A Need for Continuous Studies

There is in my country, as in the other Nordic countries, a need for substantive studies in curriculum history - including the history of school subjects. We need these kind of studies to develop grounded theories of how the content of schools develops over time in interaction with political, economic, educational and personal influences.

Up till now the main trend has been either a-theoretical narratives, or explanations linked to macro-theories (e.g. reproduction theories) like the studies from the Research Group for Curriculum Theory and Reproduction at the Stockholm Institute of Education (e.g. Englund 1980, Lundgren 1983). There is, however, a need for studies that also take into account the productive and interactive aspects of curriculum emergence over time.

The Context of the Article: 'Educational Reform through the Changing of a School Subject'

The article is based on a study of the emergence and redefining of English as a school subject from the 1880s to the beginning of the 1970s, in the Norwegian common school (folkeskole). The main emphasis is on the period between the passing of the Act on Innovation in Education (Forsøksloven) in 1954 and the subsequent set-up of the Council for Innovation in Education and the passing of the Education Act on the compulsory 9-year comprehensive school in 1969 with the subsequent curriculum development work (the Mønsterplan, 1971, 1974).(1)

Some central questions of interest are:

- What part did the school subject 'English' play as a part of and a means in the politically initiated and implemented educational reform?
- What were the main societal, political, educational, linguistic and psychological influences?
- Through which national, Nordic and international channels (organizations, institutions, groups, persons), was influence exerted?
- What were the main characteristics of the process leading to the changing and reformulating of the plan for the teaching and learning of English as part of the official curriculum? (2)

Some Major Curriculum Issues

In the context of this chapter only certain aspects can be dealt with. It was therefore decided to envisage the role and function of the school subject, English, in relation to some major curriculum issues like:

1. The introduction of a foreign language subject in the common school.
2. The establishment of the 'unbroken' 7-year common school.
3. The 'unbroken' 7-year common school as a 'prep-school' for secondary education.
4. The inequalities between both the official, the implemented and experienced curriculum in the schools of the towns and the schools in the rural areas.
5. The period of innovative curriculum experimenting from 1955 onwards.
6. The democratization of the Norwegian school system in a social-democratic direction: the establishment of the 9-year basic school.

The school subject, English, was linked to these curriculum issues in specific ways revealing extra-disciplinary influences more than innate ones to be decisive for the development of the role and content of the subject.

FROM THE 1880s TILL 1954

A Need for 'Communicative Skills'

The teaching of English as a foreign optional subject in the Norwegian common school started in the 1870s on a wave of pragmatic utilitarian interests. The Norwegian shipping towns were booming. Arendal, for instance, now a small town of some 15,000 inhabitants, was the third largest shipping town in the world. The need for certain skills in foreign languages and especially English was apparent. The local school authorities along the coast found that it was not directly against the Education Acts to introduce English as an optional, but open-to-all, extra curricular activity in the common school. Apparently, the subject flourished and the teaching was attended not only by the boys of the 'lower class' who knew they would be off to sea on leaving school at 14, but also by the greater part of the girls, who had more humble domestic or other subordinate work awaiting them on finishing compulsory schooling.

Both Skill and Knowledge

In 1885 a National Commission was set up to further reform and prepare for new educational legislation for the towns and rural areas alike. It proposed not only to 'legalize' the existing teaching of English, but also to further it as an optional extra curricular subject, especially in the schools of the towns and also in the rural areas. The main justification was still pragmatic - stressing the needs of seamen and artisans, and the interests of trade and tourism, but also the benefits to secondary schooling if the pupils had some knowledge of a modern language beforehand, was introduced as an argument. And the Education Act of 1889 consequently introduced a 'foreign language subject' as an optional subject outside the set curriculum in the Norwegian common school.

An Open Subject for All or a Subject for the Few

The term 'a foreign language subject' is symptomatic. According to the 1889 Education Acts, the school authorities were free not only to introduce (or not to introduce) a foreign language to the local schools, but also to decide if it should be

English or German. And after the Secondary School Education Act of 1896, German was the most important modern language. The conflict is apparent. English is chosen in the interest of the common school itself and of most of its pupils, and for the benefit of the wider community. If the benefits to secondary schools and to the few pupils continuing their schooling there were decisive, German would be preferred.

The Unbroken 7-Year Common School: 'English' is a Key

The egalitarian streak is very strong in the Norwegian society, and especially so in the rhetorics and practice of Norwegian educational development. The ideal from the 1880s onward sponsored by the liberals first, and later by the social-democrats, is the unbroken school where pupils are held together as long as possible and where no streaming or organizational differentiation takes place.

The immediate goal was the unbroken 7-year school, instead of a system where the 'well-to-do', often viewed as 'brighter', pupils were transferred to secondary school after class five, and in this way breaking up the classes and the 7-year compulsory school. This issue was at the core of all educational policy debates in the first two decades of this century and the pros and cons were fierce, the latter reinforced by strong support from secondary school teachers and authorities who really felt their interests threatened.

The problem was solved by a 'coup' or 'fait accompli'. In 1920, the Storting was taken by surprise and passed a law stating that only secondary schools building on the 'unbroken' 7-year school would receive state financial support. This law very effectively put an end to the old system and put into practice the 7-year unbroken compulsory school as the rule for all Norwegian children.

'English' is Paying the Cost

The coup took place at a time when several commissions were working hard to plan a new type of elementary and secondary school organization, and it became an urgent demand to make the upper classes in the common school fit for the new role as a preparatory school for secondary schooling. English had become the most important modern language in the secondary schools.(3) The demand was for a teaching of English in classes 6 and 7 equivalent to the standards of English lessons for beginners in secondary schools.

The Education Acts of 1936 made official the role of the school subject English in relation to secondary schooling, and a set curriculum was prescribed stating explicitly this end. By now the school subject English was in content and form basically shaped according to the interests of the secondary schools and primarily intended for pupils who will attend secondary schools.

A Main Function: To Serve as a Selection Agency for Secondary Schools

'English' was, by the end of the second world war, still an optional subject even if by now the teaching of it took place within ordinary school hours. It could be made compulsory according to the local school authority's decision, but this very rarely occurred. It was also predominantly a 'closed' subject - open only to the pupils who were found 'adequate' or 'fit'. A major problem became how to select pupils for admission to English classes.

The end of the nineteen-forties witnessed the blooming of American-inspired test psychology and it became accepted that an I.Q. of 90 represented somehow a limit for the intellectual capacity required. The newly established (1936) Institute for Educational Research at Oslo University, under the direction of Prof. Johs. Sandven, made adaptation of American tests possible. A special prognostic test was constructed (Dokka 1951). The score on this test, together with marks in 'Norwegian' and informal written tests by the end of class 6 and in the course of class 7, secured the standards set down by the secondary school requirements.

Striking Inequalities

The entrance ticket to secondary education in the towns and to a certain extent in the rural areas was, as noted, a passed course in English. One had, of course, also to pass 'Norwegian' and 'mathematics', but this in itself did not suffice. In the rural areas there existed, however, a few centrally located secondary schools not having a foreign language prerequisite. There were in Norway at this time two sets of educational legislation: one for the towns, another for the rural areas. (The first 'joint' Education Act is from 1959.) Even though the set curriculum for English as a result of the 1936 Education Act was the same for the schools in the towns and in the countryside, there were nevertheless strong overtones of 'discrimination'. For the towns the importance of the teaching of English was continuously stressed, especially in relation to secondary education. As regards the teaching of English in the rural area schools, warnings were given explicitly against its possible damaging effects on other subjects and it was stressed that time and effort put into that subject must not in any way make the 'normal' curriculum suffer.

And there were, of course, many hindrances not only to the introduction and implementation of English as an optional subject, but also to the implementation of schooling according to the prescriptions of the Education Acts of 1936. Scattered population, lack of communications on land and at sea, scarcity of competent teachers and lack of financial resources, did not exactly further the interests of a foreign language subject. According to statistical information from 1954, nearly 100 per cent of the towns and 27 per cent of the rural communities had by then introduced English as an optional subject. In the towns, 79 per cent of the pupils completed the English course, while this was the case for only 29 per cent in the rural areas. And within the rural areas, the geographic differences were striking. In certain communities in north-west Norway, only 1 per cent of the pupils had completed the English course, compared to 75 per cent in certain rural areas in southern Norway.

A Growing Unrest

The 'unbroken' 7-year common school for pupils up to the age of 14 in Norway was rather a unique phenomenon in Europe up to the 1950s. The idea of equality and justice through the postponement of choice and differentiation has been a non-controversial issue in Norwegian school politics. The elitist element represented by 'English' was, however, a sore thumb spoiling a much desired image. And after the war unrest was growing rapidly, starting within the ranks of the social-democratic party, with 'English for everybody' as the demand from 1952 onwards.(4) The political unrest was caused by the fact that a selection was taking place, and by the way this selection was carried out, functioning to 'reproduce' the class society and undermining what was seen as the true function of education: to further the democratization of the Norwegian society. What was needed, was a 'democratization of the teaching of English' in the compulsory school.

The 'democratization of the teaching of English' was, however, not only ideologically and politically justified. The official and main legitimation was of a pragmatic and utilitarian kind stressing the urgent needs for increased practical language skills, in particular in English, due to the growing internationalization affecting society as a whole as well as the individual person.(5) This concern was shared by everybody - teachers and educational politicians alike. By the mid-fifties, a general demand for 'English for everybody' was ideologically uncontroversial and more or less accepted within the different political parties. In addition, there were indications that it could also become pedagogically possible: the advancement of 'theories' of foreign language acquisition and new methods of teaching English as a foreign language was starting to make an impact and had some influence.(6)

Especially in Oslo, revisions were carried through from the beginning of the fifties to change the academic nature of the teaching of English and of the examination tests, making it possible for more pupils to take part and also to pass the exams. That this took place in Oslo, is due to at least two circumstances: The existence of the Oslo English Teachers' Society which, after the war, became a vigilant pressure group in relation to the Oslo school authorities,(7) and the fact that some of the most progressive school politicians of the Labour Party were, during this period, members of the Oslo School Council.(8)

So, in many ways, there existed a general consensus about the need for drastic changes as to the role and content of the teaching of English in the common school. It was therefore not unexpected that the teaching of English in compulsory education became one of the first targets for experimental innovative projects to take place in Norway during the coming period of school reforms.

INNOVATION BETWEEN SCHOOL POLITICS, RESEARCH AND PRAXIS: 1955 TILL EARLY 1960s

Like the other Nordic and European countries, Norway was by the mid-fifties facing a period of planning for and implementing long overdue school reforms. In 1954 the Storting passed the Act of Innovation in Education, opening the way for extensive experimentation by allowing the normal regulations concerning the organization and curriculum of the common school to be set aside.

The planning of different experiments in teaching English for all pupils, 'English for everybody', started immediately after the establishment of the National Council for Innovation in Education with its Secretariat in 1954.(9) From the next school year on, the first experiments took place in a middle-sized town in southern Norway, Tønsberg. More experiments followed rapidly, spread around the whole country, including Oslo, from 1958. Additional try-outs were a consequence of special circumstances: the increasing experimental set-ups with a nine-year basic school during this period making English compulsory as a consequence. Extra pressure was also put on the local communities by the Education Act of 1959, suspending the veto of the local school authorities by making English compulsory.

Aims and Means

Experiments with the teaching of English in the common school had two different objectives in mind: the teaching of English in the common school for general contact purposes, and the teaching of English in primary education as a prerequisite and foundation for secondary education. Because of this doublesidedness, two educational questions were central and imperative: the question of selection and differentiation, and the question of developing a curriculum (Laereplan) suitable for the teaching of 'English for everybody', in addition to the official curriculum existing for the teaching of English up till now.

Right from the start, different kinds of experiments were envisaged, such as experiments with:

1. Early start compared with later one (class 5 or class 6).

2. Undifferentiated teaching from Class 5 on.
3. Different selection and differentiation methods and procedures in classes 6 and 7.
4. Special programmes in the rural areas like radio and teaching 'without teacher'.
5. 'English' as part of the new 9-year compulsory school.

Some Problematic Preconditions or Background Determinants

In the different official documents preparing the Innovation Act of 1954, and the consequent establishment of the National Innovation Council for Innovation in Education, there were put down certain regulations and prescriptions as to the nature of the school research envisaged. These being the heydays of experimental school research and test psychology, it was explicitly stated that educational research was intended that was systematically planned and controlled and where the results were analysed by advanced statistical procedures.

Natural would-be partners in the large-scale research enterprise to show the future way to go in reforming the Norwegian compulsory school were, according to these documents, the Institute for Educational Research at Oslo University and the Norwegian Council for Research in Science and the Humanities, NAVF.

Steps to secure such teamwork were taken by the Council for Innovation right away. A combination of efforts, however, that seemed obvious from the Council's point of view, did not seem so in the eyes of the educational research experts or by the persons sitting on the money. The director of the Council for Innovation in Education had to resort to the top authorities in the Ministry of Education to get what he thought was needed in experimental programmes: prognostic tests for selection and differentiation, achievement tests for comparing results and statistical help for analysing research findings. Another prerequisite: a plan for the teaching of 'English for everybody' was already procured.

A Curriculum for the Teaching of 'English for Everybody'

Even if the aim was compulsory English for all

pupils, it is quite apparent that at the time the first experimental projects started up, two different types of teaching of English were envisaged with two sets of objectives and therefore different curricula or content. Consequently, a plan or prescribed curriculum for the teaching of English in the common school for 'general contact purposes' was needed to replace the old 'normal plan', except for the teaching of pupils bound for secondary schooling. Needless to say the existence of and adherence to such a plan was vital to the implementation of a teaching of English more adjusted to the capacities and potential of the greater part of the pupils.

With the starting up of the experimental classes in Tønsberg, such a plan was available to the teachers and the school authorities vouching, it was believed, for a different kind of teaching and learning of 'English as a foreign language'. Two aspects of the 'plan' are striking and must be mentioned. One is its Swedish origin. It is in fact a sad coincidence that Sweden started its innovative school experiments just in time to become a model for the same kind of experimental school research in Norway. It seems a bit 'unfair', especially as the teaching of English was concerned.

The teaching of English was never a responsibility of the Swedish common school in the same way as in Norway. The 'unbroken' common school did not exist until the reforms of the fifties and the teaching of English was till then consequently within the domain of the secondary school teachers. But, by the mid-fifties, practical experiments were getting well under way including the teaching of English, and apparently, the men in the Secretariat of the Council for Innovation in Education were looking to Sweden and they found what they were looking for: a 'plan' incorporating two different levels of teaching English - one for 'general contact purposes' and another for the more academically orientated teaching. It was the first one they 'copied' - the set national curriculum already provided for the second type.

Another aspect to be mentioned was the progressiveness of the 'plan' - not so much in teaching methods as in maintaining vocabulary control and grading of text and learning material. It also stressed the importance of practical skills of reading, understanding and making oneself understood at the cost of skills in writing and knowledge of grammar.

Some Underlying Tensions

The parents, the teachers, the school authorities and the school politicians alike, were prepared for large scale experiments as a necessary part of the democratization process of the teaching of English in compulsory education and the official reports to the Storting give evidence of general satisfaction. The archive material, however, especially the correspondence between the Council for Innovation in Education and representatives for the local communities involved, reveal serious misunderstandings, deep-rooted controversies as well as a bitter fight for power over the aims and nature of the planned and implemented experiments. Especially in the case of Oslo, there were, as we shall see, great tensions involved.

The same tensions were entailed, however, even in a milder form and more vaguely expressed, in Tønsberg and the other communities where experiments were being planned and implemented. Everybody wanted experiments carried out in class 5. But the parents, the teachers and the local school authorities wanted all the pupils in class 5 to take part - having experienced the pain of discrimination caused by the former selection and streaming procedures. The Council for Innovation in Education was, however, interested in trying out different models of different types of differentiation and teaching, and as a consequence, wanted the pupils of class 5 divided into three different groups based on the outcome of tests and teacher assessment.

In Tønsberg, the community won the battle over class 5 in the first round. Apparently, the Council for Innovation in Education feared that if they forced through their intentions on this point, it might cause such an uproar and antagonism that it might ruin the possibilities of carrying through the whole project. Tønsberg lost, however, in the second round. From 1956 there were different groupings in class 5 and they also lost the battle over differentiation in class 6. The original local plans for the project presupposed unstreamed teaching in class 6, postponing the streaming till class 7. So already from the start of the experimental period, it was apparent that the 'grassroot' notion of what democratization of the teaching of English meant, was different from that of the central school research authorities!

The situation became drastic when Oslo was involved two years later. In Oslo, experiments were wanted in order to test if three years of teaching English starting in class 5 would give the same results as starting in class 6 - keeping the teaching hours the same. In the eyes of the Council for Innovation in Education, this was not an experiment worthy of support - especially when the Oslo school authorities refused any streaming before class 7. Moreover, they refused to accept the Council's 'plan' for 'English for everybody'. On the contrary, Oslo was already moving rapidly towards an organizationally undifferentiated teaching of English for all pupils within the framework of the official curriculum for English (Normalplanen 1939). This time the local school authorities were the winners - strongly supported by the Oslo Association of the Teachers of English.

It is also clear that certain tensions were created by the different approaches represented by teachers on one side and the central authorities on the other to the experiments. The teachers were only vaguely interested in a 'democratization' of the teaching of English in a political sense. They were, however, keenly interested in a pedagogically better teaching and learning - suitable for more pupils and making more sense than a teaching and learning of English preconditioned to the needs of secondary education. Especially in Tønsberg, where a locally developed plan for the project existed beforehand, a series of pedagogical objectives were listed as the main aims of the experiments, such as the burden of homework, the changing of the academic 'tint', the effect on other school subjects, etc. These and other pedagogical or practical aims became integrated only to a very small degree in the official legitimation of the experiments.

One of the greatest difficulties for the implementation of a teaching of English according to the intentions of the 'Plan for English for Everybody', was the inability of the teachers to understand the plan and to base their own teaching on it. Going through the reports of the inspector from the Secretariat of the Council for Innovation, this is a recurrent complaint and it created at the time certain tensions between the central innovation authorities and their local implementers. It seemed to be the case for more or less all the teachers. The young and inexperienced teachers taught the way they themselves had been taught. The older and experienced ones would not change their habitual ways of teaching. The elderly teachers especially tried to make all their pupils reach the standard prescribed by the former official curriculum for entering secondary schooling. 'Everywhere it seems, the teachers have difficulties in changing their teaching from a traditional teaching of English towards a teaching in accordance with the principles of the Plan for English for Everybody'.(10)

'... on a Scientific Basis'

The demand for a scientifically based innovation made the use of an array of tests a necessity: general intelligence and maturity tests, prognostic tests for prediction, achievement tests for different stages and tests measuring interest and progress. Most of the tests were provided by the staff of the Institute for Educational Research at Oslo University. The general intelligence and maturity tests existed already. The other ones were developed by members of the academic staff.

The greater bulk of the research carried out at the Institute for Educational Research at Oslo University at this time was of an experimental psychological kind or within the area of test psychology. The general intelligence tests and the maturity tests had already been introduced as part of the services offered by the school psychology counselling centres.

There seemed to have been on the part of the teachers or the local school authorities no serious objections to the extensive use of tests in the experimental programmes. On the contrary, they appear to have been more or less convinced that this was the way to go to secure a reliable and valid foundation on which to build the future teaching of English in compulsory schooling, a belief that was shared by the school politicians and, it seems, nurtured by the experts on educational research.

The results or findings, based on the statistical analysis of the material, proved to be more or less an anticlimax giving no secure knowledge whatsoever. On the basis of the data available, it was impossible to tell when was the best starting point for English: class 5 or class 6. The Oslo experiment, as well as the Tønsberg one, seemed to indicate that intonation and pronunciation profited from an early start, but no conclusions were drawn. It was, however, very puzzling that the Oslo pupils did much better on all tests than did the pupils from other parts of the country - in spite of the fact that they had two teaching hours less (10 instead of 12).

The research interest of the experiments was, among other aspects, tied to possible correlates between the different tests. No correlates were found significant, a fact that was ascribed to deficient statistical procedures. But all the same, the early experiments with the teaching of English from class 5, with the greater part of the pupils taking part who profited from a less academic curriculum and more progressive teaching methods, were to make a decisive impact on the future development of the teaching of English for beginners. The reactions of teachers and parents were positive - even enthusiastic. The reports of supervisors, inspectors and school authorities were optimisitc and encouraging in spite of the rather dismal formal results. English from class 5 and for all the pupils had come to stay. In Oslo, at the end of the experimental period, English from class 5 on was made compulsory for everybody.

TOWARDS 'ENGLISH' IN THE BASIC 9-YEAR SCHOOL

The 1960s saw the rapid emergence of the future 'common' school: the 9-year basic school. It found its way towards realization through a two stage interim period materializing two distinct solutions: the first one dividing the pupils organizationally in two separate courses of study encompassing all subjects: the 'g' course for pupils planning to go to higher secondary school (the 'gymnas'), the second, the 'y' course for pupils going on to vocations ('yrker') not demanding higher secondary education; the second solution, a comprehensive 9-year school, where the last three years made room for organizational differentiation in certain compulsory school subjects: mathematics, Norwegian and English, and an optional one, German. The political and pedagogical intention underlying this arrangement was that all the pupils would be held together most of the teaching hours. At the same time, different groups of pupils would be given the advantage of a teaching in accordance with their abilities and potential in the more demanding subjects. Evaluation both informal and formal, like the final examinations, was to be 'relative' - that is, of an individually-referenced kind and not according to pre-set criteria. There was, however, one snag. The most demanding courses were necessary for continued schooling in the 'gymnas' and so was also German as an option. The choice of the different courses of study was, however, in the hands of the pupils themselves and their parents - the teachers and school counsellors acting only as advisers.

The starting point and the hallmark of the second part of the interim period, was the appearance of a prescribed 'curriculum' or a set of guidelines: **Laereplan for forsøk med 9-årig skole** in 1962, setting the stage for the coming period of experimental teaching to pave the way for the 9-year school. It lasted till the passing of the Education Act of 1969 which proclaimed an organizationally differentiated basic 9-year school. During this period English in class 5 and in class 6 developed into one course without any organizational differentiation taking place before class 7 and was introduced and implemented more or less all over the country causing little debate or controversy. There was, however, a growing awareness of the need for new adequate teaching material including modern textbooks. Experiments with teaching English from class 4 started in Oslo in 1967 - making the question of teaching material and progressive teaching methods even more urgent.

The main focus during the coming years was, however, on the teaching of English in classes 7, 8 and 9. There were three different courses of study for the teaching of English in these classes, differing more in expectations of mastery of skills and knowledge than in methodological approach and form of content. A new edition of the Forsøksplan from 1964 did away with the organizational differentiation in class 7 altogether. Even so, the greater part of the pupils preferred the more demanding courses in English as in the other ability-grouped subjects. There was also a growing political tension related to the fact that only pupils who had passed the most demanding courses could continue to secondary schools. This tension grew into an 'uproar' when a study revealed that the best examination results from the second demanding course were better than the lowest ones on the most demanding one. The implications were evident, and a decisive step towards an unstreamed 'comprehensiveness' had been taken.

Influencing Forces and Agents

There followed a period of intense and extensive change. Structural linguistics, behavioural psychology and instructional technology combined forces to create a new era of foreign language teaching sponsored by an enthusiastic and optimistic international climate. The catalyst in Europe was the work of the Council of Europe in the field of modern languages. Major Project-Foreign Languages and later its programme for 'an intensified policy for modern language teaching' originated from the stressing of the importance of foreign languages to further international understanding and co-operation in the articles of the convention of 1954. It was reinforced at conferences of European Ministers of Education in 1961 and 1962 where two resolutions were adopted advocating the expansion and improvement of modern language teaching. From 1962 onwards, under the auspices of the Council for Cultural Co-operation, a series of conferences took place focusing on both the political intentions as well as the curricular implications and consequences of the Council's policy.(11) As a consequence, the resolutions as well as the recommendations of the conferences were concerned with questions of starting point and access as well as the 'common-places' of foreign language teaching: aims, content, teaching methods and teaching material. The meeting of representatives of national education politicians with the linguistic subject-matter, pedagogical as well as the audio-visual or technological expertise of foreign language teaching was a unique phenomenon pertaining to these conferences.

The impact on the national level can be traced in decisions about the instalment of language laboratories and audio-visual hardware as well as in the flow of teaching material being produced especially by Swedish teacher experts attending the conferences as national representatives year after year. The aims of foreign language teaching as they were adopted at the 1966 conference in Ostia established a priority adhered to in the forthcoming curriculum development work concerning the teaching of English in the 9-year comprehensive school. These aims were as follows:

1. to enable pupils to understand speech at normal speed;
2. to enable them to speak a foreign language intelligibly;
3. to enable them to read with ease and understanding;
4. to enable them to express themselves in writing; and
5. to give them a knowledge of the foreign country and an insight into its civilization and culture.

> "The development of these aims should be integrated in the teaching at all levels in terms of the age, ability and interests of the pupils."
> (Report Council of Europe Course, 20-29 April, 1966, p.37)

THE EDUCATION ACT OF 1969 AND THE PARALLEL CURRICULUM DEVELOPMENT WORK

The Mønsterplan of 1971

The 9-year Compulsory School Education Act of 1969 laid the legal foundation for the present school system and for the six year course in English now in operation. The parallel curriculum development work was launched in 1967 by the appointment of a national commission to provide general guidelines and principles for the aims and content of the new school system. A preliminary version of the proposed curriculum was circulated and debated - even in the Storting - and by 1971, the new national curriculum, the Mønsterplan, was put into operation. A new version appeared in 1974 mainly due to necessary changes to prevent sexism and other forms of discrimination, introducing only slight alterations in the curriculum for English.

Since 1971, only one course for teaching English from class 4 to class 9 is the rule. During the first years, to help make the transition period easy, the individual or local school could decide on some limited 'ability' grouping. Today, ability grouping is strictly prohibited even if educational differentiation due to other criteria than ability is encouraged. The form and content of the 'plan' for English now in operation is more or less consistent with the Swedish one appearing a couple of years before, and very different to the one that appeared in the preliminary version of 1970 developed by three Norwegian teachers of English.(12) Once again, the Swedish 'model' proved too tempting and an easy way to procure a more professionally developed and theoretically more consistent plan than a 'home-made' alternative.

The Plan for English in the Mønsterplan is a true outcome of the liaison between structural linguistics, behaviouristic psychology and instructional technology. There is a strong emphasis on imitation and drill exercises, listening comprehension and oral competence. It is the launching of the audio-lingual method making the tape-recorder and the overhead projector indispensable as the hardware components of the 'teaching material set'.

It was 'goodbye and farewell' to the mastery of formal grammar and the knowlege of literary texts as ingredients of the teaching and learning of English in compulsory schooling. It introduced - in the eyes of the critics - an era where meaning is separated from language and where content is merely a means to acquire skill and consequently of minor interest and worth.

Today, the optimism and enthusiasm of the early seventies has given way to more reflective attitudes concerning the art of the teaching and learning of languages. The new 'bandwagon': communicative competence is already being used in the advertisements of more up-to-date textbooks than the Swedish-produced ones that invaded Norway in the 1970s. There is a revision of the Mønsterplan underway and no doubt the stressing of meaningful communication to replace meaningless imitation will be part of the theoretical framework of the revision. In what way, or if at all, it will affect the work of the teachers in the field and consequently the teaching and learning of English as a foreign language in Norway, is another question and far more difficult to foresee.

SUMMARIZING REMARKS

Using the terminology of today's educational jargon, we may say that the school subject 'English' was introduced into the centralized Norwegian common school curriculum as a consequence of first being a locally initiated curriculum project - a rather remarkable and unique phenomenon in our school history. True enough, one of the reasons for doing so was to re-establish the order of the system.

A consequence was, however, that the legitimation for English as a school subject differed greatly from that of the other school subjects in the common school. It is, however, significant that the main legitimation remained the same as the original one: a need for practical language skills. Such competence was, however, of primary interest only to the local communities where 'English' was first introduced; it was barely of secondary interest to the population as a whole. Indeed, in certain parts of the country, the needs of tourism and exchange of craftsmen might indicate 'German' instead of 'English'.

There were no moral overtones attached, as in the case of the subjects of religion and reading, nor was there the primary practical interest linked to arithmetic and handicrafts, or the general desire for enlightenment that sponsored subjects like geography. The introduction of 'English' represented a rupture with the prevalent curriculum code of the common school - a code that Ulf Lundgren (1979) would describe as a moral code. In doing so, it made room for competing influences to penetrate the common school, interests that may be ascribed to the curriculum code of secondary schooling - a curriculum code that Lundgren (1979) would characterize as 'realistic'. No wonder that the subject found itself in a difficult and fluctuating position. Implementation was slow - and the interest lukewarm.

The subject had not only great difficulties in finding its place, it was also looked upon by many as a threat to the inherent values of the common school and it did not gain status until its role and function was linked to that of secondary education. That meant that the justification of the subject changed from being practically founded to elitist orientated. In this way the entrance ticket to secondary education became a passed course in English. Thus selection for the English course became a means of controlling access to secondary schooling - a role that contributed in yielding it a status and power very unlike the other subjects of the common school.

One of the main difficulties in the implementation of a common school providing equal opportunities, has in my country been the difference between the town schools and the schools of the rural areas. The difference has been both in quality and quantity - the hours of teaching being fewer and the quality of teaching inferior in the schools of the rural areas. The introduction of English as a school subject highlights the problem, adding another dimension - that of access. The most striking feature was the absence of the possibility for pupils attending school in geographically isolated areas to take part, a fact that contributed to widening the breach between the curricula of the schools of the towns and the schools in the rural areas.

Not only did statistical information around 1954 reveal striking inequalities between towns and rural areas concerning the possibilities of access to 'English', there was also growing political unrest with the 'undemocratic' selection procedures and its 'reproductive' consequences. It is, however, worth noting that the main official legitimation for 'English for everybody' was not 'the democratization of the Norwegian society in a social-democratic direction', but the necessity for practical language skills. In the ensuing period of debate and innovation concerning 'English' in the common and comprehensive school, this political and ideological aspect was seldom brought into focus. The main legitimation was of a pragmatic kind - even if the ideological aspect of equality and equal opportunities is a strong element underpinning not only the innovation programmes, but also the tensions inherent in their planning and implementation.

There seems to be no doubt that one of the strongest reasons for the tensions was the discrepancy between the way parents, teachers and local school authorities felt about the 'democratization process' and that of the Council for Innovation in Education.

In a way, the former ones were ready to try out ways of organization and teaching that were far more progressive than were those of the central educational research authorities. The latter, on the contrary, seemed to ignore what had already happened for instance in a big community like Oslo. What they proposed felt to the teachers of Oslo like a set-back causing much dispute between the Association of Teachers of English and some of the staff of the Council's Secretariat.

In retrospect, it seems that the fatal mistake made by the Council for Innovation was use of the Swedish 'model'. The development in Norway as far as the teaching of English in the common school was concerned, was before the experimental period, way ahead of that of Sweden. The justification for introducing a separate plan for the teaching of English for everybody, in addition to the already existing plan for the teaching of English in the common school, represented a way of thinking very alien to the tradition of the common school, and counter to the efforts already made to develop a teaching of English for most pupils within the framework of the normal curriculum.

The trying out of different models of organization and different procedures of selection and streaming made little sense to the local school authorities; the teachers and parents were ready for far more drastic reforms. It may seem a paradox that the civil servants in the Secretariat of the Council, being themselves social-democrats, were not in touch with the progressive elements of the Labour Party who, for instance, to a great extent, influenced the development in Oslo as far as the teaching of English was concerned. They were, however, bureaucrats who felt that the obligations of 'English' in the common school to secondary schooling justified two different English courses. The methodological approach to the different courses were not unlike. After all, 'the direct method' was proclaimed as the method by the introduction of the Normalplan (1939). It was the aims and, to a certain extent, the content that differed, especially in that less significance was given to written work.

Today, in the light of much research concerned with the problems of innovation in school, it may seem rather strange that the existence of a plan was looked upon as more or less the 'to be or not to be' of change and innovation. The 'naivity' of the following quotation from the concluding remarks of an inspection report may seem puzzling:

> "In the end, however, all the teachers promised to make an effort and change their teaching according to the plan for English for everybody as decided by the School Council."(13)

Optimism and belief in progress was a marked

aspect of the period. It was especially evident in the trust and belief in a science of education as a foundation for educational progress and development. The idea that experiments and statistics could tell the truth about complex and many-sided problem areas, such as the teaching of English, involving a variety of teachers, pupils, schools, rural and urban areas, is symptomatic of trust in scientific methods to solve the problems of education and teaching as well as elsewhere in society.

In spite of the shortcomings, the experimental period served as an introduction to what was to come. The teachers became acquainted with the first visual-aid material, they got used to the idea of different types of English teaching - even if only 'in theory', they experienced that it was possible to teach English to all pupils and that most of them were able to master certain aspects of the language. The interim period of experimental innovation of teaching in a 9-year school was supposed to give a solid foundation on which to build for the future. The results were, however, inconclusive, as they were in the case of the experiments with English in the common school. By the mid sixties, the idea of controlled experimental innovation had given way to a looser concept of innovation development and it became accepted that decisions about future school development would be based on political decisions and not on the outcome of the trying out of different organizational models or even ways of teaching different groups of pupils. The comparative investigation of exam results from different groupings of pupils proved to be the 'cause celebre' of the period, playing right into the hands of the progressive education politicians. The latter wished to see the new comprehensive school system as a really democratic one, integrating everybody. Everybody would receive the same teaching and all the pupils would learn the same, if not by the same means and in the same time. The teaching of English was in this connection crucial, changing from being an elitist school subject to a subject to be mastered and enjoyed by everybody. For, in spite of more or less everybody having lost faith in educational research - except the educational researchers - there were great expectations tied to the possibilities of educational and instructional technology in making English for everybody a practical reality through teaching machines, tape-recorders and, if that did not suffice, there was always the language laboratory.

The scene of the foreign language conferences of the Council of Europe became the meeting place of differing interests: the political and educational-political interests of socialist progressivism, the pedagogical and subject-related economic interest of the expert teacher preparing his or her series of teaching material, the theoretic and technical interest of expert linguists or psychologists experiencing the applications of their research efforts, and the pragmatic interest of the bureaucrat seeing at last some sort of way to solving overriding problems tied to the implementation of English in a new school system.

To understand the role played by the school subject English, as part of and a means of the major school reforms, it is necessary to understand the basic nature and aims of the overriding reform as these were expressed by the education authorities, perhaps more explicitly in Sweden than in Norway. These aims have been defined as 'the furthering of a democratic society in a social democratic direction and giving equal opportunities'.(14) In a situation like this one, 'English' as an elitist subject was a serious obstacle and hindrance to the democratization of education and the furthering of the interests of a social-democratic society.

The definite non-acceptance of any kind of streaming due to intellectual capacities in the basic school is a consequence - making the Norwegian comprehensive school perhaps the most 'democratic' one in the world. The acceptance of this by all political parties may seem a paradox. It is, however, due to the general consensus in questions of education of that period - it probably would not have happened today - as well as to the strong egalitarian streak in the Norwegian society. There have been protests, especially on the part of the parents and the teachers. The latter have found teaching extremely difficult in large undifferentiated classes. The former have complained about the lowering of achievement and standards of knowledge. And there has been some political unrest while the conservatives have been in power. But the forthcoming curriculum revision will not be changing the organizational aspects of the comprehensive school. In the case of English, there will, as already indicated, probably be a change in methodological approach and also in content - re-emphasizing meaning and the subject matter of the text.

In this chapter, I have tried to show how the emerging and redefining of the school subject English was linked to certain broad curriculum issues - related to the needs of society as well as to organizational and ideological educational reforms. My study seems to indicate that research into the history of school subjects must take into account the complexity of societal and educational influences and their interacting effects, as well as the innate history of the subject. In the chapter I have treated only a few aspects of the emergence and redefining of English as a school subject. Even so, the circumstances involved indicate a rejection of the more simplistic explanations of curriculum change.

Notes

(1) Educational reform through the changing of a school subject, Institute for Educational Research, University of Oslo. Supported by the Norwegian Research Council for Science and the Humanities, NAVF.

(2) Several reports are envisaged as part of the study:

a) A survey of the main features of the emergence of the school subject English in the common school from the 1880s to 1954.
b) An account of the experimental innovation programmes and projects in the common school from 1955 onwards.
c) A description of the theoretical climate of foreign language teaching in the fifties and the early sixties from a linguistic, language learning and educational perspective, including an account of the influence exerted by organizations and institutions like the British Council (including the work of the British consultants attached to the Ministry of Education), the assocation of Teachers of English, etc.
d) An account of the rapid development from the mid-sixties till the mid-seventies with its influencing forces and agents like the Council of Europe, the Council for Innovation in Education, etc.
e) A study of the practice of curriculum development and change resulting in the English course of study in the Mønsterplan (1971, 1974).

The present paper is based on the first report: 'A School Subject Called "English"' (January 1985), and the second report, 'Innovation Between School Politics, Research and Praxis' (May 1985) and the draft of part of the fourth report.

(3) By the 1935 Secondary School Education Act.

(4) In 1952, 'the school long term programme' of the Labour Party appeared and compulsory English was one of the main issues. (Langtids-

program for skolen, Det norske arbeiderparti 1952).

(5) This aspect was especially stressed in the bulletins: 'Melding om forsøk i skolen' from the Council for Innovation in Education appearing from 1955 onwards.

(6) Influences can especially be traced through the work of the British Council representatives (from 1946) - and their British advisers attached to the Ministry of Education from 1956. There was an early influence through the writing of H.E. Palmer, especially his 'Principles of Language Study' (1921) and Michael West's 'New Method Material' (1927, 1938). The influence became stronger through the Hornby era and with the publication of 'English Language Teaching' from 1946 and his 'Guide to Patterns and Usage in English' (1954).

(7) The archive material from the association's short-lived activities and proceedings (1937-1969) (in private keeping) has been made available for the present study.

(8) One of the most influencing was Helge Sivertsen, Minister of Education in the Labour Government from 1960-63 and 1963-65.

(9) The following presentation is based on the study of the archive material from the Council's activities and proceedings 1954-62, now in the keeping of the National Archives of Norway (Riksarkivet) in Oslo.

(10) The quotation is from an inspection report, compare note 9.

(11) See for instance:
The work of the Council of Europe in the field of modern languages. Summary Council of Europe. Committee for General and Technical Education, September 1963.

(12) a) Läroplan for grundskolan, Lgr. 69, Allmän del I, Utbildningsforlaget Stockholm 1969, pp.142-145.

b) Normalplanutvalget av 1967. Forslag til Normalplan for grunnskolen, Aschehoug, Oslo 1970, pp.168-189.

(13) Compare note 10.

(14) The quotation is from the Information Journal of the Swedish School Authorities, May 1974. (Aktuellt från skolöverstyrelsen, Specialnummer maj 1974.)

References

Council of Europe,
Course on Final Examinations in Modern Languages in Secondary Education, Ostia 20th-29th April 1966. Report.

Dokka, H. (1951)
Språktest for 5. klasse. Cappelen forlag, Oslo.

Englund, T. (1980)
Medborgerlig läroplanskod för folkskola, försättningsskola och grundskola 1918/19. Forskningsgruppen för läroplansteori och kulturreproduktion, Rapport Nr. 10, Stockholm.

Hornby, A.S. (1954)
A Guide to Patterns and Usage in English. Oxford University Press, London,

English Language Teaching, a Periodical devoted to the teaching of English as a foreign language. A British Council journal from 1946 with A.S. Hornby as editor.

Laereplan for forsøk med 9-årig skole, 1960, 1962, (The experimental curriculum) Aschehoug, Oslo.

Lundgren, U.P. (1979)
Att organisera omvärlden, Liber Publica, Stockholm.

Lundgren, U.P. (1983)
Social Production and Reproduction as a Context for Curriculum Theorizing, Journal of Curriculum Studies, Vol.15, 143-53.

Mønsterplan for grunnskolen, 1971, 1974 (The curriculum for the basic school). Aschehoug, Oslo.

Normalplanen for byfolkeskolen 1939. (The national curriculum for the common school) Aschehoug, Oslo.

Palmer, H.E. (1921)
The Principles of Language Study, Harrap, London
Republished by Oxford University Press, London 1964, edited by R. Mackin.

West, M.
a) (1927) New Method Reader, Longmans Green, London 1935.
b) (1938) New Method Conversation Course, 1938. Longmans Green, London.
c) i samarbeid med J.G. Endicott, (1935). New Methods Dictionary. Longmans Green, London.

4. TENSIONS AND REALIGNMENTS: SCHOOL PHYSICS IN BRITISH COLUMBIA 1955-1980

Patricia M. Rowell
P. James Gaskell

Introduction

In British Columbia, the senior secondary physics courses are usually selected for study by students showing aptitude and interest in the subject, and by students aware that these courses are prerequisite for admission to a variety of post-secondary programs. The orientation and emphases of the secondary physics courses are laid out in government authorized curriculum guides, which prescribe the breadth and depth of the instruction. The courses can be designed so that a broad range of students are interested and successful in them, or alternatively, so that only those students intending to continue in further studies of physics are successful. This study focuses on the events and interactions which resulted in the designation of a particular orientation of school physics as the prescribed curriculum for the province, the maintenance of this official orientation, or version, of school physics for fifteen years, and the strategies employed by individuals and groups to bring about its demise.

In 1964 and 1965, curriculum guides for two sequential, year-long physics courses (Physics 11 and Physics 12) were issued by the provincial Department of Education, replacing the guide for a single one year course, Physics 91. The new courses were based on the American program developed by the Physical Science Study Committee (PSSC), with some additional topics. In order to appreciate the development of the ideas presented in the program, it was necessary for students to be enrolled in both the new courses. Whereas the old course had concentrated on description and information (Province of British Columbia, 1954), the new program intended to pay more attention to the ways in which the principles of physics are derived (Province of British Columbia, 1964). The essence of the new version of physics was that students, by engaging in inquiry-oriented laboratory work and mathematical interpretation of the observations, would develop some understanding of the nature of science and of the ways in which physicists think and work. The emphasis of the previous version had been mastery of concepts, supported by validation-oriented laboratory work. The old version incorporated numerous examples of the applications of major concepts in everyday life, a dimension almost totally neglected in the guide to the new version.

Apart from minor modifications in 1972, which did not entail any shift in orientation, the two sequential physics courses introduced in the sixties remained the guide for school physics in British Columbia for fifteen years. Not until the latter half of 1978 was any official action taken to appoint a committee to review and/or revise the descriptions.

Approval of the emphases and boundaries of school subjects is never unanimous, and as the social, educational and scientific contexts shift with time, certain groups and individuals achieve greater or lesser success in promoting alternative versions of school physics. In this chapter, we explore the influence of changing contexts on the rise and fall of a definition of school physics widely respected within the subject community.

In recent years there has been growing interest in the histories of school subjects (for example, Cooper, 1985; Goodson, 1983, 1985; Goodson and Ball, 1984). This work represents a significant response to Bernstein's remark that 'If we are to take shifts in the content of education seriously, then we require histories of these contents, and their relationship to institutions and symbolic arrangements external to the school' (Bernstein, 1974, p.156).

In the area of school science, studies by Goodson (1983), Layton (1984), McCulloch, Jenkins and Layton (1985), and Waring (1979) have analysed a variety of social influences on English science curricula in the post World War II period. These analyses are in contrast to earlier accounts of curriculum projects viewed as apolitical and essentially progressive developments (for example,

Ogden, 1976). Our study of school physics in British Columbia is distinctive in at least three ways. Firstly, the changes occur in a provincial jurisdiction with a strong tradition of centralized state control over curriculum development and examinations; secondly, provincial educational policy is constitutionally independent of federal policy while the economy is much more dependent on national economic developments; and thirdly, this study focuses on physics, a school subject that has traditionally been seen by its practitioners and by others as being the most difficult and mathematically demanding of the science disciplines.

The prescription of school curricula accompanied by the designation and distribution of school textbooks, specification of examination procedures and authorization of secondary school graduation requirements by the Ministry of Education in British Columbia represents a remarkable centralization of control. This contrasts with the decentralized and diffuse control which has prevailed in England until quite recently. The multiplicity of examining boards in England provides an array of arenas in which struggles for change have taken place. Particular groups may act to garner resources for and to influence the shape of curriculum projects (for example, the English Nuffield Schemes), but local authorities, schools and teachers must still be convinced to adopt the products of these projects. In a centralized system such as that in British Columbia, the curriculum prescriptions authorized by the state cannot be ignored in an examinable subject such as physics although there can be, and is, resistance.

In Canada, the administration and funding of secondary education is a jealously guarded provincial affair. Although there are institutions at the national level which may suggest that the school systems should move in a particular direction (for example, Science Council of Canada, 1984), federal resources are not channelled to the provinces to encourage changes. McKinney and Westbury (1975) in their study of changes in the science curriculum in Gary, Indiana between 1940 and 1970, found that the availability and adequacy of federal money was an important factor in encouraging local change.

Although the financial resources available for the construction and legitimation of school physics in British Columbia are mainly provincial, the intellectual resources available through communication with others are provincial, interprovincial and international. The revision of the B.C. physics curriculum in the sixties was not an isolated incident; similar science curricula revisions occurred throughout Canadian provincial jurisdictions, and indeed, swept across the western world.

Goodson (1983) contends that among the three major traditions within school subjects (academic, utilitarian, and pedagogic) it is the strength of a subject's academic orientation which determines its status and resources. With its early beginnings in Canada as natural philosophy, school physics has acquired a reputation as a theoretical and abstract field of study, successfully shielding itself from any suggestions of utilitarianism. The emphatic demarcation achieved by having school physics offered to university-bound students and taught by science teachers and having electronics, electricity and mechanics offered to job oriented students and taught by industrial education teachers, serves to enhance the status of school physics as an 'elite' subject. However, even for a high-status, academic school subject such as physics, there are struggles among the interested parties for a part in the shaping of the curriculum.

Conceptual Framework

People interested in shaping school subjects are intentional individuals capable of articulating their beliefs, interactions, interests and goals; they are able to describe a perspective from which they take stock of themselves and their world and from which they draw in producing and reproducing their actions. The association of individuals by virtue of shared professional perspectives is a dynamic process, constantly shifting as beliefs and interests are modified. Such modifications among the segments constituting professions are due, suggest Bucher and Strauss (1961) to 'changes in their conceptual and technical apparatus, in the institutional conditions of work, and in their relationship to other segments and occupations'. The notion that the definition of school subjects might be influenced by the character of the communication networks, material endowments, and ideologies of interested individuals and groups was put forward by Musgrove (1968), and subsequently developed by a number of theorists and investigators.

Goodson (1983) has postulated that school subject communities are not 'monolithic entities but shifting amalgamations of subgroups and traditions' (p.3), influencing and changing the boundaries and priorities for subjects. A subject community may be comprised of a variety of subject subgroups with diverse perspectives and interests in the shaping of the school subject; for example, the school physics community would include university physicists, industrial physicists, rural secondary physics teachers, urban secondary physics teachers and science teacher associations.

However, there are other professional groups such as Ministry of Education personnel and school administrators who do not have a particular subject focus but who do have a stake in the definition of school subjects (Connelly et al, 1980). The variety of subject and professional groups with an interest in a school subject can be categorized on the basis of political and professional accountability into internal and external stakeholders (Orpwood and Souque, 1984). For example, Ministry of Education personnel and science teacher groups are internal stakeholders, while university physicists, parents and business organizations are external stakeholders. Coalitions of stakeholders, either internal or external, may form what Reid (1985) has called an educational constituency, 'people who believe that they have interests in common which can be served by certain kinds of more or less uniform curricula' (p.294).

The ability of a constituency to maintain or move to change a particular version of a school subject rests on the extent of its material and cultural capital. In this study we focus on the relations existing within the subject community and in particular, on the tensions between secondary school physics teachers and university physicists around appropriate versions of, and clientele for, school physics. These tensions can be understood in terms of the interactions between individuals in these groups and the organizational structures surrounding them, and their previous life experiences. The acceptance of a version of school physics for a particular clientele is dependent on the formation of a constituency which encompasses groups beyond the subject community. Versions of school physics are modified as changing educational, social and scientific contexts influence the nature of the alliances between groups and, consequently, the power of particular constituencies.

Groups may wield power to influence the course of events through the management of various kinds of resources. These resources include not only material resources such as fiscal funds and territorial properties, but also interpretive and linguistic skills, relevant types of knowledge, status and authority. The unequal distribution of these resources provides some groups with a greater potential to direct, if not control, the course of events. This does not imply, however, that the groups with fewer resources are unable to exert any influence on the turn of events. In some instances, the alignment of groups may result in a pooling of resources to achieve a particular outcome, even though the interests of the groups in that outcome are different.

Context for Change

The need to provide 'a school for every man's child' was officially recognized in the early fifties in British Columbia when a major reorganization of secondary programs was undertaken to offer fulltime studies for all students to the age of fifteen. Students either followed the University Program which fulfilled the entrance requirements for university, or they followed the General Program. Students in both programs were housed under one roof in what had become the characteristic composite Canadian high-school. A vocational program was also offered if facilities and equipment were supplied by the school board.(1)

Secondary education began in Grade 7 (age twelve) with all students taking a common program. Not until Grade 9 (age fourteen) were students designated as being in either the General or University Program. However, there was still sufficient overlap of courses between the two programs that students could transfer between programs at the end of Grade 10 (age fifteen). Parents and students, however, viewed the General Program as inferior to the University Program and as not leading anywhere (Royal Commission on Education, 1960 p. 244), and consequently, 60-70% of secondary students enrolled in the University Program, giving rise to concerns that the standards of the program were being lowered.

British Columbia was experiencing the most

rapid growth of school population in Canada. The average increase in enrolment for the five years prior to 1956-57 was 14,000 a year; in 1957 it was 19,400 students. The demand for new classrooms was met with corresponding cost to the provincial taxpayers, and the demand for more teachers was met by recruiting from other provinces in the United Kingdom.(2) In an effort to upgrade the status of the profession, teacher training moved from the Normal Schools to the College of Education at the University of British Columbia (UBC) in 1956. The university was also beginning to expand at this time, and to pay more attention to developing research activities. Like the school system, the university science departments looked to Britain for their new appointments, and of the eight faculty members added to the physics department between 1954 and 1959, five were British emigrants.(3)

In 1957, a slowing down in construction and a sharp decline in the two principal industries, forestry and mining (Private and Public, 1958) led to increased unemployment and strain on the provincial treasury. The large and growing costs of the province's schools prompted questions about whether these were justified in terms of the results. The successful launching of the Russian Sputnik in 1957 was only one more event which focused attention on the perceived inadequacies of schools to prepare the youth of the province for tomorrow's world. Following the announcement of the appointment of a three-man Royal Commission on Education (RCE), the Minister of Education noted that 'In the light of the grim international competition that lies ahead, it is desirable to have an examination made of our courses of studies, our aims, and our methods ... with a view to strengthening our school system.' (Peterson, 1958). The Commission provided an opportunity for groups and individuals from all sectors of the community to express their views. The diversity of perspectives held by stakeholders in the provincial science curricula as revealed in the briefs to the Commission is discussed in the next section.

Community Concerns of the Fifties

Several years before the apppointment of the Commission, Dr Gordon Shrum, head of the UBC physics department, had expressed his concerns that unless the supply and quality of physics students coming to the university was increased, Canada's economic and military survival would be threatened. (Shrum, 1953, 1954). And in a 1957 talk to the Chilliwack District Teachers' Association, another UBC physicist, Dr Warren, insisted that 'the plain ugly truth is that if we do not encourage our bright your men and women to take up science at school, we shall find our way of life overtaken by one not of our own choosing' (Warren, 1957). The fears that Canada was not providing and retaining a sufficient number of scientists was supported by a survey which reported that in 1956, 54% of industrial establishments were curtailing expansion of production because of shortages in professional staff (Department of Labour, 1957) and by the report that in 1957, about 1800 scientists and engineers left Canada to work in the U.S. (National Science Foundation, 1962). The economic and military arguments of the physicists to the public provided a backdrop for the physicists' complaints to the Commission about the quantity and quality of students taking physics at the university. (RCE Brief 240, p.1).

Although more vigorous selection procedures could improve the quality of students entering physics, how could the quantity be increased? The physics professors felt that too many of the bright students were being turned away from science by uninspired and out-of-date teaching: for example, the head of the physics department of UBC concluded, 'It seems obvious that the lack of scientific training of our teachers, and particularly our science teachers, must be the main contributing factor in keeping students from choosing a career in science' (RCE Brief 145, p.2).

The thrust of the argument of the university physicists was that 'The school curriculum in science is not nearly as important a factor as the qualifications of the teachers' (RCE Brief 145, p.4). Explicit comments about the existing curriculum did not challenge its orientation. In fact, the first year course instructors said, 'Inspection of the present Physics 92 syllabus shows that a student who has mastered this course should be relatively well prepared for entry to Physics 101' (RCE Brief 240, p.2). The use of laboratories was not emphasized although it was suggested that there be more frequent labs 'in which the student himself performs the experiments' (p.2).

The perspective of the university physicists

towards secondary science teaching in the fifties focused predominantly on a perceived need to increase the quantity and quality of physics teachers in order to increase the number of academically able students studying physics at the university. The lack of criticism of the existing Physics 91 course in either its content or pedagogical style is remarkable given the revision that was about to be undertaken.

It is not surprising that the briefs (or portions of briefs) to the Commission submitted by science teacher groups showed more divergence than those of the university physicists. At the time of the Commission, there was only one university physics department in the province, whereas the teachers were scattered in locations with vastly differing economic and cultural resources and varying degrees of geographical isolation. The teachers were concerned not only about who should take what kind of senior secondary science, but also about the conditions of instruction.

Aware of the criticism being levelled at them from the university community, teachers wanted assurance that they would be working with academically motivated students. A majority of teacher groups recommended the streaming of students into alternative science courses offered to students not requiring pre-university preparation. (RCE Briefs 57, 113, 282, 299, 307). One group suggested that comprehensive examinations be employed to effect the streaming (RCE Brief 57). The idea of differentiated science courses, emanating from individuals associated with large urban institutions, must have appeared fanciful to the teachers of rural schools where the advanced science courses were often only taught alternate years because of low enrolments.

Teachers also wanted more time for instructing the science courses, and recommendations were forwarded for extending the length of study in the senior sciences to two years (RCE Briefs 163, 186, 231). Although not all science teacher groups were in favour of differentiated science courses, there did seem to be a consensus about the need for extending the length of study time. One argument in favour of longer courses was that more laboratory work could be included (RCE Brief 57). The opinion that experimental work by students should be an integral component of school science emerged in a number of briefs from local teacher oganizations (RCE Briefs 57, 112, 282, 330), balanced by concerns about the safety of such activities and the demands placed on teachers (RCE Briefs 57, 112, 327). In the late fifties, the state of laboratories in even the urban schools was cause for distress.(4) The practice of converting small classrooms to science laboratories, and the lack of up-to-date equipment was deplored by teachers (RCE Brief 112).

The suggestion that 'somewhere in the senior science courses a more militant attitude toward the moral aspect of science should be presented to the students' (RCE Brief 330, p.149) was a lone indicator that some science teachers in the province recognized the social implications of scientific advance and the possible obligations of school science.

All in all, there were few complaints in the briefs about the form of the advanced courses. However, some physics teachers were beginning to experiment with alternatives. One teacher recalls his impressions when he began teaching physics in an urban high school in the fifties: "Physics 91 - it's so anaemic that I decided not to teach it at all. I told my class they could put the book aside - we weren't going to follow the book at all" (Boldt, 1984). This teacher engaged his predominantly university bound students in individual research projects in the laboratory, using equipment borrowed from the university. Preparation for the provincial scholarship examinations was done in the couple of months preceding them. When the PSSC materials became available in the late fifties, they were incorporated into this teacher's course. A second Vancouver teacher requested that a special class of above average students be assembled so that he could teach the mandated physics program in the first part of the year, and devote the remainder of the year to PSSC laboratory activities (Ryniak, 1983). This teacher and his colleague in another lower mainland school, who was also incorporating PSSC labs into his classes for university bound students, were later to become influential members of the physics revision committee.

While physics teachers in urban schools large enough to stream the university bound, science oriented students were looking for materials to challenge the imaginations of their elite clientele, other teachers were searching for ideas which would kindle interest among students either unable or disinclined to relate to the theoretical dimensions of science. These teachers recognized that it was possible to de-emphasize reading and arithmetical skills in a course focused on the technological applications of science (Winteringham, 1984), and that students 'usually considered not capable of coping with science, could be led along lines of investigations tailored partly to his needs and partly to his interests' (RCE Brief 57, p.10). There was a widespread but unco-ordinated body of opinion supporting more science for the 'non-academic' student, although the form which such courses should adopt was rarely articulated beyond the 'practical' emphasis.

The concerns about school science expressed to the Commission were reflections of the interests of various groups. The university, anxious to expand into research, conveyed concern about the quantity and quality of an elite group of students bound for postsecondary education. The university viewed the upgrading of teacher qualifications as an important strategy for improving the quality of instruction, whereas the teachers of university bound students considered the time and facilities available for instruction to be key factors in improving the level of achievement. These teachers advocated streaming of university bound students so that the pacing of the course should not be hindered by 'average' students. Teachers of students oriented towards the 'practical' were seeking to legitimate experientially based knowledge which strained the boundaries of traditionally accepted school science.

Although the Commission found much to criticize in the B.C. public school system, its lengthy investigation did not reveal any widespread failure on the part of the schools (Royal Commission on Education, 1960, p.441). In its report, the Commission rejected the trend of progressive education, noting that trends which go too far have to be counterbalanced. Such counterbalancing was to be achieved by reasserting the value of intellectual development through the basic subjects of the curriculum, and by stemming the tide of diffuseness which characterized the multiplicity of course electives. It was one thing to make a course interesting to students, but quite another if the hard work required for mastery was dispensed with! The Commission acknowledged that the presence in the University Program of 'so many pupils whose talents are not suited for academic studies has impaired the value of the program for superior students and has tended to lower its standards' (Royal Commission on Education, 1960, p.244). In order to deal with this and related problems, the Commission recommended that the school program undergo a reorganization which would ensure effective streaming of pupils by examinations after Grade 7. The Commissioners considered that too many elective courses were offered in the secondary program, and recommended that these be reduced so that more time could be devoted to the core (English and mathematics) and inner subjects (science, social studies and languages). Moreover, those electives remaining in the program would be 'relevant to university courses, so that pupils might select their subjects in terms of the fields of study they planned to enter at university' (Royal Commission on Education, 1960, p.275). The Commissioners found the senior science courses to be 'well-designed'. The criticism that many university science undergraduates seemed to be inadequately prepared was attributed to the packing of too much content into too short a time, and the Commissioners recommended that the advanced courses be extended in length from one to two years. Although the Commissioners noted that many of the secondary science teachers they visited were 'fully qualified, well informed and interested in the recent developments in their fields' (p.314), they recommended that all secondary science teachers have at least the equivalent of a university major in some science field, and preferably an honours degree in science. The Commissioners also recommended that proper arrangements for laboratory space be made, noting that 'no other field should take precedence over science with regard to the adequacy of the facilities that are made available in the schools' (p.108).

And so, although the Royal Commission did not call for a major overhaul of any of the advanced science curricula, it did offer a framework in which specialization could be extended, and in which the highlighting of intellectual rather than applied features of the disciplines would be acceptable. The Commission endorsed the notion of selective education, in which an elite group could be specifically prepared for university admission. But neither in the briefs to the Commission nor in the Report was there any hint of the impending redirection of the physics curriculum. How this was accomplished will be explored in the next section.

Physics for the Physicists

Collaboration between city teacher and university physicist was not uncommon in the sixties; close professional and social bonds were formed during the summer examination marking sessions in the provincial capital. The experienced teachers who were invited to assist with the marking of examinations valued the stimulating discussions of the scholarship questions. In 1960, informal discussions continued long after the marking was completed, and it was from this group of concerned instructors that the Department of Education selected a committee to approve a new text for the Grade 13 course (5), since the authorized text was going out of print. Having completed its assigned task, this same committee turned its attention to the physics sections of the general science program in Grades 8, 9 and 10, and to the senior physics courses. Two of the three teachers on the committee had acquired and used PSSC materials in their classes of university bound students, and were sympathetic to the physicists' concerns for recruiting top students. The Faculty of Education member (G.H. Cannon) had attended a PSSC funded conference in Montreal in 1960 where he established contacts with the PSSC in Massachusetts. One of the three university physicist members (D.L. Livesey) had spent the winter of 1960-61 working on PSSC materials with Educational Services Incorporated (ESI) (6) in Massachusetts. Although the physics revision committee was not officially reappointed until the summer of 1962, Livesey presented a summer course for physics teachers based on the PSSC program in 1961.

Before the authorization of the new course in 1964, Livesey again conducted PSSC summer courses for teachers in 1962 and 1963, and persuaded the Department of Education to purchase PSSC films for use in the schools. Using the summer courses to evaluate the use of PSSC materials and equipment by practising physics teachers, Livesey prepared himself and a core of supportive practitioners for a redirecting of school physics. (7) The Commission Report, in recommending a two year program for the advanced sciences, opened the way for the committee to prepare two sequential laboratory-oriented courses incorporating much of the PSSC materials. Unable to obtain permission from ESI to incorporate parts of the copyrighted PSSC laboratory guide in the B.C. laboratory manual, Livesey, Cannon and Ryniak (a teacher) resigned (8) from the physics revision committee in January 1963 to rewrite the PSSC laboratory guides and to supplement them with new experimental investigations. Ten months later, Book One of A Laboratory Course in Physics (Livesey, Cannon and Ryniak, 1964) had been compiled and circulated, together with a preliminary basic equipment list. A preliminary draft of Book Two (1965) also had been prepared for review by the Revision Committee.

The composition of this physics revision committee with its four university professors, three teachers and provincial Assistant Superintendent for Schools, raised quite a few eyebrows at the time of its appointment. Although university professors had been members of former revision committees, they had never outnumbered the teachers.(9) In the context of persistent criticism from the university community, the provincial Director of Curriculum had decided to retain the university dominated committee originally set up to revise the university equivalent Grade 13 course. To the executive members of the B.C. Teachers' Federation (BCTF) this committee was something of a setback. Representation on curriculum revision committees had been a bone of contention for many years as the Federation struggled to achieve professional status. By the late fifties, the pattern of establishing a committee involved the nomination of one or two teachers by the Federation, further nominations from District Superintendents of Schools, and the selection of six or eight people by the Department of Education to form the committee. The Federation maintained that the selection of teachers for curriculum committees should be the responsibility of the Federation in consultation with the Director of Curriculum (RCE Brief 327, p.18). Moreover, the BCTF wanted the work on curriculum revision to be done during the summer, with remuneration for the work, instead of the voluntary participation of teachers during the school year.(10) Implicit in the Federation's argument was the assumption that such teachers would be acting on the committees as Federation representatives, with the responsibility to articulate Federation policy and the authority to report back.

Although the teacher organizations had gained the right to nominate some of the teachers for appointment to curriculum committees, the Department of Education maintained tight control of the flow of information, and there was no regular reporting of committee activities to the rank and file membership.(11) The B.C. Science Teachers' Association (BCScTA), a subject specialist oganization within the BCTF also had no rights to direct representation on Department of Education curriculum committees. When the BCScTA (formed in 1959) established subcommittees to examine changes occurring in biology and chemistry curricula, a similar subcommittee for physics was not set up because there was already an informal group of physics instructors in existence. It was from this group of teachers whose interests in providing challenge to the university bound students were closely aligned with the physics professors that the three committee members were selected. It was primarily the teachers' links with the university physicists and not their membership in the BCScTA which resulted in their committee appointment. The BCScTA was not formally consulted nor did it formally debate the decision to adopt a PSSC-based program offered sequentially in two year long courses.

One of the basic assumptions of the original group of discussants prior to the appointment of the physics revision committee was that a likely outcome of the Royal Commission would be the adoption of more rigid streaming in the secondary school. If this occurred, then it followed that a series of differentiated physics courses would be required.(12) However, when the Department of Education officials met with the Professional Committee on Secondary Curriculum (13) to discuss the Commission's recommendations affecting school reorganization, they received a generally negative reaction to any proposal entailing rigid streaming by examination. The character of the composite high school would remain, with the University/ General Program division replaced by a six track sequence in the final two years. The senior science courses available to students in the new academic/technical program would be designed to satisfy university admission requirements. When the curriculum committees for physics, chemistry and biology met with the Director of Curriculum to receive their terms of reference, they were instructed to give top priority to developing courses which would preserve the integrity of the disciplines, and "not to be too unduly concerned at first as to which pupils would be taking certain courses" (Meredith, 1963). However, in the minds of the physics revision committee members (Livesey, 1983), the new senior program was intended for the top 25% of the high school population, and especially for "the student who is beginning to work in physics as a discipline" (Province of British Columbia, 1965, p.7). Although the science section of the BCTF had raised the matter of science for university bound arts oriented students and non-university bound students almost every year since the 1952 reorganization, they were divided on the issue, and a motion for the retention of a second year of general science was defeated at the Annual General Meeting in 1962.(14)

Schooling of the Discipline

On the whole, physics teachers were enthusiastic about the revised program introduced in 1964 (Physics 11) and 1965 (Physics 12). Those who had attended Livesey's summer courses were converts to the cause of 'new' physics, in which teachers and students would be active inquirers. Their enthusiasm was contagious, not least because implementation of the program called for new equipment and laboratories. Instead of teaching a single year of disciplinary physics, teachers would now teach two, and in large urban schools this meant a reduction in the number of general science classes taught by the specialist oriented teachers. Since only a handful of teachers had been involved with the revision process and there had not been any piloting of the new materials in the classroom prior to the province-wide authorization, the general enthusiasm was for an unknown set of materials which promised the excitement of contemporary physics and the challenge of laboratory-based teaching.

The challenge was, in many instances, greater than had been anticipated. Responses from physics teachers to the BCScTA's questionnaires (15) in the first couple of years of the new program indicated concerns about the preparedness of teachers for instructing the 'new' physics. Although there had been several summer courses, less than half the province's physics teachers had attended them.(16) Teachers found that their workload was considerably heavier in terms of marking and laboratory preparation, and suggested that lack of time resulted in inadequate preparation for laboratory classes. With students commencing the study of disciplinary physics one year earlier than previously, the teachers found that students' mathematical skills were often insufficient for the analysis required to complete the laboratory investigations. Moreover, a number of teachers found the new approach inappropriate for the 'non-academic' student, and called for a return to the old course for such students. Some teachers actively discouraged students other than those expecting to study university science from registering in Physics 11 and 12. School administrators and counsellors were advised by physics teachers that the program was for future scientists, and 'not one for those who merely wish to acquire some knowledge of physics' (Allan, 1965).

The need to work out the difficulties associated with implementing the new program was recognized by both the university physicists and the supporting teachers. Workshop activity of the kind which had occurred in the U.S.A. some years previously was promoted thoughout the province in 1966-67, funded by a grant from ESI to Livesey and backing from the BCScTA. University physicists and teachers spoke at more than twenty weekend sessions in seventeen locations, all of which were well attended. The largest school board in the province sponsored a weekly night class for city teachers for two years following the introduction of the new courses, providing an opportunity for teachers to work through and discuss the problems of the laboratory exercises. It was not the intention of the workshops to question either the version of physics presented or the pedagogy intrinsic to the course, but rather to bolster the confidence of the teachers. As one workshop co-ordinator noted 'The workshop is not intended as a wailing wall for decrying the new physics program, but rather to seek ways of rendering these courses most effective' (Brown, 1966).

Evaluating student achievement in a laboratory-oriented course was seen to be a major difficulty in the new program. The physicists and teachers educated in the U.K. were accustomed to the idea of a 'practical' component in secondary examinations, but such a notion had never become accepted in B.C., and Livesey gave up any hope of introducing a laboratory examination as part of the government Grade 12 examinations.

The provincial examinations in 1966 were limited to a proportion of Grade 12 students and scholarship candidates.(17) Since examinations for the revised physics curriculum did not substantially reflect the inquiry approach, teachers were inclined to side-step the 'discovery' aspect, anticipating problems before students handled equipment. This teacher-guided, pre-planning of student laboratory activities was defended on the grounds that such anticipation saved time by helping students avoid mistakes; it also provided clear goals for students who lacked either initiative or understanding.(18) The labtext instructions for the laboratory investigations were frequently not understood by students, teachers claimed, and at the end of an investigation students were often left 'hanging' with no leading questions to help guide them to their conclusions.(19) And so, many teachers abandoned the inquiry approach, in which only a minority of students could perform successfully, in favour of the more traditional mastery of concepts orientation, in which a majority of students could succeed.

The enrolment pattern in the two physics courses was something of a surprise to all concerned; fewer than half of the students who completed the first year of the program went on to the second year. This pattern reflected the fact that many students studying Physics 11 were doing so for a variety of institutional and personal reasons such as the need to complete a Grade 11 science course to graduate on the academic/technical program. Most such students did not feel intellectually compelled to enrol in Physics 12 to learn the end of the story. As a consequence, the students in Physics 12 were even more elite and homogeneous in terms of their interest and aptitude in physics than had been those in Physics 91.(20)

The two year program introduced in 1964/65 was to stay in place for fifteen years. In the next section we look at the features which facilitated this stability, and contemplate the context in which change became a possibility.

Social Relations in the Seventies

British Columbia in the seventies was in a state of flux: the massive economic expansion of the previous decade had slowed, and with it the demand for technicians and scientists. School enrolments levelled off and the demand for teachers slackened. Recognition that the scientific enterprise had the potential to create as many new problems as the old ones it solved gave rise to the environmental movement and generated anti-science opinions among secondary students. As the decade progressed, the critical awareness of the role of science included the impact of technological developments, raising questions about the adequacy of student preparation for this new form of 'literacy'.

The early years of the decade had seen a relaxation of the tight governmental control of curriculum development. Legislation which permitted school districts to develop courses of interest to specific communities resulted in a proliferation of locally developed courses and adaptations of the provincial courses.(21) This transfer of initiative from central to local government was facilitated by a restructuring of graduation requirements to provide more flexibility in program selection, and by the removal of the Grade 12 government examinations. With the move towards decentralization, the BCTF saw an opportunity to further alternative definitions of curriculum. With respect to science, for example, it advocated a change in focus 'from pure science to "sciencing with a social conscience"' (Church, 1974). However, although the removal of external examinations permitted alternative definitions of school physics, the majority of physics teachers used the increased flexibility to redistribute the time available for mandated topics in terms of their own priorities. This resulted in the reduction or even elimination of some portions of the curriculum, but not in any significant reshaping of the program. The increased flexibility also resulted in a diverse selection of texts for the physics courses, in addition to the prescribed labtext (Livesey, Cannon and Ryniak, 1972) and reference text (Physical Science Study Committee, 1965).

With a declining economy and growing unemployment, the provincial school system was increasingly criticized for a perceived drop in standards. The universities were perturbed by their lack of control over the standard of admission requirements to the postsecondary institutions (now three universities and seven community colleges). The UBC physics department contemplated setting its own entrance examinations but found the prospect administratively daunting. The concerns of the university physicists were not allayed by the findings of a survey (Matthews, 1975) conducted by a postsecondary subcommittee which indicated that teachers did indeed make their own adaptations of the course. The subcommittee endorsed the laboratory orientation of the physics program, but recommended to the Ministry of Education that about 70% of the program be designated as mandatory 'core' with time allocations for instruction of specified topics. A physics review committee appointed by the Advisory Committee on the Secondary Curriculum to examine the recommendations of the postsecondary subcommittee reported that there did not appear to be any significant difficulties with the physics program, and it was not the time for modifying the physics curriculum (Naylor, 1985).

A new series of workshops for physics teachers at Simon Fraser University brought together a group anxious to keep up-to-date with developments in physics and to discuss the pedagogical difficulties encountered in the subject. Independent of, but backed by the BCScTA, the group discussed the alternative texts in use and the inappropriateness of the two year program for many students. A suggestion by a member of the group's steering committee to a Ministry of Education curriculum consultant that a revision of the secondary physics curriculum should be undertaken was immediately rebuffed on the ground that such recommendations could only be considered if put forward by the BCScTA through the BCTF (Fisher, 1985). Within the organizational framework of the BCScTA, the group solicited support for revision of the physics curriculum by means of a survey designed to illustrate the disparities existing in time allocations, texts, and espoused goals of teachers. At a time when the government was responding to calls for 'accountability' in the administration of the province's schools by reinstating centralized control in the form of a 'core' curriculum (Ministry of Education, 1976), such disparities would be hard to ignore. The BCScTA had officially opposed the decentralization trend, arguing in favour of a provincially defined core which identified major concepts in terms of intended learning outcomes, and welcomed the return to standardized curricula. Claiming that the responses to the survey indicated a necessity for the immediate formation of a physics revision committee (even though 70% of the responding teachers indicated satisfaction with Physics 11, and 80% with Physics 12), the BCScTA committee of physics teachers urged that new texts be selected, that the sequential pattern of the two courses be changed, and that more attention be paid to the 'relevance' of physics in the world of the student. It was not at all clear that the physics teachers wanted a total re-orienting of the courses, but they did want a new text.

Within weeks of the BCScTA's call for appointment of a physics revision committee, the results of a province-wide, government sponsored science assessment (Hobbs et al, 1978) were released. In this report was confirmation that student understanding of the applications of physical principles was weak, particularly among the majority of students not registered in senior physical science courses. In addition, attention was drawn to the exceptionally low enrolment of female students in physics courses. As in the BCScTA's questionnaire, teachers displayed a general satisfaction with the senior physics courses, although 63% of the teachers indicated that an alternative, more general version would be appropriate for many students. Only 13% of the physics teachers wanted to retain the existing course exclusively. The content of these two reports, released in rapid succession, highlighting the poor performance of provincial students in conceptualizing and applying physical principles, and questioning the selectivity of the clientele for the existing physics courses, was not easily ignored by the Ministry of Education. Moreover, the senior biology and chemistry programs had undergone major revisions during the seventies, entailing shifts away from the discovery approach and sequential courses. Taking into consideration the dissatisfaction of the teachers with the authorized text, the critical reports of performance and selectivity, and the governments's concern for accountability, the Ministry of Education decided that, all in all, it was 'time' to appoint a physics revision committee.

Discussion

The introduction of the 'new' physics into the secondary schools of British Columbia in 1964, and its subsequent decline fifteen years later, may be understood in terms of the educational constituency supporting school physics as a subject preparatory for university physics. Three features of this constituency must be considerered: first, what were the commonalities and differences among the members of the constituency; second, how was the constituency sustained; third, how did contextual shifts affect the effectiveness of the constituency?

School physics teachers and university physicists share a commitment to preserving the integrity, high status and viability of physics as a field of study in their respective institutions. University physicists in the past sought to protect the boundaries of the discipline by defining physics for engineering students, while school physics teachers resisted incorporation into joint physical science programs. University physicists imposed severe restrictions on the entrance to honors programs, and high school counsellors directed only the most able students towards school physics. University physicists and physics teachers share a belief that physics is the fundamental science.

However, given the different surroundings in which they work, teachers and physicists are likely to hold divergent views of other aspects of the school subject. From their occupational experiences, certain elements of their practices assume more significance than others. Assumptions about the nature of students and schooling, and the purpose of school physics are reflected in any version of school physics considered appropriate for provincial prescription. University physicists have tended to view school physics as a selective recruiting ground for the most committed and able students. Inasmuch as the quality of students entering the university physics program could be maintained by the administration of selective examinations, the physicists in the fifties were not unduly concerned about the mandated version of school physics. In comparison with other school science subjects, enrolment was low but the success rate was relatively high. The physicists were more concerned about the ability of teachers to recruit sufficient numbers of academically able students. The physicists wanted assurance that, above everything else, the secondary teachers would have more than an adequate background in the disciplinary field. In their view, the teachers' task was to transform the classroom into the exciting world of the physicist.

The physics teachers of the fifties were confronted with far from ideal conditions for challenging students with the principles of the physical world. In understaffed and ill-equipped schools they dealt with a wide range of students, teaching not only physics, but mathematics, chemistry and general science. Despite its high status, teachers were dissatisfied with the one year physics course since there was little in it which identified school physics with the activities of contemporary physicists. The teachers wanted to re-establish school physics as a subject distinctly 'science', and closely linked to the parent discipline. The 'doing' of science in the form of investigative laboratory activities was thought to be the key to this distinctiveness, and the informal availability of PSSC materials from south of the border provided support for this belief. From a pedagogical standpoint, 'doing' science was regarded favourably, although whether and what, students learned via these activities was not known.

The constituency supporting school physics as preparatory for university physics was substantially strengthened by the recommendations of the Royal Commission in 1960, which articulated the belief that the function of schooling was to develop the intellect in preparation for further training and work. The Royal Commission acted as a counter to the trend in which schools were seen to be assuming an increasingly varied number of functions. By identifying science as an 'inner' subject, by lengthening the senior science courses, and by recommending rigid streaming of senior students, the Royal Commission enhanced the perspectives of the people appointed to the physics revision committee, particularly with respect to the need for the development of a challenging version of school physics. The dominance of physics teachers with university connections and university physicists on the committee reflected the government's perception that in a decade of demand for technical and military survival, the university physicists could provide the best advice on an introductory program to the discipline. The urban teachers appointed to the committee were held in high esteem by physicists and teacher colleagues, and in their knowledge and beliefs were hardly representative of the teachers so roundly criticized in the Royal Commission briefs. The alliance of this unrepresentative group of teachers and physicists, backed by a government anxious to invest in human capital, made possible the introduction of an ahistorical, decontextual course of studies which emphasized the structure of the discipline. The physicists were satisfied that the program could challenge and select the most able students; the teachers were satisfied that the school subject could involve 'doing' physics with up-to-date materials and laboratories, and the government was reassured that it could be seen to be responding to the Royal Commission's emphasis on intellectual pursuits while deflecting the pressure for rigid streaming and selection which would put a severe strain on small, rural schools.

The introduction of a single version of physics throughout the province presented significant problems for many teachers in terms of the appropriateness of the course for their diverse clientele, many of whom were not interested in studying for two years. The committee members, anticipating that teachers would need assistance and encouragement to adopt an open-ended laboratory approach to the program, embarked on an extensive series of workshops which reinforced the school-university link and boosted the identity of school physics with the parent discipline. The annual gathering of teachers and physicists for marking of examinations also contributed to the sustenance of the constituency. But even though it had become apparent to many that the mandated version of school physics was inappropriate for all but a very select clientele, the constituency was not openly challenged until after the removal of government examinations, when teachers responded by rearranging the sequence of the course contents, modifying the experimental investigations, and incorporating alternative texts.

In British Columbia as elsewhere, the influence of the constituency which views school physics as the training ground for university physics waxes and wanes with the times. The complex interdependence of action and circumstance is not readily explicated in the case of an educational constituency. Intertwined around the actions of individual participants are lines of accountability linked in turn to the economic and cultural health of the province. When the acute shortage of scientific and technical personnel was deemed to threaten the nation's progress in the fifties, the alliance of urban teachers and university physicists was able to draw on the accountable central government to back its version of physics for the recruitment of the elite clientele. But in the seventies, in the face of a declining economy and lack of employment for scientific professionals, the call by post-secondary physics instructors to reaffirm the purpose of school physics as preparatory for further studies in the discipline was not heeded. The individuals accountable for provincial education were attending to the mounting criticism of the standards of schooling and of the lack of relevance of school curricula to society's ills. Assembling a rationale for revision which rang true with the concerns of the central authorities, teachers who wanted a version of school physics which would appeal to a broader clientele called for standardization through prescription of texts and course content, and increased attention to the applications of science in social issues. Unlike the sixties, when the BCScTA was barely established and the BCTF was still struggling for provincial representation, in the seventies a collective teacher authority was recognized by the government. The organizational and intellectual resources of the teacher organizations ensured that however well qualified, such an unrepresentative revision committee as that of the sixties could not be appointed. The absence of university physicists in the initial appointments to the 1979 Revision Committee was an indication of the apparent decline in the ability of the constituency for university physics to define the purpose of school physics. Not only did the constituency no longer mediate the perceived needs of an ailing economy, it was no longer perceived by the central authorities as the justification for mandating an elitist version of school physics as the only version for the provincial secondary school population. Given that declining student enrolments and reduced educational funding had decreased further the feasibility of differentiated science courses in the majority of provincial secondary schools, the central authorities sought to shift the legitimation of the mandated version of school physics away from the disciplinary authority of the university.

The change in economic conditions, coupled with the institutional framework of the schools, drew attention to the role of physics instruction in the schools. Groups responding to the needs of a diverse clientele, rather than to a need to preserve the 'integrity' of the discipline, challenged the interests of the prevailing constituency and raised the notion of alternative versions of school physics. The evolution of a new constituency capable of reshaping the school subject will be dependent on the working out of tensions between adherents to differing versions and the generation of shared interests.

Reference Notes

1. High school graduation in 1958 required the satisfactory completion of prescribed and elective courses to a minimum total of 120 credits in Grades 9 to 12. Prescribed courses (minimum 85 credits) included four in English, three in social studies, three in health and personal development, three in mathematics, and one in science (general science). In addition, the University Program required a second course in science (general science), and two courses in a second language. Elective subjects were chosen from the fields of agriculture, commerce, home economics, industrial arts, vocational program, and advanced courses in the academic disciplines. The latter included the senior courses in biology, chemistry, or physics.

2. In the three years 1955, 1956, 1957, more than two hundred teachers emigrated to British Columbia from the United Kingdom.

3. In the year 1954-55, the UBC physics department was staffed by fifteen faculty members. In 1959-60, there were twenty-three faculty members, of whom eleven had received their education and training in the United Kingdom.

4. In 1956, in a city high school with a student enrolment of 1,000, there was one science laboratory.

5. Grade 13 courses were the old Senior Matriculation courses, and supposed to be equivalent to corresponding courses at the university; thus Physics 101, the first year university general physics course could also be offered in senior secondary schools.

6. Educational Services Incorporated (ESI) was the non-profit organization authorized to produce and publish materials for the federally funded Physical Science Study Committee in the U.S.A.

7. In most instances, the School Boards employing the teachers attending Livesey's summer courses at UBC agreed to pay the cost of the

equipment needed for the PSSC course. The teacher returned to the school with this equipment as an example of the 'new' physics.

8. Resignation from Department committees was standard practice for those intending to author textbooks; this maintained the illusion that textbook adoption was on a competitive basis.

9. The 1953 Physics Revision Committee was composed of four teachers and one physics professor.

10. The Science Teachers' Section of the BCTF strongly disapproved of appointing full-time teachers to serve on revision committees. They recommended that committee members be given leave of absence with full pay.

11. The BCScTA was virtually excluded from the discussions on the physics curriculum change. Questioned at a February 1962 meeting, Curriculum Director, J.R. Meredith, replied that it was 'possible' that PSSC principles might be incorporated into a new course. In March 1963, the BCScTA Newsletter reported that 'a Grade 11 and 12 course along the lines of PSSC is being drawn up. The textbook and lab manual will be written locally'.

12. The idea of an alternative, broader university physics program for prospective teachers was also put forward.

13. The Professional Committee on the Secondary Curriculum was comprised of representatives from all the major organizations concerned with provincial education.

14. With little fanfare and minimal preparation, the government introduced an Industrial Science course as a compulsory component in two of the Industrial Education programs in 1965, which satisfied the expectations of neither the I.E. nor the science departments of secondary schools.

15. The chairman of the BCScTA curriculum committee constructed a series of questionnaires,

distributed to physics teachers in September 1965, January 1966 and May 1966. Questions were asked about the perceptions of, and pedagogical difficulties associated with, different sections of the new text, and also about physics instruction in general.

16. In addition to the UBC summer courses in 1961, 1962, 1963, the recently established University of Victoria offered a short course in PSSC physics in the summer of 1964, and a similar course was offered in Burnaby later the same summer by Livesey and Glover. Also that summer, Livesey instructed a course at UBC entitled Recent Developments in Physics.

17. High school meeting required standards acquired accreditation by the Department of Education. Accredited schools were allowed to 'recommend' the marks of up to 60% of Grade 12 students with a C standing or better in any course, in lieu of external examination.

18. Responses to 1966 questionnaire.

19. Workshop reports.

20. In 1953, 25% of students enrolled in English 92 were enrolled in Physics 91; in 1958, the proportion was 35% and in 1971, the proportion was 11%.

21. A large number of forestry and environmental education courses were introduced in the mid-seventies. Harvard Project Physics, piloted at a West Vancouver school in 1967, remained as an alternative Grade 11 physics course in that school. Alternative physics courses at the Grade 11 level were authorized for use in three other secondary schools.

The support of the Social Sciences and Humanities Research Council of Canada in funding this research is gratefully acknowledged.

Bibliography

Allan, E.N.G. (1965)
Comments on Physics 11 course prepared for the Principal of Lake Cowichan Secondary School.

Bernstein, B. (1974)
'Sociology and the sociology of education: a brief account' in Rex, J. (Ed.) Approaches to Sociology.
London, Routledge & Kegan Paul pp.145-159.

Boldt, W. (1984), Interview, March 15.

Brown, A.C.M. (1966)
Announcement of Physics workshop held at Shawnigan Lake, Vancouver Island, October 29.

Bucher, R. and Strauss, A. (1961)
'Professions in process' American Journal of Sociology, 66, January pp.325-334.

Church, J.S. (1974)
'Curriculum development - the role of the BCTF' B.C. Science Teacher. 16(3) pp.22-25.

Connelly, F.M., Irvine, F.G. and Enns, R.J. (1980)
'Stakeholders in curriculum' in Connelly, F.M., Dukacz, A.S. and Quinlan, F. (Eds.) Curriculum Planning for the Classroom
Toronto, OISE Press pp.44-55.

Cooper, B. (1985)
Renegotiating Secondary School Mathematics
London, Falmer Press.

Department of Labour (1957)
'Skilled and professional manpower in Canada, 1945-65'. Report prepared by the Economic and Research Branch for the Royal Commission on Canada's Economic Prospects,
Ottawa, Queen's Printer.

Fisher, N. (1985), Interview, February 18.

Goodson, I.F. (1983)
School Subjects and Curriculum Change
London, Croom Helm.

Goodson, I.F. (Ed.) (1985)
Social Histories of the Secondary Curriculum
London, Falmer Press.

Goodson, I.F. and Ball, S.J. (Eds.) (1984)
Defining the Curriculum
London, Falmer Press.

Hobbs, E.D., Boldt, W.B., Erickson, G.L., Quelch, T.P. and Sieben, G.A. (1978)

British Columbia Science Assessment Summary Report.
Victoria, British Columbia Ministry of Education, B.C.
Layton, D. (1984)
Interpreters of Science
John Murray Ltd. and the Association for Science Education.
Livesey, D.L. (1983), Interview, May 25.
Livesey, D.L., Cannon, G.H. and Ryniak, T. (1964)
A Laboratory Course in Physics. Book One
Vancouver, Copp Clark.
Livesey, D.L., Cannon, G.H. and Ryniak, T. (1965)
A Laboratory Course in Physics. Book Two
Vancouver, Copp Clark.
Livesey, D.L., Cannon, G.H. and Ryniak, T. (1972)
A Laboratory Course in Physics.
Vancouver, Copp Clark.
McCulloch, G., Jenkins, E. and Layton, D. (1985)
Technological Revolution
London, Falmer Press.
McKinney, W.L. and Westbury, I. (1975)
'Stability and change: the public schools for Gary Indiana, 1940-1970' in Reid, W.A. and Walker D.F. (Eds.) Case Studies in Curriculum Change: Great Britain and the United States
London, Routledge & Kegan Paul.
Matthews, P. (Chairman) (1975)
The Subcommittee on the High School Physics Curriculum; Report submitted to the Physics Articulation Committee and the Colleges and Universities of B.C., May 17.
Meredith, J.R. (1963)
Report of the First Meeting (1963-64) of the Science Committees.
Vancouver. October 10.
Ministry of Education (1976)
What Should Our Children be Learning?
Victoria, Queen's Printer.
Musgrove, F. (1968)
'The contribution of sociology to the study of curriculum' in Kerr, J.F. (Ed.) Changing the Curriculum
London, University of London Press pp.96-109.
National Science Foundation (1962)
'Scientific manpower from abroad'
Report H62-24, Washington, The Foundatiion.
Naylor, W.B. (1985), Interview, August 20.
Ogden, W.R. (1976)
'Contributions of major committee reports to

the teaching of secondary school chemistry: 1893-1975' School Science and Mathematics 76, pp.461-465, 599-604, 639-646.

Orpwood, G.W.F. and Souque, J.P. (1984)
Science Education in Canadian Schools Vol. 1
Ottawa, Science Council of Canada.

Peterson, L.R. (1958)
Speech reported in the Victoria Times
January 17, p.15.

Physical Science Study Committee (1965)
Physics
Lexington, Heath.

Private and Public Works aid Growth, (1958)
British Columbia Government News, 6(1) pp.1-3.

Province of British Columbia (1954)
The Sciences
Victoria, Department of Education, Division of Curriculum.

Province of British Columbia (1964)
Physics 11 (or 91)
Victoria, Department of Education, Division of Curriculum.

Province of British Columbia (1965)
Physics 12 (or 92)
Victoria, Department of Education, Division of Curriculum.

Reid, W.A. (1985)
'Curriculum change and the evolution of educational constituencies: the English sixth form in the nineteenth century' in Goodson, I.F. (Ed.) Social Histories of the Secondary Curriculum: Subjects for Study
London, Falmer Press.

Royal Commission on Education (1960)
Report
Victoria, Queen's Printer.

Royal Commission on Education (1960) Brief 57, submitted by the Lower Mainland Physics Teachers' Association.

Royal Commission on Education (1960) Brief 112, submitted by Surrey Teachers'Association, White Rock.

Royal Commission on Education (1960) Brief 113, submitted by Chilliwack District Teachers' Association.

Royal Commission on Education (1960) Brief 145, submitted by Dr G.M. Shrum.

Royal Commission on Education (1960) Brief 163, submitted by The Board of School Trustees, School District No. 44 (North Vancouver).

Royal Commission on Education (1960) Brief 186, submitted by the British Columbia Chamber of Commerce, Vancouver.
Royal Commission on Education (1960) Brief 231, submitted by the Board of School Trustees, School District No. 39 (Vancouver), with suggestions from the department heads in science.
Royal Commission on Education (1960) Brief 240, submitted by the Teachers of Physics 101 at the University of British Columbia.
Royal Commission on Education (1960) Brief 282, submitted by Southern Okanagan Junior-Senior High School, Oliver.
Royal Commission on Education, (1960) Brief 299, submitted by Penticton District Association of Teachers.
Royal Commission on Education (1960) Brief 307, submitted by Penticton District Parent-Teacher Association.
Royal Commission on Education (1960) Brief 327, submitted by the British Columbia Teachers' Federation.
Royal Commission on Education (1960) Brief 330, submitted by the Faculty of J. Lloyd Crowe Senior High School, Trail.
Ryniak, T. (1983), Interview, December 12.
Science Council of Canada (1984) Science for Every Student: Educating Canadians for Tomorrow's World, Ottawa, The Council.
Shrum, G.M. (1953) 'What about the shortage of physicists?' Physics in Canada 9(2) pp.5-6.
Shrum, G.M. (1954) 'The influence of physics' Physics in Canada 10(1) pp.7-19.
Waring, M. (1979) Social Pressures and Curriculum Innovation: A Study of the Nuffield Foundation Science Project. London, Methuen.
Warren, J.B. (1957) 'Teach more science or lose way of life' Chilliwack Program, November 20.
Winteringham, R.V. (1984), Interview, February 2.

5. PROCESS OF CURRICULUM CHANGE: AN HISTORICAL SKETCH OF SCIENCE EDUCATION IN THE ALTE SCHOOLS

Louis M. Smith

Table of Contents

1. THE PERPLEXITIES AS PROLOGUE

In the last decades of the nineteenth century, a small group of individuals in the town of Alte(1) gathered together and decided that their community needed a school. Notices were distributed to taxpayers, a town meeting was called. This spring meeting elected the first school board and voted money for a school building. By that September, a one-room frame school with forty-eight children and a teacher was in operation. Twenty-five years later, 1907-08, the high school program began in one room and the upstairs corridors of the new brick grammar school building. The curriculum was algebra, Latin, and English. Today there are a dozen buildings, several hundred teachers and professional personnel, and several thousand pupils, studying literally dozens of 'courses'.

In 1977, almost a hundred years later, the National Science Foundation (NSF) approached the Alte District to do a case study of science education: natural science, social science, and mathematics in grades K-12. Further, NSF wanted policy recommendations. Immediately, the analyst with such an agenda is faced with a series of questions: What is the status of science education today? How is it to be conceptualized; that is, what are the rubrics, the categories, that denote the regularities? Are there differences in the way participants in the system construe these regularities? Is there some better, more ultimate, way they can be achieved? Once these accurate descriptions and categorizations are in hand, how does one explain the transformation of a one-room school house as a district into the comtemporary district? Or in more particular form, at the high school, how does a three-course curriculum, only one of which is 'science', evolve into a curriculum of twelve science courses, eleven mathematics courses, and nine social science courses (one of which has five alternative components)? What seems a simple question soon becomes intriguing and a bit ironic; given NSF's broad definition of science education, is natural science explanation the same as a social science explanation? Philosophers such as Hempel argue yes; but others, Toulmin and Peters for instance, say no. And then, as we have come to find, social science in Alte High School is mostly history. Is historical explanation the same as natural science or empirical social scientific explanation? Hempel continues to argue yes while Scriven and Dray, among others, say no. To whom do we turn to provide a metatheoretical context on to which we can frame our comments?

If that were not enough of a set of problems, perplexities arise concerning the nature of educational theory. Is it a form of scientific theory or a form of practical theory; that is, where do values fit? Is educational theory mostly one or the other, or is it best conceived as a little of both? Here again, the philosophical experts seem to disagree - O'Connor argues for mostly science ('Do your ethics independently', he argues) and Hirst and Peters (and some others) argue the irrevocable integration in the key concepts - education, curriculum, teaching. On the American scene, at the level of curriculum, Schwab and Walker argue for educational theory as practical and deliberative. Interestingly, both were trained as natural scientists and have taught science. In my own view, when NSF asks for recommendations it is implicitly asking for a mix of ethical and scientific thought.

A final personal note: in the course of explaining to teachers the nature of the project, as part of the informed consent procedures, the observer found himself offering a personal rationale as part of his involvement in the project. It went like this. 'In the past I have been intensely involved in studying classrooms and individual school buildings. I've never tackled a school district. I don't even know how to think about one. To me this is the most exciting intellectual issue in the project.' Mostly the teachers responded with wry or amused smiles and grins. The social studies teachers thought the observer was out of his mind (and his depth!) and spent an hour telling him so as they quizzed him about the project. The latter was to the point of a comment a few days later from an administrator friend, 'I hear the social studies teachers gave you a bad time the other day.' In his own perception the observer felt as though, 'I gave as good as I got', and felt pleased with the initial observations of the quality of mind of the social studies faculty.

The major methodological procedure used to attack these problems was participant observation. This is a collection of techniques with a long history in anthropology and sociology and a shorter history in education. Psychology has traditionally phrased some similar research styles as case study inquiry or clinical method and has had an ambivalent and troubled relationship with it over the years. In our use of participant observation we mean essentially that the researcher participates in the ongoing events of the system - classrooms, schools, committees and individual lives. In part, he is stranger and friend. During this, he observes, talks to people, takes notes, collects documents and, most of all, attempts to understand what is happening. While we have tried to capture the methodology in numerous formal accounts, for procedural purposes a brief listing of 'Data Sources' is presented in Figure 1. This was compiled while an early draft of some of the ideas were being prepared on a sunny afternoon in early March. It is only a partial listing for illustrative purposes. It does indicate, early on, the varied settings, people, and events we tried to sample.

Figure 1 - Illustrative Data Sources: Settings, People and Events (as of 3/16)

1. Administrative interviews: superintendent, principals.
2. Extended teacher interviews with several former students and colleagues.
3. Beginning observations of classes and teacher interviews.
4. Instructional TV - program on Atomic Safety.
5. Junior High Assembly - Rural Highlands as an historical, cultural, and commercial region.
6. Meeting of sixth grade parents and junior and senior high staff in mathematics and English.
7. Open house at the Alternative High School.
8. Meetings of the steering committee for North-central visitation.
9. Luncheon conversations at several schools.
10. Before school coffee klatches at several schools.
11. Varied documents: school bulletins, newspaper accounts, local histories, etc.
12. Extended interactions with the research coordinator: shared interviews, shared observations, long substantive and methodological discussions.

From such initial questions - foreshadowed problems, to use Malenowski's term - and from such "observations" of the school and from the cumulating records, we have tried to develop a descriptive and analytic account of science education in the Alte School District (Smith, 1978).

2. THE TRANSFORMATION OF THE ALTE DISTRICT

2.1 An Overview

While we have not done a formal history of the Alte District, it seems helpful to sketch a few items on a time line over the last hundred years.(2) Such a chronicle will facilitate thinking in several ways by providing: 1) an account in the lay language of the items considered important by general historians of the Alte community; 2) some points of comparison and contrast to highlight the current program of the district; 3) some of the factual data from which we can build a more analytical and interpretive account of science education; and 4) a framework of the 'longer term large changes' into which we can incorporate some of the more recent smaller changes in science education.

In part we are trying to move toward policy issues by explicating 'naturalistic/historical' processes of change. Most of the data came from several key sources. A general account of Alte City was written by a local newspaperman and published in 1976 as part of Alte's Centennial and the nation's Bicentennial.(3) Two other accounts are secondary sources in the sense they are histories of the community; but they are also primary sources in that they were written by seventh- and eighth-grade pupils and formally published, one in the early 1930s and one in 1976. In addition, high school annuals, curriculum guides, and several reports have been utilized as primary sources. Finally, the Alte School News, in existence a dozen and a half years, published by the district for the patrons, has been consulted.

2.2 The Community and the Schools

The historical accounts are essentially in everyday lay language. In Figure 2, a one hundred year time line has been produced. The categories of events, strands, if you will, have been indicated on the ordinate. As the vignette in the prologue indicates, concerned citizens of the com-

Figure 2 - A Partial Chronicle of the Alte School District

		1880	1890	1900	1910	1920	1930	1940	1950	1960	1970	1980
COMMUNITY	Citizen Involvement	1st School Established (1880)			1st Private Residential Area Zoned 1 1/2 Acres (1910)	Executive City (1920-)		Post WW II Development Expanded Tax Base (1946)			Survey of Citizens' View of Schools (1976)	
	Size											
	SES											
	Taxes											
PROGRAMS AND BUILDINGS	Elem.	Elem. Program 1880- 1st Building Built (1880)	New Elem. School Building (1892)	Opening 2nd Elem. School		New Elem. Schools (1929-30)			Integration: Closing of Black Elem. School (1954)			
	Junior High						Junior High Program (1938) Junior High Opens			New Junior High Building		
	Secondary			H.S. Pro- Program begins 1907-08	H.S. Accredited with 23 units (1911) Opening of New H.S. (1915-19)				Current H.S. Built (1952)		Alternative High School 1972	
PERSONNEL		1st School Board Elected 1880		1st Supt. 1908		3rd Supt. 30+ years Tenure		1st Small town Supt. recognized by AASA (1940)				

munity met in 1880, picked a school board, assessed taxes, contracted for a building, hired a teacher, and began an educational program for some four dozen children. The story is an intriguing one, representing a mix of buildings, personnel, pupils, programs and community. In many ways it parallels the development of much of America.

Over the years, the community changed from a small town, almost rural, to a major suburban community with a strong commercial tax base and a citizenry of middle to upper social classes. However, the dominant or modal group is upper middle class, 'executive city' as some writers label it. With the first private subdivisions, zoned in 1910 into one-and-a-half acre lots, much of what now exists seems to have been determined. This coalescing into a community carries with it the development of a perspective, a point of view, about what is expected in the education of the children of the community. This persepctive has jelled into a demand for 'academic excellence'. In the elementary schools, 'excellence' is defined in terms of attitude (development of a desire to learn) as well as achievement (especially in reading and mathematics). The junior high is to provide a transition into the disciplinary studies of the high school. There, a program of knowledge and skills productive of learning, high college board test scores, and entrance to colleges and universities in general and Ivy League schools in particular (for the 'best' students) is demanded. In addition, the community had/has the economic resources and the political power to implement its point of view.(4) In effect the community perspective had become a mandate.

Within the last year, the school board hired an outside educational consultant to conduct an intensive public opinion study, 'How citizens in Alte view their schools.' While the report contains a number of items relevant to our later specific interests, the overall reaction is appropriate here. The question: 'On the whole, would you rate the public schools in Alte as excellent, good, fair or poor?' The responses were 68% excellent, 27% good, 2% fair, 0% poor, 3% no opinion (these latter responses came from citizens who had no children in school). According to reports from the interviewer, he had not surveyed a district with a higher rating of satisfaction with the schools. At a general level, a congruence exists between what the community wants and what the school system does. Positive sentiments are the outcome. It is important to note, however, that a vocal minority opinion does exist in the community. One of the issues on the recent television news and in brief accounts in the local newspapers is the concern about the adoption of 'untested innovations' and the children being 'guinea pigs' in the process.

Such an illustration makes an important but simple point, an oft neglected truism, relevant to NSF's interest in science education. Any kind of change in curriculum and teaching will produce positive and negative reactions in individual parents and citizens. Those reactions, as they aggregate, become direct political forces in school board elections and indirect forces in the day to day workings of the schools. Analyses, scientific, theoretical, or practical, which ignore the latent meaning in a simple illustration such as this, do an injustice to the complexity of the reality itself, and to the actors who live and work in the system.

A final word about the social structure of the community seems necessary. Religiously, the community contains a mix of Protestants, Catholics and Jews. Pre-World War II, it had a 'Jewish problem', e.g. neighborhoods with restrictive housing covenants. Those covenants and practices are gone now. Racially, the community is almost all white. As yet, there is no 'racial problem'. A story, going back a hundred years, does exist, i.e. when the original 1880 frame school was no longer large enough, a new brick school was built. The frame building was moved to a new location; it became the 'coloured school' for a number of years. After World War II, though, the black community disappeared as property was bought for commercial development. Economically, our earlier account indicated no 'social class problems'; the community is basically homogeneous, upper middle class with a strong tax base financially supporting the schools. For this report these conditions are given, a context for consideration of a particular science education program. For the social analyst and critic of American society who is concerned with broader issues of social conflict, pluralism, equality, and 'success' in the American Dream, these conditions could be taken as problematic.(5)

2.3 The Alte Schools

During the first twenty-five years at the turn of the century, the school district - that is the one-room school - was reasonably stable. In the years around 1910, a series of inter-related events occurred: 1) the population of the town of Alte increased; 2) parents at the end of the district farthest from the school wanted a school closer to home for their children - a second elementary school was built; 3) the old frame building of the first school had been replaced with a larger brick building.

Later, concomitant with the community consolidation in the twenties, thirties, forties and fifties, the school district's administration ejoyed the long-term tenure of its third superintendent. He led the district - carefully, shrewdly, some say benevolently but autocratically, and with some professional notoriety - for over thirty years. He built the elementary schools, the junior highs, and a new senior high school. The program expanded and became more complex and more specialized. He himself was one of the first nationally recognized small city superintendents. Through most of his three decades he both knew what the community wanted and helped shape concretely those expectations.

For illustrative purposes, the changes in the general school curriculum can be evidenced in the growth of the high school curriculum. Before 1907-1908, those youngsters who wanted a secondary education enrolled in one of the nearby city high schools. As the program began for the ninth graders, English, Latin and algebra were the first subjects. The program grew in size and complexity and through a series of temporary quarters. After World War I, the first high school building was built and staffed by a dozen teachers. The first high school annual indirectly describes the program by listing the subjects taught by the teachers. Currently in 1977 the program includes a dozen courses each in language arts (English, journalism, theater), social science, science, mathematics, fine arts (art and music), practical arts (industrial, commercial and homemaking), foreign language (French, Spanish, Latin and German), and miscellaneous (physical education, driver education, psychology, etc.). Figure 3 presents these in graphic form.

Figure 3
The Changing Secondary Curriculum in Alte

1907-1908	English Latin Algebra
1911	Accreditation of the high school: 23 units
1918-1920	Normal Training History Economics Science English Music and Art French Manual Training Domestic Science Commercial
1976-1977	Language Arts (English, Journalism, Theater Arts) Social Sciences Science Mathematics Fine Arts (Arts and Music) Practical Arts (Industrial, Commercial, Homemaking) Foreign Languages Miscellaneous

In the late 1970s, the environment is shifting once again. Alte, like many school districts, is faced with declining enrollments. When the few non-tenured teachers in the faculty are gone, and the district is highly tenured, what happens to the tenured faculty? What will be the role of excellence and competence, the role of age and seniority? Most certainly one of the hoped-for consequences by the administration, board, and citizenry is toning up the system, self-development by staff in overcoming 'softness and flabbiness', energizing some of the teaching core which has gone stale. Another outcome feared by many of the teachers is the chance or occasional negative phone call of a parent to a board member, or the fawning by fellow teachers to administrators or board members. In part, administrators may be faced with hard choices; in part, that's what they are paid to do and expected to do.

In brief, a variety of planned actions are underway as the district tries to cope with these changes. Most of them are outside the scope of this analysis. But the issue becomes a part of every individual's perceptions, thinking and acting. The implications for an organization such as NSF seem both obvious and obscure. The expansionist excitement, the unlimited opportunities, the predominance of hope of the late fifties and early sixties is gone. If broad scale curriculum development and implementation was difficult then, it will seem like a tea party compared to the present and immediate future. Risk-taking is precarious at best, foolhardy or dangerous at worst, in such an environment. Introspection, reflection, seeking an identity, cautious and more carefully and specifically aimed changes seems to be the atmosphere in Alte.

2.4 Initial Implications

Overall, several interesting aspects appear to be generalizable. In looking at such a brief chronicle there seem to have been implicit in this several theoretical elements:

1. Contextually, similar events had been and were going on in small communities all over America - models, legal requirements and procedures were present.
2. Citizens, acting individually and together, were defining goals, designing means and actualizing those events.
3. In what seems to be an incredible kind of social stability, a hundred years later citizens are still expressing opinions (now with the help of public opinion surveys, as well as face to face comment, criticism and support) and still acting through a local board of education.
4. The educational system which was established - governing board, curriculum, teacher, pupils, and a specified time and place - is systemic. It contains the major interdependent elements in a simplified microcosm.(6) Those basic elements persist even in the midst of overt

change.

5. In 1907-08 increasing population and a concomitant increase in complexity of the organization (three elementary schools and the beginnings of the high school) seemed to raise problems of coordination and responsibility; the first superintendent was hired, thereby making for further complexity of the organization.
6. Complexity is an intriguing concept. So far, increasing complexity refers to at least these phenomena:
   6.1 additional numbers of the same units - more elementary buildings, more teachers, more pupils;
   6.2 new kinds of units - a high school, later a junior high;
   6.3 increasing specialization of positions - individuals who don't teach but administer and coordinate; principals and the superintendent, special kinds of teachers;
   6.4 increasing hierarchy of governance and control; what originally was citizenry-board-teacher-pupils, becomes citizenry-board- superindendent- principal- teacher and pupils. Later, assistant superintendent positions and assistant principalships at the high school were created.
7. Finally, as the present social environment of the schools changes - in this case, declining enrollments - major changes begin to occur at all levels and in all parts of the system. Individuals perceive the changes as a "new ball game"; they conceptualize events differently: "a new set of rules", new interpersonal relationships, "teams" are formed.

In short, even a brief historical overview gives an observer a context of stability and change in the community and in the schools.

3. AN ANALYSIS OF RECENT CHANGE: IPI AND THE LRCs

As has been indicated, developing an understanding and explanation of the large scale transformation of the district's educational program over one hundred years would require the efforts of a serious historian.(7) We have made some tentative allusions to the shaping of the community as upper middle class with the correlated expectations for an academic college preparatory program in the schools. For a more detailed analysis of within-school changes, it seems instructive to take an instance or two of recent changes and chart them in more detail. The situations are the correlated development of the elementary school Learning Resource Centres (LRCs) and the modification of the elementary mathematics program through the introduction of IPI math, Individually Prescribed Instruction in mathematics.

3.1 The Context, Beliefs, Interaction & Sentiments

As one talks with principals and teachers in the Alte Elementary Schools, the term "individualizing instruction" appears and reappears in discussion, interviews and in classroom action. The core meaning seems to be "What can I do with/to/for each individual pupil to help him/her learn?" There is high congruence between espoused theory and theory in use in most classrooms. If individualizing instruction is the intermediate goal, teacher autonomy on how to get there is a major means. Few beginning teachers have entered the system in recent years. Most have gone through a three-tiered hiring process - paper credentials, intensive interviews, and observations of teaching. Teachers were/are hired because they have a point of view and demonstrated skill with the children.

A second belief which appears in the discussions with many of the staff is that of professional responsibility. The core meaning is wanting to be judged for actions which he/she took based upon his/her analysis of an educational problem and situation, and in which he/she made his/her best decision. The clearest accounts of this position came in discussions with teachers as they talked of the reasons they elected to teach in the district. Usually they contrasted Alte with the larger, multi-leveled, bureaucratic systems from which they had come. Usually also, they commented about interpersonal contacts in P.T.A. meetings and parent conferences as test cases for accountability in this kind of professional responsibility. From an administrative perspective this phenomenon is usually voiced as, '"District policy" has been to hire the "best" teachers and give them freedom to develop their programs'.

A third related, and more implicit factor, at least in conversations and interviews, is the 'friendly competition' among the elementary schools: that is, within the small group of elementary principals, and, in turn, between the staffs of the elementary schools. The competition seems related to the development of a 'building identity' and a favorable reputation among the immediate patrons and across the small district itself. The summary observation notes picked this up in an early discussion:

> As they talked it seemed to come out that different schools had different things going for them (as I'd heard previously). For example - one has a big outdoor education program, second grade and up, overnight camping, etc. Another is trying out some of the new CEMREL math materials in the primary grades, and so forth.

Immediately, upon these notes came the interpretive aside:

> (Obs. - All this suggests aspects of the old elementary principals' competition, identity, and place in the sun as a major issue in the dynamics of a district and efforts in curriculum, teaching, parents, etc.)

The identities engage the parents and children and are manifested in such diverse phenomena as spring festivals, flower and garden sales, and picnics. Woe to the principal and teachers who fail to perceive, to involve themselves, and to support such functions.(8) Within the buildings, the competition and identity issues flow into such diverse avenues as open space ('the big room' where a wall has been torn down), team teaching, reification of self-contained classrooms, elaboration of an outdoor education program, or, for our purposes, curricular and organizational change in the form of IPI and an LRC.

3.2 The Story of IPI and LRCs

The story of IPI and the LRCs is really a story of the confluence of several interrelated strands of development. First and foremost, some ten years ago, in one of the elementary schools, the principal and several of his teachers remained dissatisfied with what was being accomplished in mathematics instruction. The district program was a mix of innovative projects - Madison maths, University of Illinois maths, and SRA; the mathematics curriculum committee was moving toward adoption of the Addison Wesley texts. Their own concern was on problems of 'individualizing instruction'. As class size in their school was declining, the individual non-achieving pupils were less likely to 'get lost' in the crowd. The staff, in coping with this, tried several approaches.

A modified 'Joplin plan', shuffling the kids from all the primary grades into ability groups for part of the day, was tried. It foundered in part on the mix of dull third graders and bright first graders at the 'same' level of achievement. Later, the teachers moved toward developing individualized teaching materials by cutting up old work books by topic and process, collecting scattered materials from their individual files, and gathering games and manipulative materials. The need arose for some kind of centralized space and storage.

Meanwhile, attempts were underway to develop a central library in the school. Initial steps were to open a room at noon. This raised problems with lunch duty, resources, and staff. 'A lousy way to run a library', as one staff member commented. Proposals were made to the superintendent for one of the teachers to take on the task full time (in several schools), for a kindergarten room to be converted, and for parent volunteers to be solicited.

About this time a new assistant superintendent for curriculum was hired. His charge was K-12. He was looking for point of entry into the system. He found this elementary staff congenial and joined forces. He brought knowledge of the activities at the Pittsburgh R & D Center and the Philadelphia Lab, RBS (Research for Better Schools). One of their major programs was an instructional system in mathematics entitled IPI, Individual Prescribed Instruction. Several teachers and the principal visited the demonstration school in Pennsylvania. They were struck with the similarities between what they saw and what they were trying to do. They argued for giving it a try in their school. The school board agreed.

To work well, the IPI system requires something akin to a learning resource center. The Alte Elementary School LRC evolved several steps farther. In time it became a facility close to that in Figure 4. Briefly, we would note the LRC contains: a storage area for the hundreds of work sheets in the IPI program; instructional aides who check materials done by pupils, keep records, and dispense materials prescribed by the teachers; school-wide library resource (5,000 - 10,000 books in <u>each</u> elementary school library), and aides and volunteers who help out in this part of the center. In visits to the LRCs, it was not uncommon to find a half dozen adults busy with children at any one time. The facility seemed to take on a life of its own; that is, its existence and the presence of creative teachers and district resources provoked a series of alterations, additions and elaborations. As audio-visual equipment was centralized, new programs in literature, e.g. tapes of stories, were developed. Listening and study carrels were added with tape players and earphones. Possibilities in spelling were seen and the Alte individualized spelling program was developed. Special reading teachers, working with individuals and small groups, found a home and became an active part of the LRC. As several staff members commented:

> Housing is a very limited concept and many LRCs are not functional because they become central locations for materials when they should become central locations for learning activities.

The IPI program is well described elsewhere in multiple books, brochures and research reports emanating from the Pittsburgh Learning Research and Development Center, the Regional Laboratory, Research for Better Schools, Inc. (both funded by the National Institute for Education) and Appleton Century Crofts, Inc., the private publisher of the materials. Consequently, only a few brief remarks will be made here; mostly they are excerpts from several hours spent one morning in the LRC with the IPI program.

8:47 Am in the LRC. Fourth, fifth and sixth grades, in turn, this a.m. Two aides handle kids, grading and dispersing work sheets in IPI. Children in and out - four or five so

Figure 4 - Alte Elementary School LRC

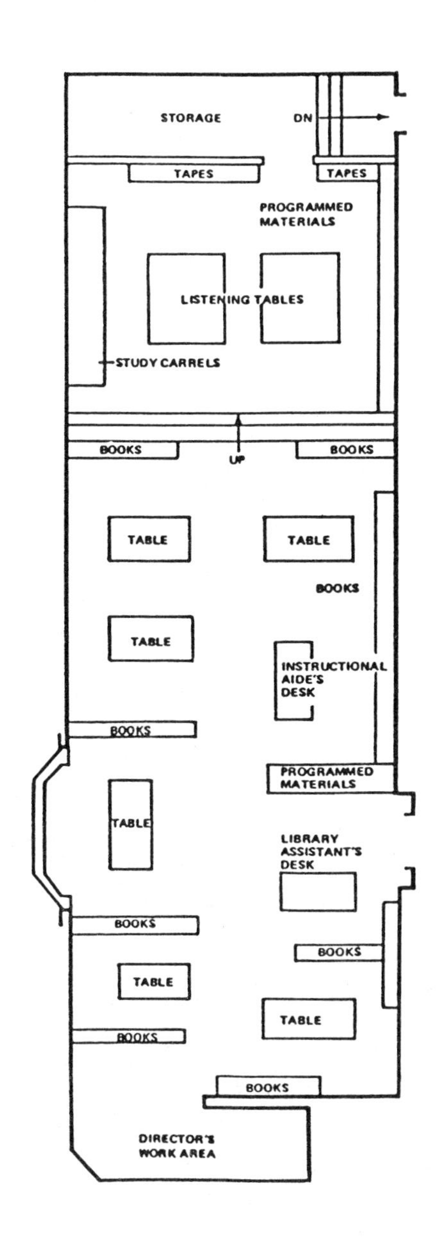

far. Each has a bright blue folder with materials. The aide, at my request, explains the system roughly:

1. a yellow sheet of Areas (numeration, add/ subt., mult., etc.) and Levels A-G (roughly grades 1-6); Figure 5 reproduces this.

<u>Figure 5 - Yellow Sheet representing IPI Scope and Sequence Summary</u>

Name: ________________

Grade: ________________

Area	A	B	C	D	E	F	G
Numeration/ Place Value	Part 1 Part 2		Part 1 Part 2				
Addition/ Subtraction	Part 1 Part 2	Part 1 Part 2	Part 1 Part 2				
Multiplication							
Division							
Fractions					Part 1 Part 2		
Money							
Time							
Systems of Measurements							
Geometry							
Applications							

2. Initial placement tests.
3. Exercises.
4. CETs (Curriculum Embedded Tests).
5. Mastery Tests.

The flow of traffic is slow enough that no one stands long in line waiting. Kids bring folders to whichever of two teachers is free. Gals grade while kids wait. Show them if there are errors. Kids correct. With current boy at least two major hints. (Obs. - Through all this I'm reminded of Brueckner's Diagnostic Tests in Arithmetic. The system seems a logical outgrowth of that point of view. Need to look at old NSSE Yearbook from 1934(?) and the Bond and Brueckner Diagnosis and Treatment of Learning Difficulties . Need to check manuals. Seems like a teaching and organizational system (aides, storage and LRC) building upon that. Need to look at IPI manuals and reference literature).
I go through Placement Test C. There are two or three pages on each area. It does look like Brueckner writ large.

9:33 The aide asks if I can understand. I take that as an invitation and go over as she corrects a couple of papers.

1. They score and record; she handles mostly exercises; the other aide the tests.
2. Have booklets of answers (keys).
3. Kids must correct and see teachers for help and clearance.
4. If kids ask re their mistake they will indicate - especially re silly mistakes. 'Teachers don't mind. We're not supposed to teach the children.' (Obs. - Apparently they handle the issues in a common-sense, reasonably deferent manner. These two gals seem bright and knowledgeable.) 'Feel stupid if you don't answer a child's question.'

A formal explication of the more generalized LRC procedures is reproduced as Figure 6. This figure is used by the staff to explain the general teaching strategy of the LRC, a part of which is the IPI program.

Figure 6 - Organizational and Instructional Strategies in Using IPI and LRC

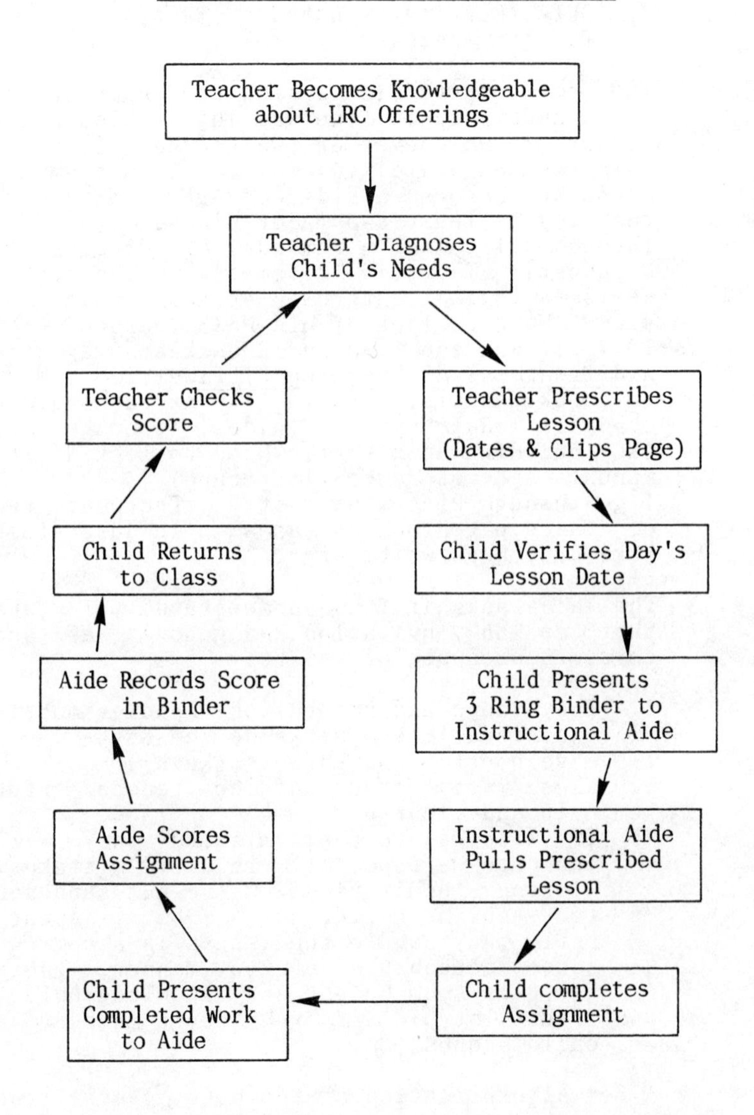

The field notes of the morning continue. They capture more of the flavor of the system and the possible slippage between the ideal and the real.

10:00 The flow continues in and out. I talk some more with the aide.

1. The individuality of kids - attitudes, temperament, 'con games' (Can my teacher OK this?) - continues.
2. Most of the grade 3 kids, as I look at a roomful of summary sheets, are in Level 3 materials. A few scattered down and up. One kid tested out of all Level 3 materials and has done only two booklets all year. To my incredulous response, the aide indicates that the youngster works very slowly, the section she's on is difficult, 'lots of problems and kids get hung up, teacher would never let her just sit'. Finally she agreed it seems strange.
3. Kids are only on IPI three days a week.
4. I haven't seen any great antipathy to the materials. Kids seem to enjoy walking and moving around. Some clowning of kids with each other - swatting and brushing each other with the bright blue folders. Seem to enjoy the aides who are calm, in good spirits, helpful, quick and efficient. Kids lean on the aides' desks, sit on a nearby table, chat while they wait, etc. (Obs. - somehow the personality, the approach and the skill of the aides seems very critical.)
5. Kids are in and out of the shelves, and in some instances the file cabinets, for materials.
6. The file cabinets contain, among other things, partial booklets - left over pages for kids who only need a section or two.

Later in the same morning, the notes picked up another strand of data, documents about the program, and initial interpretations by the observer.

> I'm amazed/struck by the seemingly flawless aspect of the system here. The aide has been with the program several years. She has no problem, works very rapidly, etc. At this end, the personnel, the facilities, the storage of materials, the plenitudes (nothing looks like it's even close to being out), the

routines are all running smoothly. Need to look at other end.

Over coffee, the observer talked independently with several teachers. The notes contain several diverse but relevant pieces for the analysis:

1. She's pro IPI, relieves the teacher of routine work, time to do more interesting things with the kids.
2. Most of this school are pro, most at school B are anti, others up and down. (Obs. - There's a funny quality re schools - principals, teachers, relationships. Don't really know as yet.)
3. She says she tends to spend remaining time following along (loosely?) a text with supplemental materials.

(Obs. - I get the feeling of multiple ways to skin the proverbial educational cat. Alte has huge array of resources, experienced teachers, able kids, low teacher-pupil ratios. Groups (schools) develop norms re how things should be done, what is good and bad, important and not, and are able to argue quite tenaciously.)

And in regard to another teacher conversation:

She has some reservations. Most of the teachers are supportive of the program. Her reservations include:

1. need group activities;
2. need togetherness versus going in fifty directions;
3. need more problems and practice than booklets provide.

(Obs. - Very complicated mix of values (togetherness), beliefs: ways of organizing the class (grouping), and what it takes to learn certain things.)

3.3 <u>The Epilogue</u>

The IPI program remains as one of the most controversial programs in the district. The essence of the epilogue is that the story isn't finished. Several items might be mentioned. The program did not spring into full bloom in the form we have recounted. It was tried for a year or two in the initial school. Presentations were made to the board, discussions were entertained, and the decision was made to implement it in all of Alte's elementary schools. From that point on, the road has been more stormy. In the eyes of one teacher, 'It was forced on the rest of the district by the assistant superintendent'.

The program has been in considerable contention since then. Some parents have been very dissatisfied. Local test scores in math were reported to be lower. Several years ago an idependent assessment of the curriculum was commissioned by the board and carried out by a local firm of evaluation consultants. They reported favorably on the program and recommended that IPI be retained as the core of the mathematics program.

Math teachers at the junior and senior high school in general look with disfavor upon the program. When the board moved recently to have the elementary math program to be half IPI and half teacher developed curriculum, one of the teachers commented, 'We've got the battle half won. It'll be totally won when IPI is completely gone.'

The LRCs have fared better, in the sense of less conflict. They've developed somewhat differently in each school, but each provides a wealth of resources and activities to supplement the teacher in her classroom.

As an illustration of curriculum change and transformation in Alte, the IPI and LRC stories present several lessons: teacher autonomy and professionalism, administrative influence, competing groups, conflicting points of views, multiple kinds of evidence, and a never-ending process with moments of quasi-stationary equilibria. That this is not atypical of the district can be seen in our current observation, e.g. the beginnings of the CEMREL's new math with its 'mini-computers' in the primary grades of one of the Alte elementary schools. Our interview and observations of outdoor education present another instance. And so on.

To determine how similar or different Alte is from other districts requires other data. Presumably other case studies will illuminate these comparisons and contrasts. Analytically, syntheses of antecedents and consequences in additional cases and from historical and comtemporaneous accounts will move toward more general models, paradigms, and theories. That is not our task here.

4. ORGANIZATIONAL STRUCTURES FOR COPING WITH CURRICULUM

The discussion of the history of the district and the items of recent change provide one perspective on science education in the Alte Schools. Another point of view arises in considering organizational structures for 'coping with curriculum'. The verb 'cope' is deliberately chosen as a label for a broad set of issues (e.g. develop, change, implement, integrate) involving 'struggling or contending with some success'. Alte has these mechanisms in place:

1. The school board reserves one meeting per month for discussion and review of curriculum. Areas are taken in rotation and/or as need arises.
2. Each major elementary curriculum area (language arts, math, science and social studies) is represented by a committee of teachers, chaired by an elementary principal. Chairmanships are rotated and allocated by choice, interest and competence.
3. Each area of the grade 7-12 program is headed by a curriculum co-ordinator, often, but not always, the chairman of the relevant high school department. The co-ordinators teach a full load during the year and work the equivalent of an extra month in the summer and weekends.
4. The curriculum chairman and co-ordinators meet once a month.
5. Over the years, resources have been available for summer curriculum work by teams of teachers and administrators.
6. Each principal is responsible for the program in his/her building.
7. Each teacher is responsible for the program in his/her classroom.

What the structures were in the past is not clear. Each superintendent seems to have developed his own arrangements. District files of curriculum committee report go back only to the late 1950s. Whether this is a function of no earlier curriculum work or lack of historical data is not clear. Other records and interviews indicate that in the recent past there have been assistant superintendents for curriculum and these individuals played influential but controversial roles in the district.

A further aspect of the system's organizational structure is the rotational review of principals. One or two are 'up' each year which means the district review cycles everyone every four or five years. This has both a formative and summative aspect. In regard to the former, discussions are held, mutual agreements are reached on self-improvement goals - for instance, science or social studies curriculum improvement in the school. Procedural steps are laid out in terms of introduction of ideas and materials, individualized work with specific teachers, and so forth. Early on in the course of one such discussion, the observer made a brief interpretive aside:

> (Obs. - Again a possible point of departure for analysis. How does a school bootstrap itself?)

With the accumulation of further data, such formative evaluation procedures seem to elaborate aspects of the district's coping with curriculum.

Several important generalizations seem to stand out from this analysis. First, and perhaps foremost, is the tension or dilemma between the bureaucratic/organizational tendencies and the individual/professional tendencies. On the one hand the organization is continually striving for rationality - agreed-upon goals and priorities, clarity of procedures and organizational mechanisms, responsible supervision. That is, there are committees with domains of activity and chairmen responsible for their functioning. On the other hand, there are highly trained, competent professionals in schools and classrooms who are selected, hired, and expected to know what to do in their own domains, to choose and decide intelligently and responsibly, and who exercise and enjoy their autonomy. As we have indicated, the dilemma is really a 'tri-lemma' in that political forces operating through citizen accolades and complaints to the board are part and parcel of the overall coping process.

If all this be true, and our data and analysis would so argue, then an agency such as NSF, or a national curriculum project, or a university department or school of education engaged in teacher education, is faced with a kind of reality not usually described in the educational change and innovation literature. The local district arrangements in curriculum and teaching - science education if you like - are not happenstance, not chance, nor accidents, but the resolutions of individual choices, contending points of view, and differential power. NSF (and the other outside groups) becomes a fourth category of contestants with its own resources and rewards, its own point of view with all the internal consistencies and inconsistencies, its own skill in persuasion and influence. The social processes continue.

5. CONCLUSIONS AND IMPLICATIONS

5.1 Conceptualizing a District Science Curriculum

Initially, and tentatively, we can define curriculum as '... a program or course of activities which is explicitly organized as the means whereby pupils may obtain the desired objective ...' (Hirst and Peters, 1970, p.60). Even a superficial unpacking of such a definition indicates the theoretical complexities and the empirical quagmire in the conception. The essential difficulties lie in the constraints provoked by intentions and plans of some agent implied in the phrase 'explicitly organized' and in the constraints provoked by the pupil learning outcomes implied in 'desired objective'. In effect, curriculum by definition contains a three step proposition:

intentions ⟶ activities ⟶ attaining desired outcome

Further complications arise, as our preceding analysis of the transformation of the Alte School District suggested, for there are several clusters of actors with intentions - board, administration, teachers, children, and parents. In general, in Alte, the intentions of these groups are congruent.

There are a number of ways one might cut into the phenomenon of curriculum. As one teacher said, 'Science education may be defined by NSF as math, science, and social studies, but no one in the Alte schools sees it that way'. In Alte High School, for instance, the administration, the teachers, and the students see three separate departments - math, science and history. That separation exists. The departments meet as departments, plan curriculum, decide (in part) who teaches what courses, what new offerings might be tried and so on. The courses tend not to be interdependent across disciplines. This is what we have come to speak of as 'formal curriculum'. Beyond an analysis into these domains of math, science and social studies, the overall program seems amenable to an analysis in terms of dimensions, aspects that cut through the program.

Formal curriculum reflects only a part of what is happening in the Alte schools in science education. We kept 'bumping into' a number of 'special events' which were occurring during the semester, which were referred to or which had left products from the past. They consumed considerable amounts of time and energy of staff and students. They seemed relevant to important educational goals. They tended to cut across disciplines. This we have called 'informal curriculum: degree of enrichment'. The two major instances which we observed were a community history project carried out by the junior high pupils and the outdoor education program implemented at all levels of the district.

Finally, a category of events, almost a latent curriculum in itself, is what we have called 'curriculum or what is taught: vignettes of teaching'. In effect, the rubrics of formal and informal curriculum miss a major element of the Alte District's program, the 'individual teacher with his idiosyncratic style'. Alte prides itself on its 'good' or 'strong' teachers. 'Living legends' might be an even more apt title. To miss this is to miss what many would see as the core element of science education in the district, or education more generally in the district.

In addition, the fact that there are separate elementary, junior, and senior high schools creates some obvious but nonetheless important distinctions. The buildings are geographically separate. By law, the elementary and secondary training programs in which the teachers have been educated are different. The organizational arrangements, departmentalization versus self-contained classes, versus open space and some teaming, are different. Such environmental events lead, quite naturally, to each building (and each department in the high school) developing its own social system - activities, pattern of interactions, beliefs, sentiments, points of view and norms. To a degree, there is differentiation within the overall district.

5.2 Processes of Change

This essay grows out of a larger project and study of the science education program of the Alte Public Schools (Smith, 1978). Our purpose here has been the more circumscribed task of a brief view of the longer term historical changes in the district and a brief view of two smaller changes in the schools; the development of the IPI math program and the LRCs, the learning resource centers. In doing this we have blended the research styles of history and ethnography. They seem to illuminate each other and seem to shed light on the micro processes of change that help explain the macro processes of historical change. Running throughout both sets of data and examples is an overriding political-cultural perspective. Individuals with their own intentions and interests, and classes or clusters of actors with their personal and professional political interests seem to be interacting interminably, sometimes co-operatively and sometimes conflictually, over the large and small aspects of education in the Alte community. Groups of parents and citizens, lawfully constituted Boards of Education, empowered central office and building administrators, and reasonably autonomous and frequently idiosyncratically powerful professional teachers seem to be a part of a 'quasi-stationary open system'. The National Science Foundation, NSF, seems to be on the fringes of that but with some powerful possibilities emanating from the national political scene.

5.3 Thinking about Educational Events

Case studies such as this one of the Alte public schools can have many consequences for different audiences. The most general one for this social scientifically oriented educationist is the continuing evolution from a more technologically and positivistically oriented kind of theoretical perspective to a more interpretive and normative kind of educational theory. Explanations are less deductive nomothetic or covering law and more configurational and concatenated as those terms are used by Kaplan (1964). As stories and narratives enter the research reports, less distinction is made between operational statements and definitions and theoretical statements and definitions. Also, as the points of view of the contending parties in the situation become more important, and as the researcher threads his way through those positions and tries to add his interpretive position to the discussion and dialogue, the detached, objective, outsider stance of the researcher seems less reasonable as a position. Finally, practical reasoning which contains value premises as well as analytical premises seems more appropriate to the phenomena under study than does the more value free statements of theoretical reasoning.

Paradigm shifts, if not revolutions, are not to be entered into lightly might be the most general consequence of the Alte case study.

Notes

1. All proper names of places and people have been coded for anonymity. In addition, slight changes in 'nonessential' elements have been made to disguise the district and its personnel. It goes without saying that our indebtedness to the Alte District is great. We were permitted free access to classes, personnel and public documents.

2. The ideas for incorporating this approach to the case study were stimulated, in part, by McKinney and Westbury's (1975) essay.

3. We have coded these documents as well; neither the problems nor the strategies and tactics re anonymity in a mixed historical/contemporaneous account have been spelled out in the social science literature.

4. Consistently, the Alte School Distict per pupil expenditures are in the highest ten percent of the metropolitan area.

5. Once again, the key role of values in a general theory of education seems evident.

6. A similar, but more philosophically grounded view is presented by Gowin (1976). He speaks of these elements as 'educational commonplaces'.

7. In a latter study of the Kensington School in the Milford School District, we attempt to do just that (Smith et al, 1981).

8. A number of stories exist of the politics of the individual schools and the district, but they are beyond our interest here.

References

Bond, G. and Bruechner, L.
The Diagnosis and Treatment of Learning Difficulties.
New York: Appleton-Century Crofts, 1955.
Diesing, P.
Patterns of Discovery in the Social Sciences.
Chicago: Aldine, Atherton, 1971.
Dray, W.
Laws and Explanation in History.
Oxford: Oxford University Press, 1957.
Gowin, Bob.
On the relation of theory to practice in education research in IDM, Relating Theory to Practice in Educational Research.
Bielefeld, Germany: Inst. fur Didaktik der Mathematik der Universitat Bielefeld, 1976.
Hempel, C.G.
Aspects of Scientific Explanation and Other Essays in Philosophy of Science.
New York: Free Press, 1965.
Hirst, P.H.
'The Nature and Scope of Educational Theory (2) Reply to D.J. O'Connor' in Langfeld and O'Connor, D.J. (Eds.), New Essays in the Philosophy of Education.
London: Routledge and Kegan Paul, 1973.
Hirst, P.H. and Peters, R.S.
The Logic of Education.
London: Routledge and Kegan Paul, 1970.
Kaplan, A.
The Conduct of Inquiry
San Francisco: Chandler, 1964.
Malinowski, B.
The Argonauts of the Western Pacific.
London: Routledge, 1922.
McKinney, W.L. and Westbury, I.
Stability and Change: the Public Schools of Gary, Indiana, 1940-1970, in Reid, W.A. and Walker, D.F. (Eds.), Case Studies in Curriculum Change: Great Britain and the United States.
London: Routledge and Kegan Paul, 1975.
O'Connor, D.J.
'The Nature and Scope of Educational Theory' in Langfeld, G. and O'Connor, D.J. (Eds.), New Essays in the Philosophy of Education.
London: Routledge and Kegan Paul, 1973.

Peters, R.S.
'Education as Initiation' in Archambault, R.D. (Ed.), Philosophical Analysis and Education.
London: Routledge and Kegan Paul, 1965.

Schwab, J.
The Practical: a Language for Curriculum, School Review. 1969, 78, 1-23.

Scriven, M.
Truisms as the Grounds for Historical Explanations, in Gardiner, P. (Ed.), Theories of History.
New York: Free Press, 1959.

Smith, L.M.
Science Education in the Alte Schools: A Kind of Case Study.
Washington DC: NSF, 1978.

Smith, L.M. et al.
A Longitudinal Tested System-model of Innovation and Change in Schooling.
In Bacharach, S. (Ed.), Organizational Behaviour in Schools and School Districts.
New York: Praeger, 1981.

Smith, L.M. and Geoffrey, W.
The Complexities of an Urban Classroom.
New York: Holt, Rinehart and Winston, 1968.

Toulmin, S.
Human Understanding, Vol. I.
Princeton, N.J.: Princeton University Press, 1972.

Van Velsen, J.
'The Extended-case Method and Situational Analysis' in Epstein, A.L. (Ed.), The Craft of Social Anthropology.
London: Tavistock Publications, 1967.

Walker, D.F.
A Naturalistic Model for Curriculum Development,
School Review. 1971, 81, 51-65.

Zetterberg, H.
On Theory and Verification in Sociology (3rd ed.).
Totowa, N.J.: Bedminster Press, 1965.

6. SCIENCE CURRICULUM CHANGE IN VICTORIAN ENGLAND: A CASE STUDY OF THE SCIENCE OF COMMON THINGS

Derek Hodson

David Layton has postulated an evolutionary model for curriculum development in which school subjects pass through three distinct phases: an initial phase propelled by the missionary zeal of untrained, enthusiastic pioneer teachers and by pupils who see immediate relevance in their studies; a development phase of growing academic respectability during which students and teachers are attracted by the subject's increasing intellectual stature and status; and a mature phase of formal scholarship, in which developments are determined by the internal logic of the subject and the judgements of its practitioners, rather than by relationships with the world outside or the needs and aspirations of the pupils (Layton, 1972a). If Layton is correct, then as a well established subject in the secondary school curriculum, science should exhibit the characteristics of a mature branch of scholarship. Amongst these characteristics are domination by examinations, remoteness from industry, commerce and the everyday concerns of pupils, and a tendency to promote in pupils an attitude of resignation and disenchantment through excessive emphasis on abstraction. Even the most generous of critics of science education in the U.K. would admit the truth of some of these charges. Such abstraction, remoteness from real life and formality of teaching methods may be inevitable consequences of the drive towards academic respectability, status and influence on the part of subject teachers. As Goodson (1983a) remarks, 'high status in the secondary school curriculum is reserved for abstract theoretical knowledge divorced from the working world of industry and the everyday world of the learner'. In a country that depends for its economic well-being on manufacturing industry, remoteness from industry is a particularly serious charge against science education and has been blamed by some for Britain's poor economic performance in recent decades: 'the general ethos and thrust of British education are, if anything, hostile to industry ... as a result too small a proportion of the national talent seeks a life in industry' (Barnett, 1979). So marked is this hostility, abstractness and remoteness that Layton is moved to declare that the secondary school science curriculum provides 'an inadequate basis for the education of all but future professional scholars' (Layton, 1972a).

Whilst there have, of course, been a number of attempts to introduce a more technology-oriented science curriculum, with the laudable goal of producing a more technologically literate citizenry, these attempts have generally failed (McCulloch, Jenkins and Layton, 1985) because of the pressures brought to bear by subject groups with a vested interest in maintaining the academic status quo. As a consequence, there must be real concern about the capacity of the secondary school curriculum to accommodate the most recent attempts at reorientation occasioned by the information technology and micro-computer revolution. Attempts to introduce courses with a social, industrial or technological bias have often been summarily dismissed or tolerated only as lower status courses for the less able. Millar (1981a) contrasts this very sharply with the situation in West Germany, where such attempts have been much more successful. In the U.K., however, the secondary curriculum continues to be dominated by the formal, abstract aspects of the subject and 'high status (and rewards) ... associated with areas of the curriculum that are (1) formally assessed, (2) taught to the "ablest" children, (3) taught in homogeneous ability groups' (Young, 1971). When attempts have been made to challenge the accepted view of school science, the result has often been fragmentation into two very different kinds of science curriculum: academic science and non-academic science - 'the former claiming credibility from the professional scientific community, and the latter through notions of "relevance" and immediate interest for the pupils' (Young, 1976). As a consequence of these differences in status and justification, 'relevance' and intellectual credibility have come to be regarded as incompatible and courses for the most able pupils (by definition, those deemed capable of passing O-level and A-level examinations in academic subjects) have become increasingly abstract and examination oriented, whilst those for the less able have been oriented towards industry and the environment. Two major consequences have usually followed: firstly, neither group of children has received a satisfactory or complete science education and, secondly, assumptions made about the scientific abilities of children at the point of selection have been reinforced by the provision of significantly different courses, with the inevitable consequence of marked differences in terminal knowledge, skills and attitudes.

Brock (1975) has identified 1839, the year of Liebig's arrival at the University of Giessen, as the 'symbolic starting point for the development of modern science education'. The ideal of the research school he founded there, which later was to attract large numbers of young British scientists, was research and inquiry for its own sake. This provided a concept of 'pure laboratory science' which was to dominate school science curricula, especially for the more able children, throughout modern times - indeed, up to and beyond the Nuffield and Schools Council courses of the 1960s and 1970s. But its emergence as the dominant conception of school science did not go unchallenged. In the mid-nineteenth century at least one other conception of what is appropriate school science was actively promoted: the Science of Common Things. That pure laboratory science eventually triumphed over the Science of Common Things and became established as the 'correct' view is not disputed. Why it became established is a rather more interesting question. It will be argued that the choice of a particular model for school science reflects the distribution of power in society and the interests and views of those in power. The science curriculum, like all aspects of education, is subject to patterns of control by dominant interest groups. As the authority and influence of these groups shift, so the nature of the curriculum changes. In the words of Bernstein (1971), 'How a society selects, classifies, distributes, transmits and evaluates the educational knowledge it considers to be public, relects both the distribution of power and the principles of social control'.

The Rise and Fall of the Science of Common Things.

> The earliest attempt to include science in the curriculum of elementary schools seems to have taken place at a school in Cheam founded by Charles and Elizabeth Mayo, whose 'Object Lessons' were designed to promote 'habits of accurate observation, correct description and right judgement upon the things of nature and art' (Mayo and Mayo, 1849). Textbooks written as aids to infant teachers wishing to adopt object lessons, including Lessons on Objects (1831) and Lessons on Shells (1832), proved highly successful and object lessons quickly became established as the basis of science education in the early years of a child's elementary schooling. It is noteworthy that the principal aim of this science education was not scientific understanding, but 'religious understanding and moral improvement'.
>
> ... and when the intelligence is awake and stirring, the teacher should gradually lead them to the moral lesson or holy doctrine connected in scripture with the object he has shown them.
>
> (Mayo and Mayo, 1849)

The significance of this motivation should become apparent later. It is interesting, too, that the major emphasis was on direct experience of objects, in order to 'cultivate the faculty of observation, this being the first faculty developed in the infant mind'. Similar work was in progress at the Edinburgh Sessional School for the Urban Poor, where John Wood promoted the study of objects as an alternative to the more traditional pedagogy based on words, symbols and abstractions.

> Never should there be too long and too scrutinizing an investigation into the mysteries of great discoveries and high science ... but rather agreeable descriptions and examinations of objects within the reach of their senses and understanding.
>
> (Wood, 1831)

In the 1840s a small but influential group of clerics, clearly influenced by the work of Mayo and Wood, promoted the teaching of science as fundamental to the moral and religious salvation of the labouring classes. Notable among these was the Rev. Richard Dawes, who became Rector of Kings Somborne, Hampshire in 1837 and, with the help of a government grant, opened a National Society school there in 1842.(1) Dawes' school quickly established a reputation for outstanding educational attainment. Two significant curriculum innovations lay behind his success: the use of reading books with a scientific rather than a religious content, and a radical approach to the teaching of science. This scheme, which soon became known as the Science of Common Things, began with a consideration of the 'everyday concerns of common life', such as clothing and its manufacture, consumer articles of various kinds, and the 'products of the parish'. The course then proceeded to explanations 'of a philosophical kind', concerning the action of pumps, the expansion and contraction of materials, and the nature of electricity, heat, light and sound.(2) Such was the success of this new curriculum that within two years of opening his school, Dawes had to plan, furnish and equip an extra laboratory in order to meet increasing demand for scientific education (Layton, 1973). Dawes' work received official recognition and lavish praise in a report by H.M. Inspectorate in 1845. Three years later, the minutes of the Committee of Council on Education (1847-8) contained a long, detailed and enthusiastic account of Dawes' curriculum organization by HMI Rev. Henry Moseley, who subsequently undertook a vigorous promotion of the Science of Common Things.

Layton (1973) identifies three conditions necessary for the establishment of science in the elementary school curriculum: well-designed and inexpensive apparatus and books, suitably trained teachers and a sound and supportive administrative framework. In 1851, a government grant scheme for the purchase of school apparatus was established, with an accompanying authorization for Moseley to prepare a schedule of science apparatus suitable for use in schools and training colleges. Standard sets of apparatus for teaching the Science of Common Things were produced by Griffin of Baker Street, well-known scientific instrument manufacturers. Two thirds of the purchase cost of these sets was recoverable in grants. Grants for the purchase of school books had been introduced in 1847 by James Kay-Shuttleworth, by then Secretary to the Committee of Council on Education, but most books available to schools were of little use for teaching the Science of Common Things. To remedy the situation Kay-Suttleworth attempted, with mixed success, to commission the writing of suitable books, which would then be included in the list of works eligible for grant. The second major resource necessary to consolidate the position of science in the elementary school curriculum was a supply of well-trained teachers. This was recognized by the Committee of Council, who gave Moseley instructions to draw up a suitable scheme for the training colleges. Moseley seized this opportunity to make science compulsory. Clearly, the kind of science he had in mind was that taught so successfully by Richard Dawes.

The third essential resource for the establishment of science in the curriculum was a sound administrative framework. Much essential groundwork had already been done by Moseley in the early 1850s, through his work for the Committee of Council. Evidence of further official support lay behind the appointment, in 1853, of Lyon Playfair (who supported the view that science should be introduced into elementary education) as Head of Science of the newly formed Department of Science and Art. With these three essential conditions necessary for the development of Dawes' scheme reasonably satisfied, and those schools already using the scheme reporting considerable success, the movement seemed poised for rapid growth.

Suddenly, in mid-decade, when all seemed set for the continued expansion of the Science of Common Things movement, several crucial changes occurred. Dawes was moved to the Deanery of Hereford and even though he retained his interest in education, most of his time had to be devoted to his new duties. At about the same time, Moseley was appointed Canon of Bristol Cathedral. He was replaced as Inspector with special responsibility for the training colleges by the Rev. Frederick Temple, who within two years had revised the scheme previously implemented by Moseley, reducing the status of physical science from a compulsory to an optional subject. By 1859 the supply of trained science teachers - the most vital condition of all for the continued success of the Science of Common

Things movement - had been virtually halted. Additionally, a significant change of priority was apparent in official thinking and Playfair, a strong supporter of the Dawes scheme in the early years of the decade, had shifted his ground regarding science in the elementary school curriculum. By 1859, with much reduced grants for science teaching, the role of science in the elementary school curriculum had been severely curtailed and with the Revised Code of 1862 all financial assistance for science was withdrawn. The result of these new regulations was that science disappeared entirely from the elementary school curriculum and it was not until 1882 that it reappeared, this time in the form of 'pure laboratory science' - a view which has persisted, despite the periodic attempts to render it more socially and technologically aware, until the present day. The question of particular interest here is why this change should have come about.

Reasons could be sought in terms of a significant shift in general educational philosophy. As Eggleston (1977) comments,

> 'A new and important feature of the time ... was the redefinition of high-status knowledge as that which was not immediately useful in vocation or occupation.'

Thus,

> 'Advocates of scientific education took care to distinguish it from technical instruction, and to emphasize its liberal and academic value rather than its industrial and commercial utility.'
> (McCulloch, Jenkins and Layton, 1985)

Given such a change of emphasis, the Science of Common Things was a likely 'casualty' in the battle for resources. Byrne (1974) observes that, in all areas of the curriculum, teachers are able to argue much more successfully for the provision of resources for high ability children and for academic courses. Consequently, school subjects have tended to follow a common development pattern, with initial utilitarian or pedagogic considerations yielding to academic considerations (Goodson, 1981, 1983a). Layton, too, seems to hint at inevitability when he argues that pure laboratory science emerged in preference to alternative approaches because the alternatives had become 'casualties in a process of natural selection as the educational environment had become progessively more sharply defined' (Layton, 1976). It would however, be a serious misrepresentation of the work of these authors to imply that they regard the processes of curriculum change as being propelled solely by 'subject factors'. Curriculum change occurs in response to decisions made by individuals and interest groups; Goodson (1981, 1983a) refers, in particular, to the activities of sub-groups of subject specialists. In explaining the evolution of the science curriculum, 'more sharply defined' is to be interpreted as 'defined by the outcomes of political interactions' (Layton, 1985). Thus, it would be more correct to describe the process of change as political selection rather than natural selection. Reasons for the change of curriculum emphasis must be sought in the interests and motives of the decision makers.

Goodson (1983b) has issued a strong warning against 'raiding curriculum history' for evidence to support theories of contemporary curriculum change. He argues that because such evidence deals with a period before the emergence of the subject groups and professional organizations which he sees as the dominant forces in contemporary curriculum change, generalizations from the nineteenth century to the present day are, at best, oversimplified and, at worst, wilfully misleading. Nonetheless, the rise and spectacular fall of the Science of Common Things graphically illustrates the Layton and Goodson views of curriculum change and the inevitable triumph of the academic over the utilitarian and pedagogic approaches and there may be some evidence that the emergence of 'pure laboratory science' as the most favoured and politically acceptable view of school science was a consequence, in part, of emerging professionalization. Certainly, it was vigorously promoted by the scientific community and by those prominent in the educational establishment, though it will be argued later that the primary motives were socio-political rather than academic.

It has been argued that far from failing, which would be a more usual reason for an abrupt change in curriculum orientation, the experiment with the Science of Common Things was showing signs of marked success (Prophet, 1980). As mentioned earlier, there was considerable official encouragement for the scheme: grants for the purchase of books and equipment, compulsory science in the training colleges and vigorous support by prominent men such as James Kay-Shuttleworth, Henry Moseley and Lyon Playfair. Evidence of grass-roots support can be found in the enthusiastic reception afforded to a lengthy session dealing with the Science of Common Things at the first annual meeting of the United Association of Schoolmasters, in 1854, in the efforts of the Mechanics' Institutes to disseminate this style of science education to the working classes (Layton, 1973) and in the many articles devoted to the discussion and further development of the Science of Common Things in influential journals such as the Educational Expositor. Typical of these articles was Thomas Crampton's (1855) eloquent support of the Dawes scheme, which concludes -

> Say not that such teaching is unpoetical and utilitarian; it directly tends to develop that true poetry which dignifies the obscure, raises the lowly, exalts the common place.

It would, therefore, be more correct to say that the teaching of the Science of Common Things in elementary schools was abandoned, rather than superseded, and that its abandonment represents a deliberate act of social control. In studying these events the motives and interests of the decision makers must be taken into account. For example, whose interests were being threatened by the success of the Science of Common Things movement and why was pure laboratory science regarded as more acceptable? It is also pertinent to enquire into the motives of those who had promoted the Science of Common Things, in particular the motives of Richard Dawes. Layton (1973) portrays him as a liberal, progressive, educational reformer, but does not ask why this wealthy, middle class cleric should have concerned himself with educating the poor of his parish. In giving an account of Dawes' early life Layton admits there was no hint of his 'passionate concern for the education of the labouring classes' which was to dominate his later life, or of his later 'powerful advocacy of science as an instrument of secular instruction', and he says, 'it is not possible to do more than speculate' on the changes which occurred in Dawes during his early years at Kings Somborne. By attempting such speculation, it may be possible to gain an insight into Dawes' motivation in developing the Science of Common Things.

Social Control Through Education

In identifying the textbook, individual teachers and the subject committee (and, in particular, the examination sub-committee) as the major sources of 'authority' about science, scientific knowledge and science teaching in the U.S.A., the U.K. and Australia (respectively) during the 1960s and 1970s, Fensham (1980) shows how different social conditions produce different notions of what is legitimate and appropriate school science. It follows that in studying events in the history of science education it is necessary to take account of the social structure and conditions in which the events took place. Otherwise there is no way of accounting for the events and no way of explaining why individuals perceived the situation as they did or acted as they did. In attempting to interpret and explain such events, it can be a major error to eliminate what *seems* superfluous and irrelevant in order to concentrate on matters which are regarded as most significant in contemporary debate. For thereby we reinterpret the past in solely present day terms and may omit from consideration the very socio-cultural factors which determined the events we are studying and wish to explain. In other words, there is no objective, theory-free historical evidence. All events are viewed from a particular theoretical position and the best we can hope to do is to *reconstruct* the events by placing ourselves in what we regard as the social and intellectual climate pertaining at the time. Educational debate is carried on in a social context and is, therefore, subject to all the usual ideological, political, cultural and ethical influences. It is important that all these aspects are taken into consideration. Whether a curriculum innovation is accepted and institutionalized depends crucially on the cultural context in which the innovation is proposed and evaluated. In attempting to characterize this 'cultural context' as it applies to the episodes surrounding the Science of Common Things movement, it is important to consider the *knowledge resources* in educational philosophy and psychology available to the curriculum decision makers. These 'knowledge resources' included the dominant views about the nature and purpose of education, about the nature of science and scientific inquiry and about children and learning. As far as these latter considerations are concerned there was a well developed 'mentality theory', which asserted that two kinds of mental types exist: those of *agnostic* mentality capable of handling complex, abstract thought, and those of a *banausic* mentality, capable only of simple, concrete thought (Shapin and Barnes, 1976). This 'mentality theory' was used to legitimate curriculum proposals for the education of different social classes throughout the latter half of the nineteenth century. In addition, it was generally held that a correspondence existed between the *social* hierarchy and the distribution of mentalities, such that the upper classes were of a gnostic mentality whilst the lower classes were of a banausic mentality. However, *all* children, whatever their social class, were regarded as being of a banausic mentality. Whilst the education of the upper classes sought to bring about the change to gnostic mentality as quickly and as efficiently as possible, the education of the lower orders sought to *fix* mentality at the banausic stage. The contrasting aims of education for the two classes are reflected in the contrasting curricular provision - facts and sensory stimulation were seen as appropriate for the lower orders, principles of manipulation and abstractions for the upper classes.

> Also it is for many reasons very important, that discriminations be made in each (subject) between what is most certainly established, and what is conjectural and doubtful, presenting to ... the lower orders ... as much as possible the first and not the second.
>
> (Wilson, 1830)

> We must not make the mistake of ... overlaying the mind of the young *aspirant to a liberal profession* with facts ascertained and the results arrived at by learned and scientific research, while he is left unacquainted with the steps and processes of the proof.... He should not be tempted to take all upon trust, on the

> ipse dixit of a lecturer, but should be put through such a course of mental gymnastics, as might enable him to climb the tree and gather the ripe fruit for himself.
>
> (Pillans, 1856)

The theory connecting mentality, knowledge and social hierarchy was not founded on any concrete, empirical evidence; it evolved as a rationalization and legitimation of the existing social order. But, once established, it was used as a resource and advocates of significantly different educational policies used it to advance their own case and to denounce opponents. Whilst, of course, a variety of viewpoints existed, a crude dichotomy will be employed here between those views which collectively advocated that the working class be given access to knowledge (the 'liberal viewpoint'), and those which opposed such a move (the 'conservative viewpoint'). The supporters of the 'conservative view' were, in general, the aristocracy and the landed gentry. Indeed, one of the most prolific writers in support of this position was the self styled 'Country Gentleman'. He described society as a pyramid built on a hierarchy of authority: the working people who constitute the base of the pyramid being required to support the superstructure of their social superiors. This hierarchy corresponded to a divinely ordained and unalterable distribution of authority, knowledge and fixed mentality. To increase the knowledge of the masses would automatically make them wish to rise in society, thus altering the balance and threatening the whole social edifice. Consequently, the best way of maintaining the existing social order was to provide no education for the lower orders. Sir Archibald Alison also expressed concern about the consequences of educating the lower orders.

> Educating the lower orders is the only possible account for the extraordinary demoralization of the lower orders and the extent to which licentiousness and profligacy press, not only against the barriers of government, but restraints of religion, precepts of virtue and even the ordinary decorum of society.
>
> (Alison, 1834)

But Alison's stance was different from that of Country Gentleman. He regarded all human beings as having an evil nature capable of misusing any knowledge unless 'restrained by the force of moral precept and sanctified by the simultaneous spread of religious instruction', so that a 'control problem' existed, which could (only) be solved by religious instruction.

> Experience has now proved that the mere education of the lower classes without any care of their religious principles, has had no sensible effect in counteracting the influence of these demoralizing circumstances ... or preventing, by the extension of knowledge ... the growth of human depravity.
>
> (Alison, 1834)

It will be argued later that those in the liberal tradition, who advocated universal elementary education, were attempting to utilize the education system for the furtherance of their own political and social goals. Whichever line of argument individuals supported, whether 'conservative' or 'liberal', one assumption was always made: that the lower orders were only to possess an inferior kind of knowledge. If social stability was to be preserved, the lower orders must be <u>less knowledgeable</u> and have <u>less useful</u> knowledge. If these analyses are correct, Victorian society may be regarded as a <u>triple</u> hierarchy of authority, mentality and knowledge in which education was seen to have a key role. Education was required both to reflect and to maintain this hierarchical structure. Any attempt to interpret science curriculum change in nineteenth century England must assume that the curriculum decision makers acted in accordance with this background of contemporary common sense belief. In considering the motives and intentions of the liberal reformers of education it is tempting, from our present day standpoint, to regard reform and educational provision for the poor as uniformly 'good' and reformers as altruistic individuals motivated by purely philanthropic ideals. However, Richard Johnson (1970) maintains that the Victorian obsession with the education of the poor is best understood as a concern about authority, power and the assertion of control. Johnson argues that those who determined the elementary school curriculum also determined 'the patterns of thought, sentiment and behaviour of the working class'. In other words, political and social control of the masses could be, and should be established through the school curriculum. Elementary schools were regarded as successful in the eyes of the dominant groups in society if the pupils emerged 'respectful, cheerful, hard-working, loyal, pacific and religious' (Johnson, 1970).

However, not all curriculum proposals reveal their underlying intention quite so clearly. It is in these cases that the refined concept of social control motivation is a useful analytical tool, providing the researcher with a means of penetrating the rhetoric surrounding the proposals. The concept assists the study of curriculum change by focusing attention on both the explicit and implicit motives and interests of the curriculum decision makers. In Richard Johnson's words, it calls into question 'the assumption ... that the development of state educational systems has been an unambiguously progressive process' (Johnson, 1977).

The concept of social control was first employed at the turn of the century by Ross, who argued that social order is established by two categories of social control instruments: ethical (public opinion, personal ideals, arts, etc.) and political (law, education, organized religion, etc.). These latter instruments are 'the means deliberately chosen in order to reach certain ends. They are likely to come under the control of the organized few, and be used, whether for the corporate benefit or for class benefit, as the tools of policy' (Ross, 1929). Some fifty years later Landis modified and extended the concept by arguing that many social control mechanisms operate independently of any conscious attempt to manipulate. In other words, in any situation social control may be operating without the controllers or the controlled recognizing the fact.

> The most deep-seated and important influences in the development of the socialized personality, and in the regulation of human institutions, come from the non-rational, unconscious, all pervasive influences that mold the individual without his knowledge. They are a part of the general culture and become incorporated

> there without any conscious attempt on the part of any particular group, or even of a society to develop or foster them.
> (Landis, 1956)

It is, as Donajgrodzki (1977) argues, as though the 'controllers _and_ the controlled are ... trained to their roles' by the socialization process. This refined concept of social control is now a powerful research tool, enabling us to take account of the social structure within which curriculum decisions are taken and to free our interpretations of those events from the self evaluations of the decision makers. Whilst a particular interest group might make deliberate, even cynical use of the curriculum to bring about a degree of social control it is just as likely that the group acts with genuine concern and apparently altruistic motives, unaware of its unconscious social control motivation. Young (1976) has argued that 'those in positions of power will attempt to define what is to be taken as knowledge, how accessible to different groups any knowledge is, and what are the accepted relationships between different knowledge areas and between those who have access to them and make them available'. If this element of socially constructed knowledge is added to the desire to effect some measure of behavioural change, then we have a refined concept of the social control process which suggests that particular interest groups (usually those in positions of power) select particular kinds of knowledge for presentation to particular groups of children, by particular methods, and that they base their curriculum decisions on what is in their interests, rather than what is in the children's interests - though, if Donajgrodzki and Landis are correct, they may do so unconsciously.

James Kay-Shuttleworth is typical of those prominent members of the Victorian middle classes who saw educational reform as a means of exerting social control and, thereby, stabilizing society. In his Manchester pamphlet, published in 1832, he presents a first hand picture of the reality of city life for the lower orders: a vivid picture of domestic squalor, collapse of family life, crime, prostitution, drunkenness, and a high incidence of diseases such as cholera and typhus. Promiscuity and debauchery, which supposedly abounded, were seen as threats to the stability of family life, resulting in poverty and child neglect; the decline in church attendance was seen as further evidence of the absence of 'suitable' moral values; drunkenness was regarded as a serious problem and public houses were seen as working class meeting places for obscene chatter, gossip-mongering and the fostering of dangerously seditious politics. Raised in such an atmosphere of intemperance, parental self indulgence and child neglect, working class children were seen to begin life predisposed to criminality, unprepared for honest hard work and potentially hostile to capitalism. Similar views were expressed very strongly by Andrew Ure.

> ... from the evil bent of human nature, the slaves of prejudice and vice; they can see objects only on one side, that which a sinister selfishness presents to their view; they are readily moved to outrage by crafty demagogues, and they are apt to regard their best benefactor, the enterprising and frugal capitalist who employs them, with a jealous and hostile eye.
>
> (Ure, 1835)

This instability in working class life was seen to pose a threat to the stable, routine behaviour required by increasing industrialization. If measures were not found to remedy the situation, industrial society and the well being of the middle classes was likely to be at risk. The solution that Kay-Shuttleworth proposed was two-fold: reform of the environment (better sanitation, better housing, a more effective police force, etc.) and educational reform.

> The poor might thus through education be also made to understand their political position in society, and the duties that belong to it, ... (that) they are infinitely more interested in the preservation of public tranquility than any other class of society; that mechanical inventions and discoveries are always supremely advantageous to them.
>
> (Kay-Shuttleworth, 1832)

With his appointment as the first Secretary of the newly formed Committee of Council for Education in 1839, Kay-Shuttleworth's views and rationalizations became official policy and the reports of the Inspectorate during the period of his administration reflect the view that the problems of the working class were largely of their own making and arose mainly through ignorance, laziness or neglect - all of which could be eliminated by personal effort. The solution was seen to lie in altering their system of values, through education: the school should take over the responsibilities of the parent and substitute its own more suitable values for the deficient values of the lower orders. Thus, schools for the lower orders were justified as instruments of socialization. In pursuing this goal he promoted the provision of libraries and Mechanics' Institutes and advocated the view that the school should become the centre for the social and cultural life of the community. The inadequacy of the working class family life had been a frequent target of attack for the liberal reformers at that time, as evidenced by these remarks by James Pillans, a strong advocate of compulsory education, and a major influence on Kay-Shuttleworth's views.

> How important it is, in particular, for the diminution of crime that the infant children of the working classes should be removed from the parental roof during the hours of labour, when it is inconvenient for the mother to tend them, even if her tendence were of any value.
>
> (Pillans, 1829)

Andrew Ure (1835) had argued that the manufacturers themselves should provide infant schools, because 'in such seminaries ... they are sure that the children learn to be obedient and orderly and to restrain their passions; and they are equally sure that, in a large proportion of cases, it is not so in their own homes'.

Another significant influence on Kay-Shuttleworth was the work of Henry Brougham. Brougham himself had been very much influenced by what he regarded as the enlightened approach of the Swiss aristocrat Philipp von Fellenberg, a friend and supporter of Pestalozzi. What was unusual about Fellenberg's approach was his concern for all classes of society: future leaders and led, future employers and employees. His original school for poor children at Hofwyl, near Berne, was expanded to include an intermediate school, for the sons of farmers, and an upper school, for the socially elite. Fellenberg regarded a practical 'agricultural education', plus a little nature study and drawing, as appropriate for the poor, because of its emphasis on observation and reasoning, and its value in inculcating habits of industry, obedience, frugality and kindliness (Fellenberg, 1839). In addition to the practical work, the curriculum for the intermediate school provided rather more theoretical work and that for the upper school included classics, modern languages, science and music. By establishing this complex of schools, which also included a training college for teachers and a summer school for in-service education of village schoolmasters, Fellenberg created Swiss society in miniature, with all its inherent class divisions. Divisions which he regarded as divinely ordained. By educating different social classes together, each could learn respect for, and understanding of the other and, most importantly of all, the lower orders could see that the lives of those above them were not an endless round of idleness and pleasure, but were subject to strict discipline, though of a different type! In reply to those who were concerned that education of the poor might lead to social revolution, Fellenberg claimed that the peasantry who were educated in the general school were, as a consequence, perfectly content and had no desire to rise above their proper station in society. Brougham saw great possibilities in adapting Fellenberg's ideas to an industrial rather than agricultural context, as a means of stabilizing the social order in England. Although much of Brougham's work was concerned with the education of the adult population of the labouring poor, through Mechanics' Institutes and his Society for the Diffusion of Scientific Knowledge, his message was basically that advocated by Fellenberg: that the better educated the people, the more tranquil and orderly in their political conduct they will be. Kay-Shuttleworth set up a school at Norwood modelled on Fellenberg's experiment at Hofwyl, using teachers recruited from David Stow's Normal Seminary in Glasgow. Stow's influence is apparent in the constant references in the school documents to training, rather than the more usual term of instruction. Training, according to Stow, includes both moral and intellectual development and is a highly skilled craft 'awakening thought, stimulating and directing enquiry and evolving the energies of the intellect' (Stow, 1836).

There would be no difficulty in seeing a social control motive in a curriculum comprising a moralizing religious education, which featured very prominently in Fellenberg's scheme. What was enterprising about the particular curriculum supported by Kay-Shuttleworth was its emphasis on science. In accordance with 'mentality theory', two conceptions of school science were advanced: one factual and unchanging (for the lower orders), one theoretical and provisional (for the higher orders). The central theme of science for the masses was to be the immutable 'laws of nature'. The world (both physical and moral) was regarded as governed by natural laws instituted by God to serve as guides to human conduct. Those who violated natural behaviour (i.e. those who broke God's laws) would be punished by God, through nature. These punishments were the social evils so vividly described by Kay-Shuttleworth. These ideas found full expression and justification in the phrenology movement, which worked them into a complex system of 'natural laws' incorporating 'mentality theory' and beliefs about the social distribution of mental types. The message comes through very clearly in the writings of George Combe, founder of the British phrenology movement.

> Natural laws do exist, and the Creator punishes if they be not obeyed. The evils of life are these punishments.
> (Combe, 1848)

Phrenology and Education

The nineteenth century science of phrenology is often regarded as mere quackery, as a peculiar Victorian enthusiasm that emerged, flourished and died within a few short years and had little significant or lasting influence. It is usually classed alongside phlogiston theory, astrology, transmutation of the elements, ideas such as Wilhelm Reich's theory of orgone energy and the speculative writings of Velikovsky and von Daniken as just another idea 'on the losing side' (MacLaren, 1974). Recently, however, there has been a radical reappraisal of the role of the phrenology movement, such that Cooter (1976) is able to claim that phrenology was 'one of the most important intellectual manifestations of the nineteenth century ...

because of the wide range of Victorian values, ideas and attitudes it appears to have mediated'. In fact, phrenologists were deeply involved in the development of many of the socio-intellectual revolutions of the Victorian era (in anthropology, biology, public health and penal reform, religion, and so on). In attempting to trace the dominant influences on the intellectual life of Victorian society Young (1980) reasserts the view that phrenology played a key role in many of these developments and constituted a major influence on many prominent figures, men such as Chambers, Spencer, Lewes and Wallace. Phrenology was promoted through the Mechanics' Institutes, the phrenological societies (which existed in many major British towns) and the host of phrenological publications, most influential of which were The Phrenological Journal and George Combe's Constitution of Man.

The basis of phrenology was the identification of the faculties of the brain. Whilst phrenologists were somewhat vague regarding the actual number of these faculties, they were clear that individuals were born with a fixed number, in proportions which fixed their characters, personalities and intellectual capabilities. Irrespective of what the particular faculties were, each individual possessed a number of 'animal propensities', 'moral sentiments' and 'intellectual faculties'. Although the animal propensities were not in themselves evil, their abuse and the neglect of the other faculties led to evil. Thus, the ignorant or uncivilized were prone to become ferocious, sensual and superstitious. If, however, individuals had the opportunity to cultivate their moral sentiments and intellectual faculties, they were able to become aware of their own constitution and to control their animal propensities. This new self perception, and with it the awareness of having to live harmoniously with neighbours and fellow workers, would lead directly to happiness. All that was needed to bring about a change in behaviour for the better was the instruction and exercise of the intellectual faculties. Once they were correctly exercised, ignorance would be overcome and development of the moral sentiments would automatically follow. Instruction, training and development of these faculties could be achieved through education, though it was important to recognize that 'the effects of education are always bounded by the natural capacity of the mind'

(Combe, 1852). Whilst modification of and development of the faculties was the prime purpose of education, the basic provision of faculties could not be altered: a 'very large' intellectual faculty could not be developed from a 'very small' one, nor could a 'very large' animal propensity be reduced to one of 'very small' dimensions. Combe clarified official thinking on this matter -

> We cannot essentially change the character of any natural feeling ... and our efforts are limited to restraining the different faculties from improper manifestations, and to directing them to legitimate and beneficial indulgence.... Different capacities are bestowed by Nature on different individuals, and after we shall have done our best to instruct and train the people, there will always remain a sufficient number of them whom no education, however much it may improve their morality, will ever raise intellectually above the humbler duties of civilised life.
>
> (Combe, 1852)

Since individuals were endowed with different faculties of varying strength, people were inherently unequal and could be classified into three mental types. The lowest class was that in which the animal propensities so predominated over moral sentiments and intellectual faculties that, if left to themselves, its members are 'extremely prone to vicious indulgences hurtful to themselves and to society'. The second class comprised individuals in whom the animal propensities and moral sentiments were well balanced. Such individuals were capable of very significant self-improvement through education and personal endeavour. The elite, upper class was made up of those in whom the moral sentiments and intellect were so greatly predominant over animal propensities that 'a perpetual serenity of temper and benignity of disposition reign within' (Combe, 1828). This mental hierarchy laid the foundation for the social hierarchy and since one's mental rank was unchangeable, so was the social structure! The inherent limits to each individual's intellectual faculties ensured that there would be no alteration to the social structure of wealth and power through education.

Rather, an uplifting of the general level of rationality, with concomitant improved morality and social behaviour, was the anticipated outcome. The higher and middle social classes were reassured that their status was not threatened, whilst the lower orders were offered a degree of self improvement, provided they obeyed the Natural Laws which constituted the core of phrenological theory. Those who followed these laws were assured of happiness and success, whilst those who did not would be punished by God through the various social evils referred to earlier. In other words, the social order was seen to be underpinned by the laws of nature, so that instruction in these laws would reinforce the existing social hierarchy. Since the lower orders had only limited mentality, the only possible means of instructing them in the laws of nature was through stimulation of the 'sensory pathways'. Thus, 'mentality theory' and phrenological theory pointed very directly to the kind of science education pioneered by Charles and Elizabeth Mayo, John Wood and Richard Dawes. Even though the Natural Laws were never clearly defined, phrenology quickly became part of common sense knowledge, influencing and shaping the opinions of the increasingly powerful Victorian middle classes. The major treatise on phrenology, George Combe's Constitution of Man (published in 1828), was one of the great Victorian best sellers: within forty years of its publication 100,000 copies had been sold, twice as many as Darwin's The Origin of Species. It is said that even homes which otherwise contained only the Bible and Pilgrim's Progress had a copy of Combe's Constitution of Man. The great success of the book derived from the almost universal appeal of phrenology: it appealed to the upper classes because it reassured them that the social hierarchy was 'natural' and enduring; it appealed to the professional and middle classes because its meritocratic overtones confirmed their attitudes regarding advancement through personal effort and achievement; it appealed to the aspiring members of the working class, who sought from its teachings practical advice on self-improvement.

> Phrenology flourished as a popular science in early Victorian Britain because of a coincidence of three factors: traditional philosophical and theological theories of mind no longer seemed adequate as scienti-

> fic explanations; rapid changes in the social structure created a sizeable number of reformers who sought an empirical grounding for their social philosophy; and the breakdown of traditional society created for many individuals a wide variety of personal opportunities which were both liberating and perplexing. For three decades phrenology appeared both to a professional, intellectual elite and also to a much wider lower-middle-class and working class audience, to be a successful solution to their scientific, philosophical and practical needs.
>
> (Parsinnen, 1974)

As Young (1973) says, 'it was offered as the key to all philosophical and social problems - a panacea for all social ills'.

In view of this widespread appeal, it would be surprising if phrenological theory had failed to influence the thinking of the liberal reformers in education and been used by them as a theoretical justification in securing their objective of social control of the lower orders. It has been argued by Hodson and Prophet (1983a) that in trying to improve the education of the working class, these reformers had strong socio-political motives and were, in reality, serving their own interests. They conclude that:

i) middle class liberalism was based on an underlying interest in stabilizing and controlling the socially disruptive forces of the lower orders in early industrial society;
ii) phrenology played a crucial role in rationalizing and legitimating these interests;
iii) school science became the vehicle by which this control was to be established.

From this theoretical perspective it is possible to analyse the work of Richard Dawes and the events surrounding the rise and fall of the Science of Common Things.

Richard Dawes and the Science of Common Things

Syllabus details of the Science of Common Things can be found in Layton's (1973) classic work *Science for the People*. Of more significance here are the teaching methods Dawes employed, his underlying philosophy, his motivation and his actions.

Realizing how few teachers possessed the knowledge and expertise necessary to implement his proposals, Dawes produced a teacher's guide: Suggestive Hints towards Improved Secular Instruction making it bear upon Practical Life (1854). This book, which might lay claim to be the first curriculum development package in science, contained a powerful argument in favour of teaching science 'bearing upon the arts of life and of everyday things' and an abundance of practical illustrations. This emphasis on direct experience, though not necessarily on individual practical work (as advocated by his great contemporary John Stevens Henslow at Hitcham in Suffolk), was a powerful and significant element in Dawes' scheme and derived directly, as indicated earlier, from 'mentality theory'. 'Mere verbal explanations ... are of no use whatever', he argued, and words and other abstractions only become useful when accompanied by practical illustration. The overriding aim of schoolmasters ought to be 'to make children observant and reflective; to make them think and reason about the objects around them' (Dawes, 1857). By using examples that were familiar to them, and by providing opportunities for the use of reason, Dawes was providing instruction in science which proved spectacularly successful. As will become apparent later, it was this very success that sowed the seeds of the scheme's own destruction.

It was suggested earlier that speculation about Richard Dawes' early life at Kings Somborne might provide an explanation for his concern with the education of the poor and his development of the Science of Common Things. A concern with social control and a commitment to phrenological ideas together constitute such an explanation. Social stability was a predominant concern of the mid-nineteenth century middle classes and in Dawes' case this concern was made more immediate by direct contact with the poor, through his parish work at Kings Somborne, described by Layton (1973) as an 'especially poor parish of some 1,100 people'. Such experiences inevitably lead to conflict: on the one hand, genuine concern for the lot of the labouring poor and, on the other hand, a deep anxiety that their struggle for self-realization, improvement and advancement might destroy the stability and order of society. Phrenological theory would have provided a ready rationalization of this conflict and a possible solution: self improvement for the masses and stabilization of the social hierarchy via education. The poor would be shown that whilst they might improve their lot considerably, they could not expect to alter their natural place in society. Understanding and acceptance of the laws of nature, and their justification of the existing social hierarchy, was to be achieved through studying the Science of Common Things.

A more concrete link between Dawes and the phrenology movement may be found in his association with William Ellis, a leading figure in the development of secular education and an influential phrenologist. De Giustino (1975) describes how Ellis's schools quickly became established as 'the working models for other phrenologists interested in education'. Because of his vigorous promotion of phrenological principles and his concern to remove religious instruction from the curriculum, Ellis was strongly criticized by the clergy for fostering a 'Godless education'. Given their contrasting backgrounds, social connections and personal reputations, it is rather surprising that Dawes, the clergyman, should agree to edit and to write the preface to a book written anonymously by Ellis, the 'Godless educationist'. It is even more surprising that this work (Lessons on the Phenomena of Industrial Life) should have been promoted by Dawes and Playfair for adoption by the Church Training Schools. Layton does not question the apparent contradiction in this collaboration, nor does he note Ellis's strong phrenological commitment, but he does point to a certain similarity of views.

> Ellis and Dawes were, in fact, old allies who had discovered much common ground in their discussions within the Society of Arts on the subject of schools for the labouring poor.
>
> (Layton, 1973)

Through contact with Ellis, Dawes must have been familiar with phrenological philosophy, and the act of lending his name to a phrenologically-based treatise on the laws of social economy indicates his acceptance of much of this philosophy.

Thus, it would seem that Dawes and his contemporaries in elementary science education were engaged in the articulation and development of an education for the poor designed to fit them for their industrial occupations and to develop in them attitudes of obedience and orderliness. The intention was to teach them that personal shortcomings were responsible for their present unhappy situation and that the opportunity for improvement lay in their own hands. Through individual efforts, learning to rely on one's own hard work, the improvement of diet, ventilation and cleanliness in the home, and through constant practice of habits of prudence, sobriety and self-denial, the general condition of the lower orders would be improved - although their overall station in life would not.

In drawing attention away from the economic and social demands of capitalism as the cause of their current deplorable quality of life, and presenting the idea of self-help through science, the liberal reformers can be seen to be inculcating the values of the newly powerful and industrially dependent middle classes into the labouring poor, thus stabilizing the social structure and furthering their own vested interest. In arguing that the move to establish the Science of Common Things in the elementary schools was an attempt to establish some measure of social control to counteract the problems created by early industrialization, Hodson and Prophet (1983a) identify four key objectives.

1. To gain acceptance by the lower orders of a pre-ordained social hierarchy and their low position in it.
2. To foster the idea that the poor physical and economic state of the lower orders was of their own making and not the fault of the capitalist system.
3. To encourage them to improve their social conditions, but not their social position, by the application of simple scientific principles to their everyday lives.
4. To inculcate a set of moral values which were the dominant values of the new middle class and were seen as essential for the ultimate success of industrialization.

A fifth and closely related objective was the fostering of the orderly behaviour and obedience necessary for the smooth operation of the industrial enterprise. In other words, the production of a compliant force of factory workers.

In the early 1850s this experiment with the science curriculum appeared poised for success, but by the end of the decade it had lost its momentum so completely that the Revised Code of 1862 contained no proposals at all for elementary school science. The reasons for the rapid decline of the Science of Common Things movement lie in the power struggle between the liberal reformers and the conservative establishment. Again, concern with social control is seen to have motivated the curriculum decision-makers.

The Emergence of Pure Science

The declared goals of the Science of Common Things were the general intellectual development of children, the improvement of reading skills, the acquisition of scientific knowledge related to the child's immediate environment, and the provision of experience for the exercise of reason, speculation and imagination. It was assumed, in accord with the views of Charles and Elizabeth Mayo, that once self-confidence and clarity of thought had been achieved, improvement in the moral and religious condition of the children would follow. The emphasis on applied sciences, such as mechanics and agricultural chemistry, ensured that education could be related to that which was familiar to the labouring classes and that this familiarity would ensure that the restricted linguistic experiences of so many elementary school children was no longer an insuperable obstacle. The Science of Common Things was to be the vehicle by which the lower orders were equipped to think for themselves.

> Here was no crumb of upper-class education charitably dispensed to the children of the labouring poor. Instruction was related to a culture which was familiar to them and provided opportunities for the use of reason and speculation by drawing upon observations which pertained to everyday life. Understanding and the exercise of thought were not the prerogative of the upper and middle classes.
>
> (Layton, 1973)

The significance of this last sentence cannot

be overemphasized. As a consequence of the spectacular success of the Science of Common Things in achieving this goal, influential scientists of the day - men such as Owen, Hooker, Lyell and Faraday - advanced the view that the ruling class was in danger of losing its dominant position through lack of scientific knowledge and that the introduction of science into the curriculum for the children of the upper classes was an urgent priority. The science they considered appropriate was 'pure laboratory science', as practiced at Liebig's research laboratory at Giessen University, which in recent years had been attracting large numbers of British students. The ideal of this research school - research and enquiry for its own sake - provided a concept of pure science which was a ready-made candidate for inclusion in the curriculum for the education of the higher orders, with its traditional emphasis on abstraction and social distancing. Robert Hunt (1854), Secretary to the Society of Arts, argued that whilst the practical aspect of science was of 'some importance', it was the study of abstract science that 'refined and elevated human feelings' and was the true mark of a gentleman. Science was to be admitted to the curriculum of the public and grammar schools provided that it conformed to the principles underpinning the traditional classical education. In other words, it should emphasize academic and cultural matters rather than commercial and industrial concerns. This view of science as a rigorous form of mental training gained ready support from the scientific community and from the universities (Barton, 1981).

Under the chairmanship of Lord Wrottesley, the parliamentary committee of the British Association for the Advancement of Science sought the opinion of many eminent scientists about the most appropriate form of science education for the upper classes. The report clearly indicates a strong belief in the educational value of pure laboratory science. It could be argued that the report also implicitly reflected the growing awareness of a serious problem: that science education at the elementary level was proving highly successful, particularly as far as the development of thinking skills was concerned, and that the social hierarchy was under threat because there was no corresponding development for the higher orders. Giving the labouring poor access to a particular form of knowledge, and a particular set of skills, whilst denying it to their superiors, was seen as a very dangerous state of affairs. Wrottesley, himself, drew attention to this matter when he commented on the impressive grasp of scientific principles by children in schools for the labouring poor compared with those in grammar and public schools. He described in detail an incident in which he asked a class for the explanation of the principle of a pump.

> ... a poor boy hobbled forth to give a reply; he was lame and humpbacked, and his wan emaciated face told only too clearly the tale of poverty and its consequences ... but he gave forthwith so lucid and intelligent a reply to the question put to him that there arose a feeling of admiration for the child's talents combined with a sense of shame that more information should be found in some of the lowest of our lower classes on matters of general interest than in those far above them in the world by station.
>
> (Wrottesley, 1860)

Wrottesley's conclusion on the incident reflects the fears of the upper classes concerning the possible consequences of such education of the lower orders.

> It would be an unwholesome and vicious state of society in which those who are comparatively unblessed with nature's gifts should be generally superior in intellectual attainments to those above them in station.
>
> (Wrottesley, 1860)

Similar views, showing the depth of the disquiet, were expressed by many other influential individuals. In an article in the Edinburgh Review, A.C. Tait (who followed Arnold at Rugby and later became Archbishop of Canterbury) expressed concern that the education of the poor was making such good progress that the higher orders were being left behind. Consequently, it was 'absolutely necessary for government to attend to the education of the rich' (Tait, 1854). He predicted a complete overturn of the social order if 'the son of a labourer possesses better knowledge than the son of the squire'. It is interesting to note that he also made direct reference to Dawes at Kings Somborne and to the undesirability of the children of labourers being educated alongside the sons of the higher orders. It would seem that Dawes had acted very directly on Fellenberg's ideas. By the time of the publication of the Report of the Public Schools Commission (1864), this anxiety had reached epidemic, almost hysterical proportions.

> It is not only an unhealthy but also a dangerous state of things in some respects, that the material world should be very much better known by the middle classes of society than by the upper classes.
>
> (H.M. Commissioners, 1864)

If it was considered such a 'dangerous state of things' that the new middle class had access to a form of knowledge denied to the upper class, how much more serious must have seemed the situation described by Wrottesley, in which the lowest social group was seen to be becoming superior in scientific knowledge.

By the late 1850s a campaign, backed by _The Times_, had been mounted on two levels. On the _one hand_ it advocated the merits of pure science as an essential component of the curriculum for the higher orders and, on the other hand, it advocated a _halt_ to the scientific education of the lower orders, whom it saw as being dangerously over-educated. The higher orders had realized that those below them in the social hierarchy were gaining access to scientific knowledge, and its attendant critical thought processes, and that such a valuable resource might be used in future socially and politically undesirable activity. It has been suggested that this, and not the appearance of what Layton (1973) calls 'better alternatives', was the reason behind the abandonment of the Science of Common Things (Hodson and Prophet, 1983b) and that the Revised Code of 1862, which removed science from the elementary school curriculum, was the institutionalization of these beliefs, justified on administrative and financial grounds. Prominent amongst the advocates of the 'new' elementary school curriculum was Joshua Fitch, appointed Principal of the British and Foreign

School Society Training College in 1854, and promoted to the Inspectorate in 1863. His curriculum proposals comprised reading and writing, arithmetic, English grammar ('the classics of the poor'), a little geography and history, scripture, but no science. Instead of a thorough working knowledge of common and everyday things obtained by the direct study of science, as in Dawes' scheme, there were to be 'country walks, star gazing and domestic experiences' (Fitch, 1861).

When science eventually reappeared in the curriculum of the elementary schools, some twenty years later, it was in a very different form from that advocated by Dawes. A watered down version of pure laboratory science had become accepted as the correct view of science, a view which has persisted, largely unchallenged, to the present day. Roscoe (1874), a vigorous campaigner for this conception of school science, argued that the goal of pure science is 'personal communication with nature for its own sake'. Through this type of scientific enquiry, which was value-free and disinterested, 'habits of independent thoughts and ideas of free enquiry are thus at once inculcated'. In arguing that schools exist primarily to select and supply future scientists of talent, he described the teaching of science in schools as 'the means of sifting out from the great mass of the people those golden grains of genius which are too often lost amongst the sands of mediocrity'. This view of science was designed to develop an elite who conformed to the image of the pure scientist rationalized by the higher orders. Science had been allowed into elementary education once more, but this time on the terms of the ruling order, which effectively excluded the mass of the population from any meaningful scientific education. In this way it was ensured that the resource of scientific knowledge was available to all in principle, but only accessible in practice to the elite. Thus, it no longer constituted a threat to the existing social order.

Michael Young (1976) claims that science teachers continue to see the main purpose of science education as the supply of future scientists, with the consequent neglect of the science education of the less gifted. Curriculum decision makers, he argues, have social control motives in wishing to create a large, scientifically illiterate workforce, 'who see themselves as dependent upon experts in more and more aspects of their life'. He further claims that those in power see it as desirable that 'except in the specific context of their work, and possibly in leisure pursuits such as car maintenance, our increasingly technologically dominated world remains for the majority as much a mystery as the theological mysteries of feudal times'. Whilst these latter claims may be extravagantly overstated, there is little doubt that in presenting science as an abstract, theoretical study, little provision is made for the future non-specialist. Alternative, non-academic courses, for those less successful in passing examinations, rarely provide a genuine consideration of scientific methods and issues. As a consequence, few would claim that contemporary British science education produces a scientifically and technologically literate citizenry.

What of the Future?

The thesis developed here is that the way in which school science is perceived is _not_ the end result of inevitable progress in the disinterested search for 'curriculum truth'. Rather, it is _socially constructed_, being the product of particular sets of choices made by particular groups of people, at particular times, in furtherance of their particular interests. Thus, it represents the triumph of a particular interest group. In the words of Karl Marx:

> The ideas of the ruling class are in every epoch the ruling ideas: i.e. the class which is the ruling _material_ force of society is, at the same time, its ruling _intellectual_ force. The class which has the means of material production at its disposal has control, at the same time, over the means of mental production, so that thereby, generally speaking, the ideas of those who lack the means of mental production are subject to it.
>
> (Marx, 1845)

An attempt has been made in this article to explain the rapid rise and equally rapid fall of the Science of Common Things in terms of social control motivation on the part of the liberal reformers who supported it and the conservative 'establishment' which removed it from the curriculum. It may be possible to discern interest group conflict and implicit social control intent in many other episodes in the history of science education - for example in the nature study movement in the early years of the century (Jenkins, 1981), in the general science movement in the years immediately following World War One (Jenkins, 1979), in the Nuffield developments of the 1960s (Waring, 1979a, 1979b) and in the proposals of the Scottish Education Department (Millar, 1981b). Consequently, it is important that teachers are alert to implicit as well as explicit messages in proposals for new science curriculum initiatives (ASE, 1979, 1981; SSCR, 1984). In confronting such proposals, it is important to ask:

1. Whose view of what is appropriate school science is being advanced?

2. Whose interests are being served by the particular proposals being promoted?

3. Whose view of society is being projected?

These questions become even more relevant when confronting the increasing number of calls for children to consider science in its socio-economic context (HMI, 1979; DES, 1982, ASE; 1984). It is not by coincidence, and certainly not without historical precedent, that current proposals for science courses for the 'less able' are considerably more socially oriented and, therefore, susceptible to social control influences than the abstract, 'pure science' courses proposed for the high fliers.

Notes

1. More detailed information about the life and work of Richard Dawes may be found in Ball (1964), Henry (1867) and Layton (1972b).

2. Details of Dawes' teaching strategies and course content are provided by Layton (1973).

Acknowledgement

This chapter draws extensively on the historical research of R.B. Prophet (1980) and the author's debt to Bob is gratefully acknowledged.

References

Association for Science Education (1979)
Alternatives for Science Education
Hatfield, ASE.

Association for Science Education (1981)
Education Through Science
Hatfield, ASE.

Association for Science Education (1984)
Rethinking Science? Teaching Science in its Social Context
Hatfield, ASE.

Alison, A. (1834)
'Progress of Social Disintegration No 1. The Schoolmaster' Blackwoods Edinburgh Review 35 pp.228-248.

Ball, N. (1964)
'Richard Dawes and the Teaching of Common Things' Educational Review 17 (1) pp.59-64.

Barnett, C. (1979)
'Technology, Education and Industrial and Economic Strength' Journal of the Royal Society of Arts CXXVII (5271) pp.118-127.

Barton, R. (1981) 'Scientific Opposition to Technical Education' in Stephens, M.D. and Roderick, G.W. (Eds.) Scientific and Technical Education in Early Industrial Britain
Nottingham, Department of Adult Education, University of Nottingham pp.13-27.

Bernstein, B. (1971)
'On the Classification and Framing of Educational Knowledge' in Young, M.F.D. (Ed.) Knowledge and Control
London, Collier Macmillan pp.47-69.

Brock, W.H. (1975)
'From Liebig to Nuffield. A Bibliography of the History of Science Education, 1839-1974' Studies in Science Education 2 pp.67-99.

Byrne, E.M. (1974)
Planning and Educational Inequality
Slough, NFER.

Combe, G. (1828)
Constitution of Man
Edinburgh, J. Anderson.

Combe, G. (1848)
What Should Secular Education Embrace?
Edinburgh, MacLachlan, Stewart and Company.

Combe, G. (1852)
On Secular Education
Edinburgh, MacLachlan, Stewart and Company.

Committee of Council on Education (1847-8)
Minutes pp.7-27.
Cooter, R.J. (1976)
'Phrenology: the Provocation of Progress'
History of Science XIV pp.211-234.
Crampton, T. (1855)
'The Teaching of Common Things'
Educational Expositor 3 pp.161-164.
Dawes, R. (1853)
Suggestive Hints Towards Improved Secular Instruction
London, R. Groombridge and Sons.
Dawes, R. (1854)
Lessons on the Phenomena of Industrial Life.
Written anonymously by Ellis, W.
London, R. Groombridge and Sons.
Dawes, R. (1857)
Effective Instruction
London, R. Groombridge and Sons.
De Giustino, D. (1975)
Conquest of Mind. Phrenology and Victorian Social Thought
London, Croom Helm.
Donajgrodzki, A.P. (1977)
'Introduction' in Donajgrodzki, A.P. (Ed.)
Social Control in Nineteenth Century Britain
London, Croom Helm.
Department of Education and Science (1982)
Science Education in Schools
London, DES.
Eggleston, J. (1977)
The Sociology of the School Curriculum
London, Routledge and Kegan Paul.
Fellenberg, P.E. von (1839)
What Fellenberg has done for Education
London, Saunders and Otley.
Fensham, P.J. (1980)
'Books, Teachers and Committees - A Comparative Essay on Authority in Science Education'
European Journal of Science Education 2 (3) pp.245-252.
Fitch, J.G. (1861)
Public Education Why is a New Code Wanted?
London, Bell and Daldy.
Goodson, I.F. (1981)
'Becoming an Academic Subject: Patterns of Explanation and Evolution'
British Journal of Sociology of Education 2 (2) pp.163-180.

Goodson, I.F. (1983a)
School Subjects and Curriculum Change
Beckenham, Croom Helm.
Goodson, I.F. (1983b)
'Subjects for Study: Aspects of a Social History of Curriculum'
Journal of Curriculum Studies 15 (4) pp.391-408.
Hodson, D. and Prophet, R.B. (1983a)
'The Influence of Phrenological Theory on the Science Curriculum in Victorian England'
European Journal of Science Education 5 (3) pp.263-274.
Hodson, D. and Prophet, R.B. (1983b)
'Why the Science Curriculum Changes - Evolution or Social Control?'
School Science Review 65 (230) pp.5-18.
H.M. Commissioners (1864)
Inquiries into the Revenues and Management of Certain Colleges and Schools, and the Studies Pursued and Instruction Given Therein.
London, HMSO.
H.M. Inspectorate (1979)
Aspects of Secondary Education in England
London, HMSO.
Hunt, R. (1854)
'On Familiar Methods of Instruction in Science' in Lectures in Connection with the Educational Exhibition of the Society of Arts, Manufacturers and Commerce
London, Society of Arts pp.175-179.
Henry, W.C. (1867)
A Biographical Notice of the Late Very Rev. Richard Dawes, M.A., Dean of Hereford.
London, William Clowes and Sons.
Jenkins, E.W. (1979)
From Armstrong to Nuffield
London, John Murray.
Jenkins, E.W. (1981)
'Science, Sentimentalism or Social Control? The Nature Study Movement in England and Wales, 1899-1914' History of Education 10 (1) pp.33-43.
Johnson, R. (1970)
'Educational Policy and Social Control in Early Victorian England' Past and Present 49 pp.96-119.

Johnson, R. (1977)
'Educating the Educators: "Experts" and the State 1833-9' in Donajgrodzki, A.P. (Ed.) Social Control in Nineteenth Century Britain London, Croom Helm.

Kay-Shuttleworth, J.P. (1832)
The Moral and Physical Condition of the Working Classes reprinted in Kay-Shuttleworth, J.P. (1862) Four Periods of Public Education London, Harvester Press (1973).

Landis, P.H. (1956)
Social Control: Social Organization and Disorganization in Process, revised edition, Philadelphia, J.B. Lippincott and Company.

Layton, D. (1972a)
'Science as General Education' Trends in Education 25 pp.11-15.

Layton, D. (1972b)
'Science in the Schools: the First Wave - A Study of the Influence of Richard Dawes (1793-1867)' British Journal of Educational Studies 20 (1) pp.38-57.

Layton, D. (1973)
Science for the People London, George Allen and Unwin.

Layton, D. (1976)
'The Educational Work of the Parliamentary Committee of the British Association for the Advancement of Science' History of Education 5 (1) pp.25-39.

Layton, D. (1985)
Private communication.

MacLaren, A (1974)
'Phrenology: Medium and Message' Journal of Modern History 46 (1) pp.86-97.

Marx, K. (1845)
The German Ideology quoted in McLellan, D. (1971) The Thought of Karl Marx: An Introduction London, Macmillan.

Mayo, C. and Mayo, E. (1849)
Practical Remarks on Infant Education London, Home and Colonial School Society.

McCulloch, G., Jenkins, E. and Layton, D. (1985)
Technological Revolution? The Politics of School Science and Technology in England and Wales Since 1945 Lewes, The Falmer Press.

Millar, R.H. (1981a)
'Science Curriculum and Social Control: A Comparison of some Recent Science Curriculum Proposals in the United Kingdom and the Federal Republic of Germany' Comparative Education 17 (1) pp.23-46.

Millar, R.H. (1981b)
'Curriculum Rhetoric and Social Control: A Perspective on Recent Science Curriculum Development' European Journal of Science Education 3 (3) pp.271-284.

Parsinnen, T.M. (1974)
'Popular Science and Society: The Phrenology Movement in Early Victorian Britain' Journal of Social History 8 (1) pp.1-20.

Pillans, J. (1829)
Principles of Elementary Teaching Edinburgh, Adam Black.

Pillans, J. (1856)
Contributions to the Cause of Education Edinburgh, A. and C. Black.

Prophet, R.B. (1980)
'A Sociological View of Science Education in Elementary Schools in Nineteenth Century England'. Unpublished MEd thesis, University of Manchester.

Roscoe, H.E. (1874)
'Original Research as a Means of Education' in Essays and Addresses by Professors and Lecturers of the Owens College, Manchester London, Macmillan pp.21-57.

Ross, E.A. (1929)
Social Control: A Survey of the Foundations of Order. Cleveland, The Press of Case Western Reserve University.

Secondary Science Curriculum Review (SSCR) (1984)
Towards the Specification of Minimum Entitlement: Brenda and Friends London, Schools Council.

Shapin, S. and Barnes, B. (1976)
'Head and Hand: Rhetorical Resources in British Pedagogical Writing, 1770-1850' Oxford Review of Education 2 (3) pp.231-254.

Stow, D. (1836)
The Training System Glasgow, Blackie.

Tait, A.C. (1854)
'Government Education Measures for Poor and Rich' Edinburgh Review 99 (201) pp.158-196.

Ure, A. (1835)
The Philosophy of Manufacturers
London, Charles Knight.

Waring, M. (1979a)
Social Pressures and Curriculum Innovation. A Study of the Nuffield Foundation Science Teaching Project
London, Methuen.

Waring, M. (1979b)
'The Implementation of Curriculum Change in School Science in England and Wales'
European Journal of Science Education 1 (3) pp.257-275.

Wilson, J. (1830)
'Education of the People'
Blackwoods Edinburgh Magazine 27 pp.1-16.

Wood, J. (1831)
'Edinburgh Sessional School'
Quarterly Journal of Education 1 pp.78-83.

Wrottesley, Lord John (1860)
Thoughts on Government and Legislation
London, John Murray.

Young, M.F.D. (1971)
'An Approach to the Study of Curricula as Socially Organized Knowledge' in Young, M.F.D. (Ed.) Knowledge and Control
London, Collier Macmillan pp.19-46.

Young, M.F.D. (1976)
'The Schooling of Science' in Whitty, G. and Young, M.F.D. (Eds.) Explorations in the Politics of School Knowledge
Driffield, Nafferton Books.

Young, R.M. (1973)
'The Role of Psychology in the Nineteenth Century Evolutionary Debate' in Henle, M., Jaynes, J. and Sullivan, J.J. (Eds.)
Historical Conceptions of Psychology
New York, Springer pp. 180-204.

Young R. (1980)
'Natural Theology, Victorian Periodicals and the Fragmentation of a Common Context' in Chant, C. and Fauvel, J. (Eds.)
Darwin to Einstein. Historical Studies on Science and Belief
Harlow, Longman/Open University pp.69-107.

7. THE DEVELOPMENT OF A SENIOR SCHOOL GEOGRAPHY CURRICULUM IN WESTERN AUSTRALIA, 1964-84

Colin J. Marsh

Introduction

This study investigates how a geography curriculum for senior school geography students was initiated and evolved over the period 1964-84 in Western Australia. There are a number of forces at work in any curriculum development activity and this case study is no exception. In the first section, major factors are outlined and considered within a decision-making model. Occurrences over the period 1964-1984 are then examined in some detail, in terms of two phases of development.

The Content

(a) West Australian Education System

There is a tripartite system of secondary schooling within the state of Western Australia and this mirrors a similar pattern which occurs in all other states of Australia. The major system is the state education department which provides secondary education for 70% of the school population. The Catholic Education system provides secondary schools for 14% of the school population, and independent private schools account for the remaining 16%. Schools are provided in urban and rural centres, often widely dispersed, over the one million square miles comprising the state of Western Australia.

The state education department teachers tend to be selected from those locally trained at the four institutions in Western Australia offering a four-year teacher education programme leading to a Bachelor's degree and a Diploma in Education.

Their employment can take them into all areas of Western Australia, both rural and urban. The majority are members of a strong teachers' union which has had considerable success so far in obtaining specific conditions of work such as those relating to number of teaching periods, preparation time per week.

Non-state education department teachers are often selected from all states of Australia and even overseas, although there has been an increasing tendency to attract local graduates judged to have very high potential in teaching. There is a tendency for many of these teachers to have high academic qualifications, such as a Bachelor with honours degree, or a Master's degree. In some cases, it has been possible for teachers with high academic qualifications but no teaching experience to obtain teaching positions in these schools. School staff in these schools tend to be less mobile than their colleagues in state education schools. The non-state schools are predominantly situated in the one metropolitan city (Perth) and promotional opportunities are far more restricted. An association of non-state education department teachers is in existence but it has not been able to demand the specific guidelines about teaching duties accorded to their state school teaching counterparts.

(b) The External Examination

External Examinations can have a major influence upon the levels of implementation of a curriculum in both direct and indirect, positive and negative ways. The announcement that a curriculum will be subjected to an external examination may elicit feelings of fear and trepidation among students but it might equally produce strong support from teachers and parents. Many teachers may prefer teaching toward an external examination because they can gain definite ideas about the level of content and range of topics to be covered. Parents may be very desirous of their children sitting for external examinations because of their role as entry-certificates into tertiary level institutions.

Curriculum developers often take steps to include their new curriculum within existing external examination frameworks. A recognized external examination for their product is one sure way to guarantee large-scale adoption and implementation, and also credibility and status for the personnel involved in the curriculum development. The Schools Council project, Geography for the Young School Leaver, appears to have been one of the most successful of the Schools Council projects, largely due to its incorporation in O level, Mode II and Mode III CSE examinations (Stenhouse, 1980, pp.173-175).

But there are some negative aspects about external examinations. It is undoubtedly true that external examinations can provide unintended directions and emphases for a curriculum. It may be that certain concepts included in a curriculum (for example, dealing with attitude issues) are difficult to incorporate within the traditional objective test items or essays. Teachers, students and examiners all try to play the system. The previous examination papers provide cues for teachers and students about the areas of emphasis and topics to ignore or at least cover in summary fashion. Examiners also make subjective judgements, often based upon unwarranted assumptions about what should be included as examination questions. Too often, they will avoid, as Higginbottom (1980, p.117) lamented with regard to Geography for the Young School Leaver, important aspects such as value and attitude clarification questions. Cameron and Hill (1977), suggest that if there are not clearly stated objectives for an examiner to follow, examiners will either ask their own favourite specific questions or ask very general questions which would allow practically any content matter to be used to answer them.

Curricula for the final two years of secondary school (Years 11 and 12) in Western Australia are dominated by the pressures of external examinations. The Year 12 examination results are most important for students intending to proceed to tertiary studies, as an aggregate of these examination results is used as a basis for determining whether or not a student will be admitted to a tertiary institution. A Joint Syllabus Committee, a formal body comprising academics, education administrators and teachers, operates for each examinable subject offered to students in their final two years of secondary schooling. It is their task to initiate and legitimate a specific syllabus and to formulate a Year 12 examination associated with it.

Each Joint Syllabus Committee is an advisory committee of the Board of Secondary Education (BSE). The BSE is responsible for certification of all senior school students. The certificate made available to all students at the end of year twelve reports student achievement based upon 50% moderated school assessments and 50% external examination results. The four tertiary institutions in Western Australia require external examination results totally from all students intending admittance. No allowance is made for school assessments in their calculation of an aggregate score for each student.

A Model of Curriculum Decision-making

The above contextual details provide a preliminary basis for understanding the forces affecting curriculum development. However, there are other factors which have to be considered and this is where models of curriculum decision-making can provide useful insights.

Rogers and Shoemaker (1971) have developed a model, the Authority-Innovation-Decision-Making system, which enables other forces to be considered and which appears to be remarkably relevant to the state education system in Western Australia. Rogers and Shoemaker claim (1971) that Authority-Innovation decisions are crucial in such formal organizations as educational systems. They developed a five-function model to explain how decisions are made about an innovation, emphasizing the pressures placed upon individuals within organizations to comply with the new demands implied by its adoption and implementation.

Rather than all individuals partaking in curriculum adoption, planning and implementation activities, Rogers and Shoemaker suggest that, empirically, there are two distinct groups of decision-making individuals, the <u>superordinate</u> group and the <u>subordinate</u> group. The major decisions are made by the superordinate group, who initiate and direct the curriculum development and its dissemination. In terms of their paradigm, the authors suggest that members of the superordinate group are chiefly concerned with the functions of Knowledge, Persuasion and Decision. By contrast, members of the subordinate group are chiefly concerned with implementing decisions made by the higher status group; as a result, their functions are confined to Communication and Action. Each of these functions involve some dissemination activity which usually varies from discussing and exchanging ideas ('knowledge', 'persuasion') to distributing actual products, reports and evaluations ('communication', 'action').

Applying the Authority model to a specific educational setting, such as a state education system, reveals that, in fact, there can be various superordinate and subordinate groups in operation.

Within a state education system, there is a head office staff with its specialists and senior officials. Teachers, by contrast, along with principals, constitute the subordinate group.

Figure 1 also identifies another important decision-making group: the examination board. The executive committees of the examination board, comprising mainly administrators and senior academics, formulate examination policies and legitimate specific syllabi. Apart from junior staff of the examination board who distribute information about examinations to the general public, the teachers (and students) in schools can again be viewed as the subordinate group who implement the examination practices. This dichotomy is somewhat crude, in that many examination boards do, in fact, have teacher representatives on their executive committees, but their influence on decision-making within those bodies appears to be modest.

Professional associations can also be influential within a state education system. For example, subject associations typically influence the initiation and direction of curriculum innovations and can also affect levels of adoption and use by teachers. As Table 1 shows, there is a tendency in many professional associations for the executive committees to be composed chiefly of senior educators (academics, administrators). An executive committee, as the superordinate group, will in turn determine the association's involvement in in-service activities, in the production of materials and in required working arrangements, while the rank and file members, many of whom are classroom teachers, will be involved as recipients of the planned activities.

Textbook publishers and authors are another influential group; Cohen (1978) includes them in his reference to the "political power of private and politically accountable agencies" (p.429). Multinational book publishers, for example, have

Table 1
Curriculum Decision-makers and Processes in a State Education System

	CURRICULUM DECISION-MAKING PERSONNEL: KNOWLEDGE/PERSUASION/DECISION PROCESSES		ADOPTERS/IMPLEMENTERS: COMMUNICATION/ACTION PROCESSES
Education Dept. or System	Head Office, Senior Staff	direct influence →	classroom teachers, students
External Examination and Certification Boards	Administrative Senior Staff, Senior representatives from academic positions	direct influence →	classroom teachers, students, indirectly on parents, employers
Professional Associations	Office bearers, who are typically senior academics, educational administrators	differential influence →	classroom teachers indirectly on students
Tertiary Institutions	Professional staff who establish prerequisites for tertiary study directly, or via examination committees	differential influence →	classroom teachers and students, indirectly on parents
Textbook Publishers and Authors	Senior administrators, experienced authors determine range and scope of curriculum materials to be published	direct influence →	classroom teachers and students

Figure 1
An Authority Model for a State Education System

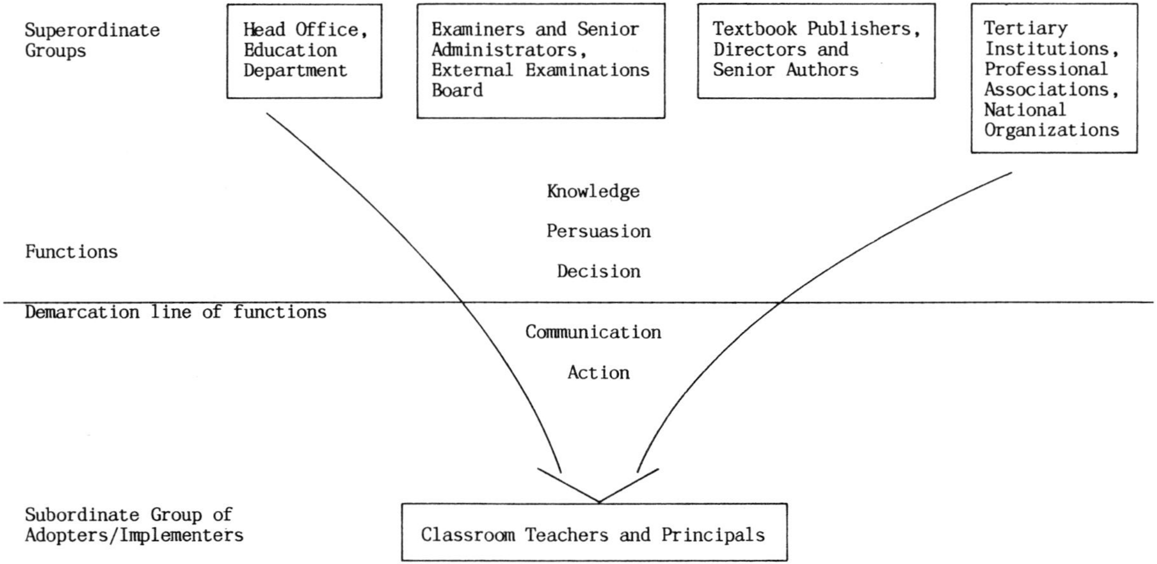

(Adapted from Rogers and Shoemaker (1971))

definite policies with regard to the range, direction and level of textbooks they intend to publish. Although they have to be fully aware of market interests and demands, their actual publications may not meet the demands of specific education groups. Teachers and their students are again the subordinate group in that they must select from the textbooks available. In fact, in subject areas with little available reference material, commercial textbooks can become, by default, the actual curriculum.

The Authority Innovation Decision-Making model thus has implications for all these groups, although some are clearly more important than others. Teachers, as employees in an educational system, will be bound by regulations established by the decision-making group within the same system. But they will also be strongly influenced by the guidelines established by the decision-making group from the external examination boards. This can lead to conflict. For example, head office education directives might stress student enquiry and self-evaluative unit tests while the external examination might favour content-oriented examination questions.

The Five Functions of the Model

The first function, Knowledge (see Fig. 1) is clearly the province of the superordinate group, whose members are the focal point for receiving information about new educational products and techniques from outside agencies and commercial firms. How that information is processed however, is a key variable. Selective perception will operate within any decision-making group, with certain directions favoured over others, often due to the distortion of information en route. Knowledge acquisition depends upon the accuracy of messages received from external and internal sources. The breadth and range of these inputs will determine the amount of selective screening. Likely activities by decision-makers at this point include requesting information via documents and papers, visits to firms and reliance on experts.

However, the major thrust for decision-making groups is at the 'Persuasion' stage. Officials will have gone beyond initial familiarization with an innovatory technique or product, and will now be interested in seeking out detailed information.

Perhaps feasibility surveys will be initiated. More important, internal lobbying may occur between various 'power elites' over their support for a particular innovation. Decision-makers may elicit information about needs from school personnel to help them in preparing their case. Alternatively, some school principals and staff may have heard about an impending decision and will submit written requests for a particular stance.

An Innovation might be initiated by the examination board decision-making group, as in the case of revised school assessments. In this case, similar in-house bargaining will be occurring, with the likelihood of some spill-over to other decision-making groups such as the head office group, several of whose members might be part-time officials on the examination board.

The entrepreneurial skill of head office personnel is needed to get curriculum projects initiated. This may require intensive discussions to persuade others. There is good evidence that central office administrators, by dint of their drive and enthusiasm, are often able to steer decisions to adopt an innovation with little resistance (Emrick and Peterson (1978); Huberman and Miles (1982)).

The Decision stage is the culmination of all formal and informal meetings arranged to persuade colleagues. Informally, the decision may have been reached much earlier, but formal meetings and notifications are required to ratify and legitimize.

The model suggests that with regard to these three functions - knowledge, persuasion and decision - there is little interaction between the head office and classroom teachers. Rather, it is at the Communication and Action stages that the employer decision-making group disseminates information about its curriculum decisions, and in particular, provides details about how the curricula are to be implemented. Dissemination can take various forms: personal contacts, inservice days, advisory teacher visits, official pronouncements, news releases and official publications. These techniques are all used to transmit the culture of the new curricula, with the intention of transforming the existing culture of the recipient groups of teachers, in terms of Rudduck's (1980) terminology.

This applies also to the other decision-making groups who are able to wield superordinate influence over the teacher/implementer group. Examination boards will distribute manuals and handbooks about new syllabi. In some cases, moderators are appointed to visit schools to monitor standards of student achievement. Examiners appointed to a new syllabus might call special meetings of interested teachers to discuss the implications of their new approach.

Textbook publishers undertake similar, but less hierarchical, dissemination activities through their press releases, cocktail parties to launch a new publication, visits by travelling salesmen and the distribution of leaflets, brochures and complimentary copies.

As mentioned above, the decision-making groups are not only communicating information about a new curriculum, but in many cases are specifying how it is to be implemented. Prescriptive instructions about how a curriculum innovation is to be used by teachers has been termed "fidelity of use" approach (Fullan and Pomfret (1977)) and is variously justified. For example, some curricula have been developed to follow a set sequence; making changes could reduce the project's real impact. Then again, decision-makers might have agreed to introduce curricula into schools on the assumption that only minimal resources (materials, staff) were required to support them. Teachers not following these procedures might then require more resources than was actually available to each school. In other instances, senior members of the decision-making group, such as Directors, might well have elaborate and strongly held ideas about how a new curriculum should be implemented. In some educational systems, they can "police" follow-through by visitations to local schools from inspectorial staff.

The above details set out the major functions of the Rogers and Shoemaker decision-making model. In the following section actual occurrences between the decision-making groups are elaborated for the period 1964-1984.

Phase 1 (1964 - 1976)
Historical Account

The 1960s in Western Australia provided an educational setting in which the only tertiary institution, the University of Western Australia, maintained a closed and restricting influence upon secondary school students via the annual examinations and selection procedures for tertiary study. The Public Examinations Board of the university fixed the curricula/syllabi which were the basis for the examination papers. Successful secondary school candidates at these examinations were accepted as first year students in the following year at the University of Western Australia.

Geography was one of the subjects examined. In fact, during the 1960s it was an extremely popular subject, attracting the major number of students for an individual subject, after English and Mathematics. But there was concern among teachers about the emphasis of the curriculum upon physical/regional geography and about the restrictive influence of the Public Examinations Board.

The creation of the first chair in geography in 1964 and the establishing of a separate department of geography at the University of Western Australia, was a change of considerable significance. The new group of geography academics, not unexpectedly, advocated different emphases in the teaching of geography, in keeping with geographers in other universities. The new thrust was for systematic studies of contemporary world problems, and in particular, the use of scientific method to develop and test specific theories and generalizations.

Teachers were also wanting changes to the geography curriculum but their perspective was attuned to new educational emphases such as the teaching of process skills rather than content, the use of inquiry-methods to acquire and build concepts and a greater emphasis upon values topics.

Educators in Western Australia were also agitating for general reforms in secondary education. A major report published in 1969, the Dettman Report, recommended a move toward school-based curriculum development and the removal of external examinations. Sound educational reasons were advocated in the report for increasing the opportunities for teachers to develop curricula in the final two years of secondary school, but it was a far from easy task to remove, or even downgrade the importance of the external examinations.

Various skirmishes erupted between members of the Public Examinations Board, especially between academic geographers and educators. Matters appeared to come to a head in 1969 when conflicting pressures from the university, state education department and some vocal, concerned senior teachers, led to the formation of the Geography Teachers' Association of W.A. (G.T.A.W.A.) which was formed in December of 1970 with syllabus reform as one of its main tasks.

Of considerable importance was the one day conference hosted by G.T.A.W.A. in June 1971. As G.T.A.W.A. was formally affiliated with geography associations in other states, especially New South Wales (N.S.W.), it might have been expected that powerful individuals from these sister organizations would be requested to lend support. At the June 1971 conference, vigorous denouncement of the existing geography curriculum was made by a local university academic and alternative approaches and paradigms were presented by a well known geography educator from N.S.W. The overall effect seems to have been that a small group of executive members of the G.T.A.W.A., with positions of influence in the university and in the state education department, rose to the challenge of producing an alternative curriculum. This document was in turn adopted by the newly formed Joint Geography Syllabus Committee (part of the new Board of Secondary Education administrative structure after the demise of the Public Examinations Board).

The new document, according to Hill (1976, p.20)

> "... was put together by the two leading members of the Committee in the relatively short time of 8-9 months, during 1972, circulated in draft form in April 1973, disseminated through circulars and in-service courses and introduced with minor amendments into the school system in 1974".

Without detracting from the initiatives and drive of the authors of the new document, it would appear that this development and dissemination period was incredibly brief, as revealed by the two comparisons below. It appears overly hasty by comparison with a recent curriculum change in Queensland. In this case, the Queensland geography committee attempted to develop a process, inquiry-oriented geography curriculum using Australian content. The curriculum, entitled Australian Geographical Inquiries (A.G.I.), was developed during the period 1976-1977, trialled in 1978, and retrialled in 1980, prior to it becoming generally available to Queensland schools (Bartlett, 1981). Although direct comparisons can't be made with the Secondary Geographical Education Project (S.G.E.P.) in Victoria because it spans six years of high school, the elaborate strategies for the trialling, dissemination and take-up of S.G.E.P. units (Hartnell, 1977) further highlights some of the deficiencies in the processes undertaken in implementing the Western Australian geography curriculum.

The West Australian curriculum document contained ten concept clusters which reflected the structure of the discipline, as espoused at the time by prominent goegraphers such as Haggett (1965) and Chorley and Haggett (1965). As indicated in Figure 2, the ten concepts can be typified by the three dominant paradigms of that period, namely the Man-Land View, the Area Studies View and the Spatial View.

Also included in the document were five major approaches to the teaching of geography, intended to foster a spirit of inquiry in students. They referred to preferences for a study of patterns and processes of the natural environment, a study of the emergence of the cultural landscape and an emphasis upon contemporary problems and geographical principles. No content was prescribed in the document although it might have been assumed by teachers (and reinforced by subsequent examination papers) to still refer predominantly to Australia and Monsoon Asia.

Research Study 1

In order to explore teachers' reactions to the new curriculum and to attempt to gauge the extent to which they accepted, rejected or modified it, data on geography teachers and their perceptions of the new document were obtained by means of a questionnaire sent to all (163) teachers of geography in government high schools in W.A. This study by Hill and Marsh (1979) was carried out towards the end of November, 1976. A total of 102 (62.6%) completed questionnaires were returned.

Of relevance to the topic here are questionnaire items which focused upon teachers' judgments about the advantages and disadvantages of the new geography curriculum.

In an open-ended question, teachers were asked to list what they considered to be the three main

Figure 2
A Structure of Geography Based on Ten Concept Clusters

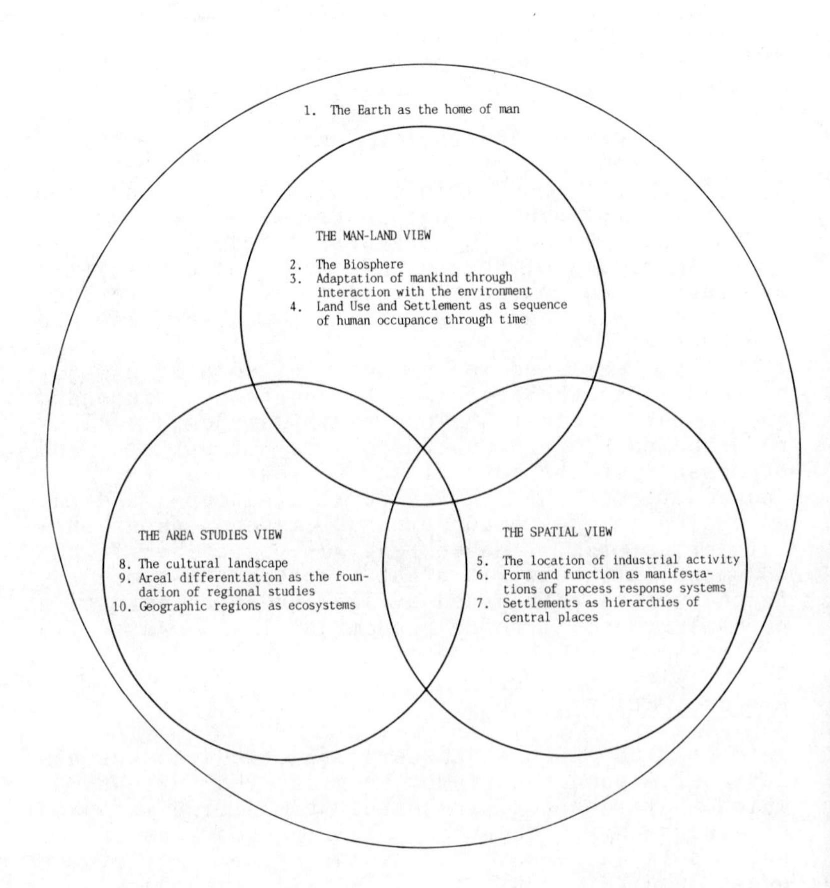

(after Hill and Cameron 1977, p.99)

advantages and the three main disadvantages of the new curriculum. The most frequently cited advantages were:

1. It allows flexibility and freedom to select content appropriate to the interests and strengths of both staff and students.
2. It is based on the understanding and application of concepts as opposed to the memorization of factual information (mentioned by 26.5% of respondents).
3. It places much more emphasis on practical work, field-work and local area studies (mentioned by 26.5% of respondents).

Some 35 disadvantages were mentioned, though the most frequently cited were:

1. The lack of direction with regard to programming and required depth of treatment of topics and uncertainty regarding content, especially in relation to examination requirements (mentioned by 40.8% of respondents).
2. Too much to cover in a two-year course (mentioned by 20.6% of respondents).
3. Constraints imposed by the need to externally examine it (mentioned by 13.7% of respondents).
4. It is too academic for many, requiring a high level of conceptualization beyond the capacity of less able students (mentioned by 13.7% of respondents).

The results are particularly interesting in highlighting the consequences of the compromise which the Joint Geography Syllabus Committee made between having to fulfil the formal requirement to produce an examination syllabus and meeting the anticipated need for a framework for a curriculum within which teachers could develop their own courses. As a number of respondents pointed out, the chief advantage of the new curriculum is also its main drawback. The positive aspect of an open curriculum is that it allows freedom to select content. In the context of an examination syllabus, however, the negative aspects of an open curriculum emerge, for then freedom and flexibility become a lack of direction and uncertainty as to the content to be covered and examined. The list of most frequently cited advantages seems to indicate that teachers welcomed the changes in favour of school-based curriculum development and a concept-based mode of study with learning activities involving pupils actively exploring their immediate environment. The list of disadvantages are all related to the openness of the curriculum in the context of the examination requirements.

Phase II (1976 - 1984)
Historical Account II

The research results described above revealed some teacher difficulties in the teaching of the new geography curriculum, especially problems relating to how to gauge the range and depth of content to be used to teach the new concept clusters. Because there were no objectives in the new document, teachers had to infer content from sample examination papers and from references and textbooks cited as being important.

The Geographical Association tried to provide assistance to their members. The association ran a series of in-service courses and workshops on the new curriculum. 'Enrichment' sessions were provided on an annual basis for final year geography students. As can be seen in Table 2, the association provided an extensive range of in-service activities during the 1970s - activities which might normally be expected to be undertaken by the teacher employer authority.

However, by the end of the 1970s it was clear to teachers and administrators that all was not well with the new geography curriculum. The concept clusters incorporated in the document had been stated in broad terms so that teachers might have considerable freedom in selecting specific content of special relevance to their local area. This was based on the assumption that individual schools would be permitted to progressively increase their proportion of school-based assessment from 20% in 1975 to 50% within a few years. This move to school-based assessment was summarily terminated in 1977 by the Board of Secondary Education (the overriding authority for all Joint syllabus committees) when it announced that external examinations would count for 100% from henceforth when determining tertiary admission places. Through their subject association, geography teachers began clamouring for more specific details to be included in the two-year

Table 2

In-Service Courses in Geography Available to Geography Teachers 1976-80

	Sponsored by Geographical Association of W.A.		Sponsored by W.A. Education Department
1977			
Duration	Series of 6 x 2 hr sessions	2½ days	2 days
Eligibility	Members and non-members	Members and non-members	Senior Masters
Major Emphasis	Specific Topics on the TAE Syllabus	Fieldwork topics	Programming based upon the syllabus
Venue	Metropolitan	Country	Metropolitan
1978			
Duration	2½ days		2 days
Eligibility	Members and non-members		Senior Masters
Major Emphasis	Fieldwork Topics		Programming based upon the syllabus
Venue	Country		Metropolitan
1979			
Duration	2½ days	Series of 5 x 2 hr sessions	
Eligibility	Members and non-members	Members and non-members	
Major Emphasis	Fieldwork topics	Specific topics on the TAE syllabus	
Venue	Country	Metropolitan	
1980			
Duration	2½ days		2 days
Eligibility	Members and non-members		Senior Masters and Teachers in charge
Major Emphasis	Fieldwork topics		Specific topics on the syllabus
Venue	Country		Metropolitan

curriculum, as it was now to be wholly determined by students' achievements at a final year external examination.

Research Study II

A follow-up research study was undertaken by Marsh (1982) in 1980 to obtain data about the degree to which some major implementation problems perceived by geography teachers in 1976 had ameliorated or deteriorated after a period of four years. Indirectly, the follow-up study attempted to gauge the effectiveness of some dissemination strategies, and the support activities and materials available to geography teachers from both state department sources and the Geography Teachers' Association.

The original study was undertaken in November 1976 and involved a questionnaire being sent to all (163) teachers of geography in state high schools in W.A. The follow-up study undertaken in November 1980 used the same questionnaire and it was sent to all (162) teachers of geography. The return rate of 56% was a little lower than the first study which had a 63% return rate. It was not possible to ensure that the original sample of geography teachers were the only ones who completed the follow-up questionnaire. However, because all geography teachers were surveyed on both occasions it might be assumed that a sizeable number of teachers who returned questionnaires in 1980, had also been involved in the study in 1976.

An open-ended item was included in the questionnaire used in both the 1976 and the 1980 surveys and which requested teachers to list what they considered to be the three main advantages and the three main disadvantages of the T.A.E. syllabus. The results are listed in Table 3.

There appears to be a contradiction between the major advantage and the major disadvantage as listed in Table 3, yet the contradiction may be a pragmatic solution to the influence of the external examination.

Some additional perspectives are provided by the results listed in Table 4, which summarize the major problems cited by teachers in the 1976 and 1980 surveys. In the 1976 survey, teachers appeared to have considerable difficulty covering the many aspects of the syllabus, and the 1980 survey reveals that this situation had not improved. It may have been exacerbated by the

Table 3
Perceived Advantages and Disadvantages of the T.A.E. Geography Curriculum

	1980 %	1976 %
Advantages		
1. It allows flexibility and freedom in choosing content. A wide choice of options are available to the teacher.	37	68
2. It is based on understanding and applying concepts which have application to everyday situations.	23	27
3. It enables an integration of the subject matter with practical field work activities.	13	27
Disadvantages		
1. It gives little direction with regard to programming, depth of coverage of topics.	56	41
2. It is beyond the capability of many students.	18	14
3. Too much emphasis on Monsoon Asia to the exclusion of Europe, the Middle East and U.S.A.	12	-

Table 4
Major Problems Associated with Teaching the T.A.E. Geography Curriculum

	1980 Results*	1976 Results*
1. Finding time to cover all that you want to.	4.11	4.05
2. Students lack basic skills.	3.97	3.91
3. A wide range of student ability.	3.93	3.77
4. Deciding upon depth of treatment of topics.	3.63	3.89
5. Reconciling the freedom allowed by the syllabus with the constraints imposed by the T.A.E. Examination.	3.58	3.64
6. Availability of resource material on W.A. and the local area.	3.40	3.76

* Means given on a 5 point scale ranging from 0 = no problems to 5 = a major problem

problem of less academically inclined students now staying on into senior high school because of limited job opportunities. As revealed in Table 4, "catering for a wide range of student abilities" was a problem in 1976 but it had become acute in 1980. A related problem was the "availability of resource materials on W.A. and the local area". Presumably teachers perceived that there was a very limited range of local resource materials available in 1980. Finally, it should be noted that teachers in the 1980 survey had not overcome the problem of "deciding upon the depth of treatment of topics".

Historical Account III

The concerns by geography teachers were eventually taken up by the Joint Geography Syllabus Committee after intensive lobbying by prominent geography educators and academics. The proposed solution was for a subcommittee of the Joint Geography Syllabus Committee to be established, comprising two academics, a senior education administrator (state education department) and a senior teacher (state education department) to establish a modified curriculum which clearly stated the areas to be examined. The subcommittee reorganized the previous concept clusters and more importantly, produced specific content details which would henceforth be examinable.

The educators on the subcommittee were especially concerned that teachers would be given specific details on the content to be examined. They did not seek elaboration of other curriculum elements such as a detailing of aims and methods, although this would have involved them in going beyond the terms of their brief from the Joint Geography Syllabus Committee.

The academics on the sub-committee seized the opportunity to reorient the geographical paradigms included in the earlier curriculum. An ecological approach to geography was advocated most strenuously to replace the Man-Land perspective.

From interviews carried out by the author with the sub-committee members, it appears that the academics "traded" a reduction in total content and an increase in the specification of details about the remaining areas, for an acceptance of their ecological perspective. Further, it seems that the press of the external examination was sufficient reason for them not to embark upon considering other major deficits of the curriculum, such as detailing and integrating of objectives and methodology.

This revised curriculum was accepted by the Joint Geography Syllabus Committee in 1980 and became officially accepted and introduced into all West Australian secondary schools in 1981.

Research Study III

Another study was undertaken by the author in 1982 to ascertain how teachers were using this revised version of the curriculum. The earlier studies (Hill and Marsh 1979; Marsh 1982) highlighted continuing (and new) problems for geography teachers but did not provide information on their actual levels of implementation. This data was obtained in a related study (Marsh 1984) by the author using the Levels-of-Use (LoU) interview procedures developed by Hall et al (1973). The LoU instrument is based on the premise that a teacher will move along eight levels from "non-use" through to a "mechanical" level, a "routine" level, and in some cases, to "refinement" and "refocusing" levels. Hall et al (1973) have identified and operationally defined each of these eight levels and these are listed in Table 5.

Table 5
Level of Use Distribution

		State Education Department Schools	
		N	%
Non-Use	0	-	-
Orientation	I	-	-
Preparation	II	-	-
Mechanical Use	III	11	25
Routine	IVA	26	59
Refinement	IVB	5	11
Integration	V	2	5
Renewal	VI	-	-
		44	100

LoU interviews were undertaken with a sample of 44 senior geography teachers out of a total of 162 teaching in state education secondary schools during 1982.

The proportion of teachers at the different LoU levels is listed in Table 5. As all geography teachers are required to teach the curriculum the non-user levels (0 to II) do not apply. The data provides a snapshot of teachers' levels at this point in time and, of course, further inverviewing would be required to establish the degree to which teachers changed their LoUs over a period of years.

The number of teachers at level of Use III Mechanical Use was 25%. These results are not unexpected as interviews revealed that many of the teachers were teaching senior school geography for the first time. Because the revised curriculum was only in its second year of operation, it might be considered surprising that so few interviewees were in this category. The comparatively low figures might be explained by the fact that some teachers have been using the new curriculum since 1975, and they have been able successfully to interpret examination requirements despite the vagueness of the concept clusters in the original document. It might also be conjectured that some teachers have made very few changes, if any, to their mode of teaching since the introduction of the 1981 curriculum, and so they are not exhibiting typical Level III behaviours of "disjointed and superficial use of the innovation" (Hall et al, 1973).

The majority of the interviewees (59%) were assessed at Level of Use IVA Routine. This level is typified by teachers who have stabilized their activities and who give little thought to improving the use of the innovation or its consequences. It is also interesting to note that teachers at this level "make no special efforts to seek out information as a part of ongoing use of the innovation" (Hall et al, 1973:8).

This data might be interpreted in different ways. From one point of view it could be viewed as highly satisfactory that approximately two-thirds of the teachers in the sample have reached a stable, routine pattern of teaching the geography syllabus. But it could be inferred that teachers are so overwhelmed by the external examination that they are content to establish a pattern that merely ensures a reasonable standard of examination success for their students. That is, they are not motivated to adapt the syllabus in any way, to extend or develop particular concepts or learning activities.

Very few interviewees (11%) were assessed at Level of Use IVB Refinement and even less (5%) at Level of Use V Integration. In the Western Australian context, it appears that the external pressures are so great that teachers have little motivation to experiment with changes of any kind, whether they are experiments to improve student outcomes emanating from formal feedback from students (Level IVB) or group collaborations with colleagues to increase student outcomes (Level V). In circumstances where a curriculum is to be implemented according to precise guidelines, it could be viewed as undesirable for teachers to be operating at IVB and V Levels of Use. This might explain the low numbers of LoU IVBs and Vs when it might be expected under normal evolution for a sizeable number of teachers to progress to higher levels as they became more experienced and competent (Hall, 1978).

During 1984 a major report into primary and secondary education was released and it is likely that this will have major effects upon secondary school curricula in ensuing years. The Report of the Committee of Inquiry into Education in Western Australia (Beazley Report) recommended in particular that:

(a) external examinations to apply to the final year (Year 12) of schooling rather than the final two years (Years 11 and 12);
(b) the number of externally examined subjects per student in Year 12 for those intending to enter tertiary institutions be reduced to a minimum of 3 and a maximum of 5 subjects. Scores on each subject will consist of 50% external examination and 50% school assessment;
(c) students studying non-tertiary entrance subjects will be subject to school-based assessments;
(d) the Board of Secondary Education will be replaced by the Secondary Education Authority consisting of a majority of teacher members.

Some of the recommendations have already been implemented for the 1985-86 cohort of senior school students but it will be some years before the full impact of the Beazley Report will be felt in schools. It is likely to usher in a very different phase of secondary education in Western Australia.

Discussion

After a period of twenty years (1964-84) it is instructive to reflect upon curriculum development activities associated with the school subject of geography in government schools in Western Australia.

In phase one, the developments might be characterized as having been avante-garde. Senior academics in the newly established university department of geography clamoured for substantial changes in the content to be examined and they were largely successful. Educators who supported the new content paradigms, saw opportunities for reducing the control of the examination boards. What eventuated by the end of the 1970s was a compromise situation whereby a potentially exciting, new curriculum had to be modified for use by teachers because the powers of the external examination were not able to be diminished to any significant degree.

The second phase was characterized by a period of consolidation and a "coalition of forces" (Goodson 1984) to effect some changes of emphasis and changes in content details. It may be that the implementation of the Beazley Report recommendations will bring about a vastly different pattern in the late 1980s and beyond.

It appears that two factors in particular were most influential during the twenty year period, namely:

(a) external examinations;
(b) superordinate groups.

By the mid-1980s the powers of the external exam continues to loom large for geography teachers. To a very large extent, the examination successes of their students provides an indicator to their fellow teachers and to parents about their status as an effective teacher. Small wonder then that the geography teachers' perceived concerns about the new curriculum were about such matters as whether they could "cover" the course in the time, or whether their less-academic students had the necessary skills to cope with the academic orientation of the subject.

It is interesting to note that the geography teachers were not opposed to the academic orientation of the curriculum. The data obtained by Hill and Marsh (1979) and Marsh (1982) did not contain references by teachers to the alternative Board of Secondary Education curriculum which had an applied geography/vocational/utilitarian focus. Teachers accepted the need for an academic orientation - the examination board and university academics advocated it - and teachers were prepared to work within this orientation (as noted also by Goodson (1983) with reference to geography and environmental studies in secondary schools in the U.K.).

Perhaps this ready acceptance by geography teachers reflects their socialization into an academic tradition, as advocated by their university teachers (Cooper 1984). Since the university department of geography was established in 1964, it is likely that the majority of teachers currently teaching geography would have completed their geography major at this institution. For example, the survey undertaken by Marsh (1982) indicated that 88% of the geography teachers had completed geography majors since 1966.

The influence of the external examination also affects teachers' commitment to particular modes of teaching. Surveys by Hill and Marsh (1979) and Marsh (1982) noted that teachers welcomed the opportunity to use inquiry teaching methods but that their use of didactic, expository methods seemed to increase over the period 1976-1980. Perhaps many of the teachers resigned themselves to the task of being "examination coaches". The LoU data collected in 1982 (Marsh 1984) certainly indicated that the majority of teachers were concerned with achieving only a minimal "routine" level of implementation.

Further, it should be noted that teachers and academics appear to have assumed that geography students were disposed toward a rational, academic orientation to geography (as noted by Reid (1984) with regard to U.K. teaching). Attempts to include applied geography problems in the curriculum (the section titled Contemporary Wórld Problems) were opposed by teachers because they were purportedly too difficult to teach. It appears that no surveys of senior students were undertaken to obtain data on their interests. The assumption seems to have been that students and their parents accepted, without question, the need for an academic orientation to the study of geography, as a school subject.

Another dominant factor during the period 1964-84 was the influence of several superordinate groups, especially the examination board and the subject association, as outlined in the Rogers and Shoemaker model.

The Joint Geography Syllabus Committee and the Board of Secondary Education dictated the terms by their insistence upon an examination syllabus and their disinterest in a comprehensive curriculum document. Within two years of the inception of the new curriculum, the Board of Secondary Education reversed the decision of a gradual introduction to school-based assessment and announced in 1977 that the external examination would henceforth be the total and only assessment.

The subject association, like its predecessors elsewhere (Bucher and Strauss 1961) was borne out of a period of intense conflict between academics, examination board officials and educators. The Geographical Association of W.A. commenced its activities under the banner of examination reform. In the first few years it agitated strongly for change and was influential in accelerating the acceptance and implementation of the 1975 curriculum. It also provided strong support for teachers via in-service courses and workshops.

By contrast, its influence over recent years has been far more modest. There has not been vociferous demands by geography teachers for change. Further, a survey of teachers' views by the Board of Secondary Education (Waugh (1981)) concluded that a majority of teachers (84%) were very positive about the present examination system. As a result, the Geographical Association has not had a clear mandate for change and it has concentrated instead upon recommendations for minor revisions (for example content amplification documents, and workshops on computer applications to the teaching of geography.

Head office officials of the state education department maintained a moderating rather than a leadership role during the period 1964-84. Education department officials have always been well represented on the examination board (B.S.E.) but they were disposed to support the existing external examination structure even though their departmental report on secondary education (Dettman

Report (1969)) recommended a change to school-based assessment.

The superintendent (inspector) responsible for the teaching of geography in state government secondary schools did not play a dominant role. Various reasons might be advanced for this stance, such as his lack of recent academic qualifications in geography or his pre-occupation with the development of a new kindergarten - Year 10 curriculum in social studies.

Whatever the reasons for the lack of leadership offered in official committees, it was also evident that the department provided minimal support for teachers faced with the task of implementing the new geography curriculum in 1975. As indicated earlier (Table 2) the state education department provided very few in-service courses for teachers. A field centre for geography teachers was provided for several years but then changed its focus to provide services for social studies teachers. It would seem that the state education department officials had so many financial needs for lower secondary school curricula that they tended to minimize their involvement and financial support for senior school curricula (which were so clearly dominated by university academics and examination board officials).

Unlike situations in the United Kingdom, geography teachers in Western Australia did not have the opportunity to opt for one of several geography courses. Senior academics and educators formed coalitions of influence to persuade others about the form and direction of the new curriculum. Details of the new document were communicated at a much later stage to teachers and the latter were given very little opportunity or time to react to it. Once the new geography curriculum had been produced and accepted by the Joint Geography Syllabus Committee, it became compulsory for all geography teachers in Western Australia. It was up to the teachers to accommodate to the new structure with its attendant pressures upon academic understandings and knowledge.

References

Bartlett, V.L. (1981)
Australian Geographical Enquiries: An Evaluation Report
Brisbane, University of Queensland.

Bucher, R. & Strauss, A. (1961)
"Professions in Process"
American Journal of Sociology, 66.

Cameron, J. & Hill, P. (1977)
"Reconstructing the Curriculum in Western Australia", Teaching Geography, 2, 3, 128-130

Chorley, R.J. & Haggett, P. (1965)
Frontiers in Geographical Teaching
London, Methuen.

Cohen, D.K. (1978)
"Reforming School Politics",
Harvard Educational Review, 48, 4.

Cooper, B. (1984)
"On explaining change in School Subjects", in Goodson, I.F. & Ball, S.J. (Eds.)
Defining the Curriculum
London, Falmer Press.

Education Department of Western Australia (1969)
Secondary Education in Western Australia (Dettman Report), Report of the Committee on Secondary Education appointed by the Minister for Education in Western Australia. Perth, Education Department of Western Australia.

Emrick, J.A. & Peterson, S.M. (1978)
A Synthesis of Findings Across Five Recent Studies in Educational Dissemination and Change
San Francisco, Far West Laboratory.

Fullan, M. & Pomfret, A. (1977)
"Research on Curriculum and Instruction Implementation",
Review of Educational Research, 47, 335-397.

Goodson, I.F. (1983)
School Subjects and Curriculum Change
London, Croom Helm.

Goodson, I.F. (1984)
"Subjects for Study: Towards a Social History of Curriculum", in Goodson, I.F. & Ball, S.J. (Eds.) Defining the Curriculum
London, Falmer Press.

Haggett, P. (1965)
Locational Analysis in Human Geography
London, Arnold

Hall, G.E., Wallace, B., Dossett, B. (1973)
"A Developmental Conceptualization of the Adoptive Process within Educational Institutions"
Austin, University of Texas.
Hall, G.E. (1978)
"Concern-based In-service Teacher Training: An Overview of the Concepts, Research and Practice". Presented at the Conference on School-focus In-service Training, Bournemouth, U.K.
Hartnell, R., Pollard, G., Worthy, R. (1977)
"The Adoption of a Curriculum Development Programme". Paper presented at the ANZAAS Conference, Melbourne.
Higginbottom, T. (1980)
"Response: Geography for the Young School-Leaver", in Stenhouse, L. (Ed.) Curriculum Research and Development in Action.
London, Heinemann.
Hill, P.W. (1976)
"Change and the new Geography Syllabus in Western Australia". Unpublished manuscript.
Perth, Murdoch University.
Hill, P.W. & Cameron, J.M.R. (1977)
"Syllabus Change in Geography: A Western Australian Example", Geographical Education, 3, 93-100
Hill, P.W. & Marsh, C.J. (1979)
"Teachers' Perceptions of the Diffusion of an Authority-decision Framework: A Senior School Geography Case Study"
Australian Journal of Education, 23, 1, 32-44.
Huberman, M. & Miles, M. (1982)
How School Improvement Works: A Field Study of Twelve Sites.
Andover, Mass., The Network.
Marsh, C.J. (1982)
"Teachers' Perceptions of TAE Geography Syllabus", Western Geographer, 6, 1, 21-30.
Marsh, C.J. (1984)
"Implementation of a Curriculum Innovation in Australian Schools"
Knowledge: Creation, Diffusion, Utilization, 6, 1, 37-58.
Marsh, C.J. & Hill, P.W. (1984)
"Implementation of a Syllabus Innovation in Western Australia"
Studies in Educational Evaluation 10, 135-147.

Marsh, C.J. & Huberman, M. (1984)
"Dissemminating Curricula: A Look from the Top Down" Journal of Curriculum Studies, 16, 1, 53-66.

Reid, W.A. (1984)
"Curricular Topics as Institutional Categories: Implications for Theory and Research in the History and Sociology of School Subjects", in Goodson, I.F. & Ball, S.J. (Eds.)
Defining the Curriculum
London, Falmer Press.

Rogers, E.M. & Shoemaker, F.F. (1971)
Communication and Innovations: A Cross-cultural Appoach
New York, Free Press.

Rudduck, J. (1980)
"Curriculum Dissemination as Planned Cultural Diffusion". Paper presented at the Annual AERA Conference, Boston.

Stenhouse, L. (1980) (Ed.)
Curriculum Research and Action
London, Heinemann.

State Government of Western Australia (1984)
Education in Western Australia: Report of the Committee of Inquiry into Education in Western Australia (Beazley Report)
Perth, Government Printer.

Waugh, R. (1981)
"Teacher Receptivity to the CSE System"
Perth, Board of Secondary Education.

8. A HISTORICAL PERSPECTIVE ON JUSTIFYING THE TEACHING OF MATHEMATICS

George M.A. Stanic

The *sine qua non* of the curriculum field is the struggle to answer the question of what we should teach. As Herbert Kliebard (1981) has said, 'If human mental capacities were so great that everything could be known or if the amount of knowledge available were so small that it could be known to everyone, then we would have no need for the study of curriculum' (pp.2-3). Given the fact that human beings are faced with an almost unlimited amount of available knowledge and a limited capacity to know, it is of no small import that the subject area of mathematics has universal support for a place in the school curriculum.

But why should we teach mathematics? Although at first glance the question may seem trivial because the importance of mathematics for individuals and society as a whole seems so obvious, it is actually a question of vital importance. The question of why we should teach mathematics is one which must be constantly addressed because the way the answer is formulated and reformulated provides a valuable lens for viewing the questions of content, method, and quality of teaching that tend to be the greatest concerns of mathematics educators.

When the answer to the question of why we should teach mathematics is viewed as an ongoing process, the value of historical perspective becomes apparent. In the United States, the early years of the 20th century provide a particularly valuable historical moment to study, for it was during this time that the traditional place of mathematics in the school curriculum was, in fact, being threatened. By the 1930s, mathematics educators such as Earle Hedrick (1936) were speaking of a 'crisis that ... [threatened the] extinction [of mathematics] as a required subject in major curricula of secondary schools' (p.112).

So I want in this chapter to look at justifications for teaching mathematics that were being offered in the early years of the 20th century. This chapter is not intended to be the definitive response to the justification question. It is merely an attempt to raise the question, to link our struggles with those of our professional forebears, and to live up to the belief that our response to the question should be an ongoing process. A study of the justification question points to the issue of whether different areas of mathematics require different justifications. Furthermore, the question of why we should teach mathematics raises the issue of exactly what mathematics is. These issues will not, however, be explicitly addressed. Instead, the purpose of the remainder of the chapter is to highlight aspects of the historical data and tentatively to suggest certain implications for our own historical moment. The historical data do not tell us what to do today because each historical moment is unique, but they do point to possible consequences of some of our actions.

Justifications for Teaching Mathematics Offered During the Early Years of the 20th Century

Curriculum Interest Groups

In response to the decline in the influence of 19th century mental discipline theory and to societal changes brought on by intense industrialization, urbanization, and immigration at the turn of the century, four curriculum interest groups emerged during the early 20th century (Kliebard, 1981). The humanists, led by people such as Charles William Eliot and William Torrey Harris, emphasized the importance of the traditional disciplines of knowledge. The school curriculum, according to the humanists, should consist of those subjects which reflect our Western cultural heritage and which help to develop reasoning power. The humanists defended tradition; but they, too, played an important role in changes taking place in the American curriculum. They did not, however, suggest reform to the same extent as did the members of the three reform interest groups - the developmentalists, the social efficiency educators, and the social meliorists.

At the turn of the century, the developmentalists were led by Granville Stanley Hall. They argued that decisions about what should be taught could only be justified based upon an understanding of the natural order of development in the child. Impressed with studies conducted by Joseph Mayer Rice and led by David Snedden, the social efficiency educators promised to respond to the changes taking place in the school population and in the wider society while holding the fabric of society together. Their ultimate goal was a smoothly functioning, efficient society which would be based on predetermining the most appropriate societal role for each individual. They insisted that school subjects be directly functional; that is, the curriculum of the social efficiency educators was to include only that subject matter which was demonstrably useful for people's future societal roles. If the social efficiency educators sought through their reforms to hold together the fabric of society through efficient planning, the social meliorists sought to weave a new fabric. With roots in the writings of Lester Frank Ward, the social meliorists saw in schools and the school curriculum a way to alleviate the suffering of individuals by eliminating harmful inequalities in access to knowledge. For the social meliorists at the turn of the century, a just society was to be based on the equal distribution of knowledge.

Mathematics Educators and the Interest Groups

Mathematics educators in the early years of the 20th century could argue for the important developmental experience that the study of mathematics provided, could substantiate the usefulness of mathematics to individuals preparing for various societal roles, and could even point to the need for all children to have access to mathematics in order to overcome unjust societal inequalities; however, it was in the humanist interest group that these mathematics educators found the greatest support for the place of mathematics in the school curriculum. And it was in the social efficiency interest group that they found their strongest critics. One clear message in the historical data is that all the interest groups recognized the importance of mathematics to our society. Even David Snedden advocated offering rigorous high school mathematics courses. However, Snedden and other social efficiency educators believed that not all people needed to study mathematics in high school; one needed to study only as much mathematics as was required for daily living and for one's vocation. Snedden went so far as to suggest that most people needed no mathematics beyond sixth-grade arithmetic. Therefore, a basic issue seems to have been not whether rigorous high school courses in mathematics should be available but who should be required and encouraged to take such courses (Stanic, 1983/1984b).

Humanist educators such as David Eugene Smith of Teachers College, Columbia University, and Jacob William Albert Young of the University of Chicago were appalled at the thought of mathematics being looked upon only from a limited utilitarian (or directly functional) viewpoint. Young (1906), for instance, provided a long list and description of justifications for teaching mathematics (pp.13-46). His two main classifications of justifications related to the importance of mathematical subject matter and the importance of mathematics as a mode of thought. Under the former, he included the value of mathematics to civilization as a whole, to individuals in their daily activities, and to individuals in their chosen vocations. Furthermore, under this first category, Young saw the teaching of mathematics as important because mathematics is 'so essentially characteristic of the human mind, so little influenced by environment, so uniformly present in every civilization' (p.14) and because mathematics 'is equally ingrained in nature, at least in nature as seen and interpreted by the human mind' (p.15). But, according to Young, 'the facts of mathematics, important and valuable as they are, are not the strongest justification for the study of the subject by all pupils. Still more important than the subject matter of mathematics is the fact that it exemplifies most typically, clearly and simply certain modes of thought which are of the utmost importance to everyone' (p.17). More specifically, Young referred to the importance of 'understanding statements, noting facts, and making inferences' (p.46). Furthermore, said Young 'the skill gained from the study of mathematics ... is available beyond the bounds of mathematics, whose form of reasoning is the ideal towards which all other reasoning strives; owing, however, to the simplicity and narrow range of mathematical inferences, mathematics can only give the beginning of the requisite practice' (p.46). Of fundamental importance to Young, then, was the idea that 'mathematics properly studied tends to strengthen, does strengthen, the power of thinking independently and accurately' (p.40), a position consistent with the basic humanist viewpoint.

This humanist position was challenged during the early years of the 20h century. The educational world of the humanists was changing most drastically, and they responded to the challenge and change in a variety of ways. Even Young and Smith, clearly humanist in their basic orientations, were affected by the other interest groups, particularly the developmentalists. Smith, for example, wrote an article entitled, 'Mathematics in the Elementary School' in 1903 with Frank M. McMurry, a colleague of Smith at Teachers College and one of the early members of the Herbartian movement (a movement which in part reflected developmentalist thought). In the article, Smith and McMurry stressed that 'the child's interest in the quantitive side of life should be the highest immediate aim of the teacher of mathematics in the grades ... [A]nd the nature of the child, together with the needs of society, should constitute the main standard in selecting subject matter. This signifies that these two ideas should be given a fuller control in mathematics than has thus far been allowed' (p.94). However, in a later piece which was described in its preface as necessary because the 1903 article with McMurry was out of print, Smith (1909), writing alone this time, cautioned his readers about the 'tendency throughout the country to make arithmetic, as other subjects, more interesting to children'. Although he saw a benefit in making arithmetic 'interesting and even attractive to children', he was concerned that educators would offer children 'a sickly substitute for the vigorous subject that has come down to us' and even felt that school arithmetic had already become 'anaemic' (p.39).

The 1909 article indicates that the impact of the developmentalists on Smith, while apparent, was not as great as a reading of only the article written with McMurry might lead one to believe. In the follow-up article, Smith's humanist orientation was clear, as was his growing concern about the ideas of the reformers. The concern on the part of many mathematics educators about the ideas of the reform interest groups continued to grow. In the

1920s and especially the 1930s, the mathematics education literature was characterized not simply by a defense of the role of mathematics in the school curriculum, but also by solemn warnings of a crisis in mathematics education. In most cases, the fear was not so much that mathematics would be eliminated as a subject area, but that it would be eliminated as a high school requirement for all students (Stanic, 1983/1984b). These fears were not unfounded. Both in terms of requirements for high school graduation and in terms of percentage enrollments in traditional mathematics courses, mathematics as a school subject was in a state of decline during the early years of the 20th century (Stanic, 1986).

It is clear that the social efficiency educators had much to do with the state of affairs in education, generally, and mathematics education, specifically. Yet is is not clear whether social efficiency educators created this atmosphere or responded (and gave direction) to an already prevailing mood. Social conditions in the early part of the 20th century had much to do with the fact that social efficiency thought became prevalent. The growth of industrialization, urbanization, and immigration at the turn of the century was related to the significant increase in the high school population. Between 1890 and 1940, enrollment in American high schools grew from 359,949 to 7,123,009 students. In 1890, only 6.7% of 14- to 17-year-olds attended high school; by 1940, 73.3% of America's 14- to 17-year-olds were attending high school (James & Tyack, 1983). That some change in the American high school curriculum took place as the population of the high school increased twentyfold is not unexpected; indeed, it would have been remarkable if there had been no change in the school curriculum during this period of unprecedented growth.

It is also important to recognize that although social efficiency thought became prevalent during the early years of the 20th century, the views of the social meliorists, developmentalists, and humanists did not disappear (Kliebard, 1981). The views of the social meliorists, while never really dominant, flourished for a time during the years of the Great Depression; and Lester Frank Ward's advocacy of 'equality of opportunity' became embedded in the ideology of American education. Developmentalist ideas were an important part of change taking place in the American school curriculum, particularly in the elementary school; furthermore, a coalition of sorts formed between the develomentalists and the social efficiency educators. And the humanist tradition remained strong among mathematics educators (Stanic, 1983/1984b).

The reform milieu faced by mathematics educators in the United States was complex; this complexity is exemplified in the formation of the National Council of Teachers of Mathematics in 1920. Among the reasons for establishing the council were to 'help the progressive teacher be more progressive' and to 'arouse the conservative teacher from his satisfaction and cause him to take a few steps ahead' (Austin, 1921, p.3). Yet the council clearly was formed in response to what the founders saw as attacks on mathematics by people they referred to as 'so-called educational reformers' (Austin, 1921, pp.1-2). That the NCTM was able to define 'progressives' as supporters of mathematics and label foes of mathematics as 'so-called educational reformers' is a reflection of the confusing mix of reform ideas to which mathematics educators had to respond. The confusion was, however, at least in part of their own making, as, in their attempt to defend the place of mathematics in the school curriculum, some mathematics educators unwittingly may have given support to the social efficiency educators who most threatened the traditional role of mathematics. The responses to the reform milieu of William Betz and William David Reeve, both prominent members of the mathematics education community, exemplify some of the attempts to justify the teaching of mathematics in a society and school curriculum undergoing significant change.

The Response of William Betz to the Reform Milieu

William Betz (1913), like many other educators of his era, expressed concern about the 'lowering of standards' brought about by the 'policy of extending every educational opportunity to the masses' (p.220). Responding to the views of the social efficiency educators, he said the 'demand' for 'efficiency' in the high school 'should be welcomed enthusiastically by all teachers'; he warned, however, of 'loose thinking' and claimed that 'the work of a school ... [cannot] be gauged like the output of a factory' (pp.222-223). By 'efficiency' Betz meant the ability to use acquired knowledge, not the economy of time and effort and the elimination of waste referred to by the social efficiency educators.

Betz described 'five important aims of mathematical teaching', which he classified under symbolism, applications, the function concept, space intuition, and logic (p.226). He concluded that no other high school subject had better reason to be included in the school curriculum. 'Mathematics', he said, 'meets a fundamental human need'. He saw mathematics as 'essential from either a purely ideal or a narrowly utilitarian standpoint'. And in the opportunity mathematics provided 'to acquaint the minds of the young ... with reliable standards of intellectual certainty', Betz saw the 'highest moral value' (p.227).

Betz wrote with a spirit of compromise, saying that 'the mathematical curriculum of the future must meet the wants of all types of students. For some of these types only actual experiment can determine the most desirable selection and sequence of topics' (pp.229-230). But he also said that the 'five aims cannot be fully realized unless every student in the general course is required to become familiar with the elements of algebra, of plane and solid geometry, and of plane trigonometry' (p.230).

In defending the latter claim, Betz, to a certain extent, turned the social efficiency educators' belief that school subjects must be directly functional back on them. 'If America wishes to compete with Europe along industrial, technical, or scientific lines', he said, 'it cannot ignore the increased educational opportunities given to European secondary students' (p.230). As opposed to the social efficiency educators who viewed high school mathematics as essentially useless for most people and suggested that few students needed to study mathematics in depth, Betz was suggesting that as many people as possible should take a reasonable amount of mathematics in the high school to help us compete with other nations. According to Betz, all students should study mathematics in depth in order to make certain that all potential mathematicians and scientists could be discovered. On the one hand, Betz was rejecting a basic belief of certain social efficiency educators that future societal roles could be predetermined early and easily. In essence, he was suggesting that an educator can never be certain, especially early in a child's school years, of an individual's ability to become a mathematician or a scientist. On the other hand, Betz was implicitly accepting the goal of 'social efficiency' by arguing that national security concerns made mathematics directly functional in a way not completely recognized by the social efficiency educators. That is, Betz was suggesting that mathematics was directly functional not just in the lives of individuals but for society as a whole. The need for a secure society capable of competing with other nations was, according to Betz, too important to take a chance on losing potential scientists and mathematicians by restricting educational opportunities in mathematics (or, more accurately, by not requiring high school students to take a sufficient amount of mathematics).

It was difficult to justify the secondary school requirements in mathematics based solely on the immediate and obvious usefulness of the mathematics being studied. Betz and other mathematics educators were confronted with the social efficiency educators' belief that school subjects had to be useful to justify their place in the school curriculum. Despite the decline in the influence of mental discipline theory, mathematics educators clung to the idea that mathematics had disciplinary value, that it exercised the mind and improved one's thinking in some general sense. No one doubted that high school mathematics was useful for some people. Many people, however, began to doubt the need to require mathematics of all high school students, regardless of their intended careers. Betz's national security argument was one attempt to justify its place in the required school curriculum.

But the attempt brought with it problematic consequences. The national security argument implies that the primary goal of mathematics teaching is to prepare and find those talented few (as difficult as they may be to identify) who can lead the country in competition with other nations; therefore, more people should study more mathematics in order to assure that the talented few are found. The argument also implies little real value of mathematics for the majority of students who must sit through the classes in which the future mathematicians will be nurtured and eventually discovered. Furthermore, even for the talented few, the importance of mathematics is tied only to its usefulness in their future vocations. So the use of a national security argument has problematic consequences for those who actually believe that studying mathematics in high school is good for everyone.

Betz did not base his belief that mathematics should be a required subject in the high school only on the national security argument. Yet the fact that he felt compelled to make such an argument is evidence of the growing criticism faced by mathematics educators. And the fact that he responded to the social efficiency educators on their terms by attempting to convince them of the usefulness of mathematics even may have provided implicit support for their cause. Furthermore, despite his national security argument, the number of mathematics courses required for high school graduation and the percentage of students enrolled in traditional secondary school mathematics courses continued to decrease during this era (Stanic, 1986).

The Response of William David Reeve to the Reform Milieu

Betz may have given implicit support to the cause of the social efficiency educators, but he also explicitly stated a broad view of the role of mathematics in the school curriculum and was careful to warn of the dangers of social efficiency thought. Other mathematics educators did not express such a broad view and were less critical of social efficiency ideas. Some even attempted to use the language of the social efficiency educators (and the developmentalists) to advance reform ideas with their own history inside mathematics education. The best example of this comes from some of the advocates of unified mathematics. Since at least the turn of the century, a number of mathematics educators advocated 'breaking down the walls' between mathematics and other subject areas and between the various areas within mathematics itself. In the United States, William David Reeve was among those educators.

Reeve saw in the reform ideas of the developmentalists and, particularly, the social efficiency educators a chance to argue for unified mathematics. More specifically, Reeve attempted to use to the advantage of unified mathematics the reform ideas of curriculum critics such as Henry Morrison,

Abraham Flexner, and David Snedden. While Reeve (1916) was calling the work of, for example, Morrison 'friendly and constructive' and not at all an attempt 'to discredit the place of mathematics as a part of the child's educational equipment' (p.204), other mathematics educators saw in the work by Morrison 'a severe criticism' (Minnick, 1916, p.61) against the place of mathematics in the school curriculum.

The work by Morrison referred to by Reeve as 'friendly and constructive' was published in 1914 in the Thirteenth Yearbook of the National Society for the Study of Education: Part I and reprinted in 1915 in the Mathematics Teacher. Morrison, then superintendent of public instruction for New Hampshire, discussed 'Reconstructed Mathematics in the High School'. In rejecting the 'disciplinary argument' and in expressing his concern with the 'needs, interests, and capabilities of children' and with the 'social needs which high schools must meet', Morrison espoused ideas which represent an interesting mixture of developmentalist and social efficiency thought. The differentiated curriculum he suggested was a reflection of the social efficiency goal of preparing people for their predetermined societal roles, and he claimed that his vision of 'reconstructed mathematics' would 'save time and increase teaching efficiency'. Furthermore, he looked upon 'the scientific management people in industry' as models of the 'scientific spirit' (Morrison, 1914, p.30).

Morrison's call to reorganize the college preparatory curriculum 'in both content and method' (Morrison, 1914, p.20) was especially appealing to Reeve. In describing the benefits of a unified mathematics program, Reeve (1916) emphasized the vocabulary of the social efficiency educators, pointing to, for example, the assets of unified mathematics from the 'social standpoint' (p.209) and to the 'economy of time and efficiency of effort' (p.211) that unified mathematics would bring. Reeve admitted (pp.211-212) that he was linking a reform movement with its own history inside mathematics education with the suggested reforms of critics outside mathematics education, but he clearly made the decision to take advantage of the reform atmosphere of the early 20th century.

Reeve's advocacy of general mathematics exemplifies another attempt on the part of some members of the mathematics education community to justify the teaching of mathematics based on the belief of social efficiency educators that school subjects must be directly functional, and his somewhat forced marriage of external and internal reform movements may have had negative consequences for the place of mathematics in the school curriculum. One could not claim that the early acceptance and use by Reeve and others of the rhetoric of the social efficiency educators 'caused' the crisis that many mathematics educators, including Reeve, spoke of by the 1930s. Certainly, much more was involved than the use of problematic rhetoric by certain mathematics educators. However, Reeve's uncritical acceptance of the curriculum reform rhetoric may have exacerbated the crisis to a greater extent than did Betz's national security argument. Uncritically accepting the language of social efficiency gave support to a movement that threatened the traditional place of mathematics in the school curriculum. Reeve's use of the social efficiency metaphor meant that the social efficiency educators could, in a sense, define the situation. The school curriculum was viewed through the lens of social efficiency, and using such a lens restricted the possible outcomes for Reeve's general mathematics program. Instead of the rigorous college preparatory course of study he originally wanted, general mathematics became almost a remedial course for students deemed incapable of handling the traditional coursework (Stanic, 1983/1984b, 1986). Reeve had failed to recognize the possible consequences of describing his program through the eyes of social efficiency; and this failure may have had an effect not just on general mathematics, but also on the entire mathematics curriculum.

Ironically for people like Reeve who attempted to use the criticisms of mathematics education made by David Snedden and the social efficiency educators to support changes, Snedden scorned most attempts at compromise. In fact, he even rejected the idea of requiring general mathematics in the ninth grade, calling 'composite mathematics' an attempt 'to preserve old prescriptions in a new guise' (Snedden, 1919, p.136).

Conclusion

Again, history does not tell us what actions we must take today because every historical moment has factors that make it qualitatively different from other moments in history. On the other hand, we should not (and cannot afford to) be ahistorical as we deal with present-day issues. History may not tell us how to act, but it does provide valuable perspective as we make decisions about how to act. And, as I view events occurring in the 1980s, I am a bit concerned that, at least in the United States, educators have not taken advantage of historical perspective. Let me cite two examples. The first involves the 1980 response of the mathematics education community to 'back-to-basics' reformers of the 1970s; the second involves the more recent crisis in education discussed in a number of reports by national committees and individuals.

In 1980, the National Council of Teachers of Mathematics published An Agenda for Action: Recommendations for School Mathematics of the 1980s. I believe that it is an example of the problematic use of external reform rhetoric (in this case, the rhetoric of back-to-basics reformers) to advocate internal reform.

The NCTM's first and foremost recommendation was that 'problem solving be the focus of school mathematics in the 1980s' (p.1). In arguing for this recommendation, the authors of the Agenda attempted to characterize problem solving as a vital 'basic skill'. While clearly expressing some criticism of the 'back-to-basics movement' (p.6), the authors also expressed sympathy for the idea of 'teaching basic skills with greater effectiveness' (p.5) and attempted to use the rhetoric of back-to-basics reformers to advocate a focus on problem solving.

Although the back-to-basics movement reflects a certain amount of diversity of ideas, many back-to-basics reformers have advocated the social efficiency educators' belief that school subjects must be directly functional. Given that this justification for including a subject in the school curriculum has a long and controversial history, accepting the rhetoric of the back-to-basics reformers has potentially negative consequences for mathematics educators.

Generally, when people talk about basic skills

in mathematics, they are referring to computational skills with whole numbers, fractions, and decimals. The authors of the Agenda challenged the common meaning of 'basic skills' and accepted the view expressed by the National Council of Supervisors of Mathematics (1977). Ten basic skill areas were listed in the Agenda, one of which was problem solving. Essentially, the NCTM was saying that it, too, supported the emphasis on basic skills, as long as everything it wanted in a mathematics program was called a 'basic skill'.

Placing the problem-solving recommendation within the context of back-to-basics rhetoric (i.e. classifying problem solving as simply one of ten basic skill areas) makes it difficult to respond to someone like Thomas Good (1979), who, using a more limited definition of basic skills (one that did not include the NCTM's view of problem solving), stated: 'The first step may be to improve basic skills. There is no reason to be excessively defensive about increasing students' performance in national achievement tests' (p.61). If problem solving is only one of ten basic skills to be learned, there is nothing wrong with wanting students to focus first on developing skill in the fundamental operations with whole numbers, fractions, and decimals. According to this view, the skill of problem solving can be taught after the fundamental operations are mastered. This violates the spirit of the NCTM's problem-solving recommendation, yet the acceptance of the language of 'basic skills' limits the NCTM's response to this view.

Clearly, and perhaps particularly in mathematics, not just what skills should be learned but the way such skills should be taught is crucial; that is, there is a danger that students will conceive of skills as ends in themselves, rather than as means to achieve other ends. As John Dewey (1910) said, 'practical skill, modes of effective technique, can be intelligently, non-mechanically used only when intelligence has played a part in their acquisition (p.52).

It is also clear that the authors of the Agenda would agree with Dewey; in fact, their recommendation that problem solving be the focus of school mathematics indicates this agreement that skills must be acquired with intelligence in order to be used with intelligence. However, the NCTM's argument is contradictory; or, at the very least, the NCTM diminishes its argument for permeating the mathematics curriculum with problem solving by characterizing what appears to be a general approach to the teaching and learning of mathematics as simply one of ten technical skills to be learned.

The point here, as it was in Reeve's advocacy of general mathematics, is that the acceptance of external reform rhetoric to advocate internal reform is problematic because such an action supports the external reform (with all its implications) and has the potential to distort the true meaning of the internal reform. In the case of the Agenda, the use of the back-to-basics rhetoric lends a form of support to the movement which contradicts the explicit criticism provided in the Agenda. Furthermore, acceptance of the language of 'basic skills' has the potential of distorting the problem-solving focus intended by the NCTM. The claim here is not that the NCTM would want its argument characterized in this way; the claim is that its use of back-to-basics rhetoric has potentially negative consequences that must be dealt with.

Now consider the recent crisis in education in the United States. Among many reasons for improving education in the United States, the need for national economic and military security has been prominent (Stanic, 1984a). Even before A Nation at Risk (USDE, 1983), the first and most widely read and discussed of the recent reports, was published in 1983, the president of the National Council of Teachers of Mathematics in 1982 began his reign with a statement entitled, 'In Support of Military and Economic Strength' (Willoughby, 1982). His introduction is particularly revealing:

> The next two decades will be critical for the United States. Our ability to defend ourselves militarily is in doubt. Our presence in the marketplace for manufactured goods has already been seriously compromised in such important fields as communications and transportation, and we are rapidly losing our grip on areas such as computer and space technology. It is entirely within the realm of possibility that the United States will manage to become a second-rate power in the next 20 years.

> There are many reasons for this decline. Some such causes are broadly economic or political and must be addressed in those domains. However, a remarkable fact that is hard to ignore is the relatively great emphasis placed on the teaching of mathematics, engineering, and the natural sciences in both Japan and the Soviet Union - our major competitors, respectively, in economic and military strength. (p.2)

There is nothing necessarily wrong with being concerned about national security. And the issue here is not whether those who emphasize increasing high school requirements in mathematics in order to ensure the security of the United States are right or wrong about their facts regarding the state of the economy and the national defense; nor is it whether they are right or wrong in assuming such a direct relationship between the level of military and economic strength and high school requirements in mathematics. Furthermore, the fact that the national security issue did not appear to impress William Betz's contemporaries does not mean that it will have little impact now. Indeed, it appears as though states and communities are increasing the number of courses in mathematics required for high school graduation (although the cause of this change is complex anbd cannot be attributed simply to the recent reports). However, the issues associated with the national security argument are the same for us as they were for Betz. Preparing and identifying the talented few is implied as the most important goal of mathematics education. Those that have emphasized mathematics for national security, including some mathematics educators, may believe that there are other justifications for teaching mathematics and may be interested in more than simply finding those talented students who will lead the United States against its economic and military foes. What we have today, however, are the problematic consequences of Betz's national security argument without his broader vision of why we should teach mathematics.

Different justifications for teaching mathematics arise from different assumptions about what mathematics is, who should be encouraged or required to take how much mathematics, and what it means to be an educated human being; and they have different implications for the mathematics curriculum. Invoking a particular justification for teaching mathematics should mean that such assumptions and implications are recognized and accepted. I believe the examples show that we are not as aware as we should be of the consequences of our beliefs and actions. As we attempt to better understand such consequences, history can provide perspective - but no answers.

An earlier version of this chapter was presented at the International Conference on 'Foundations and Methodology of the Discipline Mathematics Education (Didactics of Mathematics)' Bielefeld, Federal Republic of Germany, July 1985.

References

Austin, C.M. (1921)
'The National Council of Teachers of Mathematics' Mathematics Teacher 14 pp.1-4.

Betz, W. (1913)
'What Mathematical Subjects Should Be Introduced in the Curriculum of the Secondary School?' Mathematics Teacher 5 pp.218-233.

Dewey, J. (1910)
How We Think
Boston, D.C. Heath.

Good, T.L. (1979)
'Teacher Effectiveness in the Elementary School' Journal of Teacher Education 30 pp.52-64.

Hedrick, E.R. (1936)
'Crises in Economics, Education, and Mathematics' Mathematics Teacher 29 pp.109-114.

James, T. and Tyack, D. (1983)
'Learning from Past Efforts to Reform the High School' Phi Delta Kappan 64 pp.400-406.

Kliebard, H.M. (1981, April)
Education at the Turn of the Century: A Crucible for Curriculum Change
Division B Invited Address presented at the annual meeting of the American Educational Research Association, Los Angeles, CA.

Minnick, J.H. (1916)
'Our Critics and their Viewpoints' Mathematics Teacher 9 pp.80-84.

Morrison, H.C. (1914)
'Reconstructed Mathematics in the High School: The Adaptation of Instruction to the Needs, Interests, and Capacities of Students' in The Thirteenth Yearbook of the National Society for the Study of Education: Part I
Chicago: University of Chicago Press pp.9-31.

Morrison, H.C. (1915)
'Reconstructed Mathematics in the High School' Mathematics Teacher 7 pp.141-153.

National Council of Supervisors of Mathematics (1977) 'Position Paper on Basic Mathematical Skills' Arithmetic Teacher 25 pp.19-24.

National Council of Teachers of Mathematics (1980) An Agenda for Action: Recommendations for School Mathematics of the 1980s Reston, VA, Author.

Reeve, W.D. (1916) 'Unification of Mathematics in the High School' School and Society 4 pp.203-212.

Smith, D.E. (1909) The Teaching of Arithmetic New York, Teachers College, Columbia University.

Smith, D.E. and McMurry, F.M. (1903) 'Mathematics in the Elementary School' Teachers College Record 4 pp.91-160.

Snedden, D. (1919) 'Mathematics in the Education of Youth from 12 to 18 Years of Age - Some Proposals for Further Study' Educational Administration and Supervision 5 pp.125-144.

Stanic, G.M.A. (1984a) 'Un Esprit Simpliste' Journal for Research in Mathematics Education 15 pp.383-389.

Stanic, G.M.A. (1984b) 'Why Teach Mathematics? A Historical Study of the Justification Question' (Doctoral dissertation, University of Wisconsin-Madison, 1983) Dissertation Abstracts International 44 p.2347A.

Stanic, G.M.A. (1986) 'The growing crisis in mathematics education in the early twentieth century' Journal for Research in Mathematics Education 17 pp.190-205.

United States Department of Education (1983) A Nation at Risk: The Imperative for Educational Reform. Report of the National Commission on Excellence in Education Washington, DC, Government Printing Office.

Willoughby, S.S. (1982) 'In Support of Military and Economic Strength' NCTM News Bulletin 18 (5) p.2.

Young, J.W. (1906) The Teaching of Mathematics in the Elementary and the Secondary School New York, Longmans, Green.

9. WHO CONTROLS THE CURRICULUM? THE STORY OF 'NEW MATHS' 1960-80

Bob Moon

Introduction

Charles Bourbaki, a rather unsuccessful General in the French army very nearly became King of Greece at the age of 46. For reasons now unclear he declined and subsequently suffered exile to Switzerland after the debacle of the Franco-Prussian war. Depressed by circumstances he attempted suicide, survived a poorly directed shot and lived eventually to the age of 83, dying in the last years of the nineteenth century.

To understand the New Maths invasion of European classrooms in the 1960s and 1970s it is important to know about Bourbaki. His name was chosen as a publishing pseudonym by a group of mathematicians loosely grouped around the University of Nancy. Their papers, and a major treatise, was to revolutionize teaching and research about mathematics in Universities throughout the world. The Bourbakists were a secret society, about twelve in number, with a changing membership because retirement from the group at fifty was compulsory. Titles of the publications, Set Theory, General Topology, Topological Vector Space, whilst obscure at the time, were to become familiar terminology for thousands of primary school teachers all over Europe.

The exploration of the five case studies reported here was an attempt to observe the ways in which different national systems of education responded to pleas for a reform of the mathematics curriculum, pleas in large part inspired by the activities of the Bourbakists. In particular concern centred around:

> Would the account of a particular change working through the formal system confirm or question the existing categorizations of differences between systems?

> Is the attention paid to national styles of curriculum development appropriate, given the international phenomena of the curriculum development movement - particularly the 'project' approach which characterized an early period of reform?

> How do the formal systems respond to changes in the social and economic conditions prevailing at different periods?

These initial ideas implied a questioning of some of the taken for granted assumptions about educational systems and curriculum development. Curriculum study has led to the growth of a considerable literature describing the way in which countries had evolved different systems for curriculum development and control. The focus of analysis had been the nation state. In many related disciplines this had become an inescapable framework of analysis. Shafer (1955) attempted to explain this:

> 'The customary method of historians in our times, and for the last two centuries, has been to write national histories, to study national institutions, to attempt solution of national problems. It is easier and more convenient, the material can be more readily collected and synthesized, they themselves are nationalists, it is politic, and it has become a tradition. They also do it because the nation has become the most important social unit and the most obvious one to study. People in our time live in nation states and possess national consciousness; most of their vital activities are carried on within the framework of the nation state. Moreover, as practitioners of the scientific method, scholars are bound to look for distinctions, for differences based on kind, level and function; and nationality is the most significant contemporary group distinction.' (p.215)

Rowlinson (1974), taking a global perspective, provides a basis for modifying nationalistic viewpoints when he suggests:

> '.... the different national reforms of European education, so much determined by historical, political and social developments within the separate countries, show a striking homogeneity when viewed from a non-European perspective.' (p.29)

Broadfoot (1980), pursues the theme more directly when she makes a plea for

> '.... the importance of looking beyond the rhetoric of control in an education system to the reality that underpins it', (p.119)

and she suggests that observation of the complex relationships involved in curriculum innovation is best demonstrated by detailed case study in areas to identify

> '.... the actual rather than the theoretical controls which affect the impact of research and development'. (p.119)

The first generation curriculum projects had created an interest in national styles of curriculum change in West European countries. International organizations such as UNESCO, OECD and the Council of Europe had a particular concern to look at dissemination strategies. Towards the end of the nineteen seventies, however, in a number of countries, the role of government in relation to the control of the school curriculum had become increasingly controversial. Debate of these issues has often been informed by categorizations of style or tradition in the ordering of national affairs. Terms such as centralized or decentralized, for example, were and are, frequently used to create concern or hope, according to individual persuasion, in the political polemic of the day. The extra significance of this rhetoric, to use Patricia Broadfoot's phrase, became more and more significant in policy discussions related to the different approaches to curriculum development.

At the same time researchers began to look beyond formal accounts of change in different systems. The compromises, and personalized interventions and trade-offs that were so characteristic of curriculum reform came under close scrutiny. Accounts of particular reform intiatives attempted to express the rich complexity within which different groups worked to promote or inhibit innovation. The practical realization that change was less simple than some, in an earlier period had imagined, was manifest in theoretical terms, in a more developed understanding of the different processes at work. The relationship of these processes to the formal systems established for curriculum development provides, therefore, one particular focus for this enquiry.

Curriculum study, which developed in parallel with the controversies surrounding New Maths, drew inspiration from a variety of disciplines. A number of theorists have advocated the use of comparative case study as a way of further understanding the way events unfolded. Stenhouse (1980) in a Presidentail Address to the Comparative Education Society in Europe, said

> 'I am mounting a like criticism of the tradition in comparative education of studying and writing about the _systems_ of other countries, and asking that we develop in our field a better grounded representation of day to day educational reality resting on the careful study of particular cases'. (p.10)

and Westbury (1980) echoed this view in proposing that

> 'What is clear is that variety .... is a prerequisite for the abstracting that is an essential part of the search for an understanding of how systematic curriculum change can be conceptualized. And if we are to seek to gain intellectual control over this problem, if we are to draw upon the experience that has been secured by the reflexive test of our understanding of this problem that the last two decades have offered, conceptualizations based on a _variety of cases_ is perhaps the only way forward. Comparative analysis thus becomes an important way of moving forward toward a more comprehensive understanding than any of us can secure based on our own

inevitably limited experience'. (pp.521-2)

In these vignettes, therefore, of curriculum reform a variety of data was sought, much of it going beyond the formal record of curriculum change. Interviews with those who participated in, or observed, the events of the period; media evidence where available; reports of parliamentary proceedings and the activities of educational publishers all represent examples of the sort of information collected. Assembled, the data would provide case records from which an analysis of the period could grow.

Theoretical Perspective

The early evidence from the case studies raised questions about many of the assumptions that pervade the established literature.

Firstly there are the ideas that arose from the activities of collaborative international research during this period most significantly sponsored by UNESCO or OECD. A number of publications explored the impact of curriculum reform initiatives on national systems of education. The Handbook of Curriculum Development (OECD/CERI 1973) and the four volumes Case Studies of Educational Innovation (OECD/CERI 1973) represent two examples. Assumptions within these works include a recognition that subject based development had its origins in the USA and was subsequently grafted onto different national systems. Equally it was repeatedly asserted that

> descriptions and categorizations of the control of curriculum development are broadly related to the traditional structures of the national systems of education. In particular, although the reports recognize the conceptual difficulties associated with the terms centralized and decentralized, they repeatedly stress the significance of this distinction for understanding curriculum control and development.
> 'Over and over again we are faced with the issue of "centralization" versus "decentralization"'
> (OECD/CERI 1975 Vol. IV p.258)

From the outset, therefore, national traditions had been seen as of significance in understanding curriculum control and change. The CERI and Council of Europe publications, although supporting this view, also began to introduce a questioning note which later observers reinforced. The lack of data, noted by a number of theorists, made further speculation difficult. As the curriculum work of CERI was coming to an end, new developments in the sociology of education began to make an important impact on curriculum study.

The sociologists of education, symbolized at that period, most notably by Michael Young's collection of papers 'Knowledge and Control' (Young et al 1971), raised as problematic the nature of academic knowledge and the school curriculum. He and others set out to ask what implicit assumption had led sociologists to ask certain questions, for example about selection, whilst treating others, for example about academic education, as given. The interest in concepts such as dominance and power was to provide a marked change of emphasis from the systems analysis approach of the international publications of a few years earlier.

The lack of empirical evidence from this debate was, however, to lead to a more historical approach to the understanding of curriculum change. In parallel with and related to the theoretical viewpoints of the sociologists there was a growing interest in the studies of History and Sociology as major disciplines (Jones, 1976). The creative tensions between historians and sociologists are long established and well documented. The declining influence of functionalist theory and the awakening interest in the historically rooted ideas of Weber or Durkheim is one representation of this. In the study of history the strength and influence of the French annales school had pushed debate strongly towards a more social perspective, providing a clear methodological lead for those wishing to explore the theoretical ideas advanced within the sociology of knowledge. In a review essay, Warwick and Williams (1980) described the relationship between history and the sociology of education as one, until recently, of benign neglect. They went on to describe a range of work that was changing this. Curriculum, therefore, had an opportunity to become central to the debate around what had been called 'The New Criticism'; and curriculum history had direct relevance to the ideas advanced about power and control.

The growing concern about the effectiveness of the curriculum reform strategies pursued in the period after 1960 was also beginning to influence research. The lack of an historical perspective within which to assess new forms of theory building was noted by a number of critics. Tanner (1982) cites various authorites to support his assertion that

> 'The ahistorical character of curriculum reform efforts has been identified as a substantive problem in the curriculum field by curricularists and educational historians alike.' (p.405)

The debate in the pages of Curriculum Inquiry (Volumes 7-8) between Franklin and Davis testifies further to the interest in this area.

In 1977 one symposium of the Annual Meeting of the American Educational Research Association in New York was given over to the theme 'Retrospective Analysis as a Source of Knowledge about Curriculum Development'. Robert Wise of the National Institute of Education presented a paper entitled 'A Case for the Value of Retrospective Accounts of Curriculum Development'. A year later in Britain, the History of Education Society devoted a conference to the theme 'Post-war Curriculum Development: An Historical Appraisal' (Marsden, 1979). Out of this activity, case studies in journals and more extensive reports in book form began to appear. The development project was a prime focus for this (Waring, 1979; Stenhouse 1980) as was the historical development of subject within the school curriculum. This latter interest has provided the most recent research. Ball, (1982), Goodson (1981 and 1983), for example, carried out investigations into English, Environmental Studies, Geography and Biology. This work is in part based within a socio-historical tradition reflected in the earlier work of Ben-David and Collins (1966) and Layton (1972).

There are in the themes put forward ideas that link directly to the issues raised in the CERI publications. The case studies of projects, however, tend to eschew a comparative approach, looking at development in terms of take up and impact (the most critical of evaluative criteria during the period) rather than in terms of the links between the project methodology and the institutional structure within which the reform had been conceived. This is less true in the investigation of subject histories, although it is for the most part carried out within national contexts.

Further assumptions, therefore, can be observed in the ideas of the sociologists of and the historians of school curriculum.

> .... the concept of power has been introduced, particularly by reference to the dominance of high status institutions (especially the universities). Control is exerted directly, for example, through public examinations, or indirectly by providing the academic respectability to support subject status within the curriculum. This broadens the concept of authority and responsibility for change implicit in the approach of the CERI publications.
> .... the exercise of power within institutionalized arrangements is seen as mediated through the interaction of different groups, and in particular those that constitute the professionalized clusters around subject areas and/or curriculum movements.

Explorations of curriculum change moved, therefore, from the whole systems approach, represented in the CERI formulations, to an interest in case study and subject histories. Concern with the macro level continued, however, motivated not only by theoretical controversy but also by broader political issues which had come to prominence by the end of the 1970s.

In 1979, Margaret Archer published her major study of the Social Origins of Educational Systems. She used the concept of centralized or decentralized systems as the focus not only for an historical appraisal of how systems change but also to prophesy how they might develop in the future. The study marks an important contribution to the debate and will be considered before the evidence of more recent work in political science.

Archer set herself the ambitious task of answering the question 'How do education systems develop and how do they change?' (p.1)

Using a macro sociological approach illustrated and supported by evidence from France, Russia, Denmark, England and Wales, she advances a theoretical model which explores both the origins and development of educational systems as well as proposing possible ways in which they may change over time.

She distinguishes between centralized and decentralized educational systems in terms of development from a common origin within the churches. Centralized systems developed where freedom from the old orthodoxy was achieved through political action and the restriction of the activities of the church by law. Decentralized systems were more likely to originate where financially powerful groups, disadvantaged by religious control, established educational institutions outside the influence of the church and state. Her focus was historical looking at national developments in France, Russia, Denmark and England and Wales. In an important passage, she argues

> 'The supreme importance of political manipulation in the centralized system had two consequences for analysis. Firstly, it was possible to describe educational interaction as a political story, with character, plot and outcome, which could be told chapter by chapter and volume by volume for both France and Russia. Secondly, it was possible to explain educational interaction in terms of the changing interrelationships between the political structure and the structure of educational interest groups. When dealing with decentralized systems the nature of both description and explanation differs considerably. On the one hand interaction cannot be described as a story (political or otherwise) because three different kinds of negotiations are going on simultaneously and are taking place at three different levels (those of the school, community and nation) instead of being restricted to the last of these .... This is no historic saga, but only a vast collection of short stories in which some of the same characters reappear and some of the same problems are tackled by different personae in different ways .... (pp.396-7)

Overall it is a long and detailed argument and not without some subsequent criticism. King (1979), for example, suggests that the conceptual structure takes insufficient account of situational reality.

> 'Anyone knowing the way in which multifarious systems of education and/or schooling are "worked" by those expert in taking advantage of the local scene is constantly struck throughout this book by exceptions and objections which bring into question its "overworking" theory.'

Warwick and Williams (1980) speculate whether the theoretical approach chosen by Archer led to inadequate choice or weak interpretations of the data and they take her to task for creating an inadequate dialogue between theory and experience. Her conceptual framework does, however, underpin assumptions previously noted.

> .... development within centralized systems is seen as linear. Description is possible within the narrative form. Development, however, within decentralized systems is seen as more complex requiring description that extends beyond the political arena.
>
> .... the style of development is characterized by a stop-go pattern of events in centralized systems and an incremental process in decentralized systems.
>
> .... the availability of resources is seen as critical in determining the power different groups can wield in any educational negotiation.

Political scientists writing in the late 1970s were equally concerned with the analysis of system styles and decision making processes. Some writers (Castle and McKinlay, 1979, Benoit, 1975) presented arguments for bringing politics back into the unravelling of events despite the theoretical strength of the prevailing sociological concerns.

And Kogan (1982) supports the themes advanced for

> '.... a political model describing how educational institutions may control, legitimate and perhaps change society .... nothing is automatic. Changes occur, sometimes accidentally, when the right configurations of feelings, ideologies and power coincide.' (p.6)

Arthur Wise (1979), focusing on developments in the USA, addresses the issue of increased state intervention by a critical examination of bureaucratic activity. Using a Weberian framework he suggest that every act of the bureaucratic machine involves either weighing the relationship between means and ends or ensuring that a practice conforms to norms.

> 'When the relationship between means and ends is not known and the bureaucratic rationalization persists, we shall say that we are witnessing the phenomenon of hyper-rationalization - that is an effort to rationalize beyond the bonds of knowledge.' (p.65)

The relevance of this phenomenon to the public control of the curriculum is then developed. Such a process inevitably, says Wise, leads to increased centralization with an excess of prescription from outside the local setting.

Wise's analysis is important in looking at the perceived changes in nature of central control that occurred after the OPEC oil crisis of 1973 and the contraction in resources (see Papadopolous, 1980). Out of this two further assumptions can be discussed:

> the characteristics and needs of educational bureaucracies are seen as major elements in describing the process of educational change;
>
> the post-1973 period is seen as characterized by an increase in bureaucratic activity and in centralized control.

It is in the context of ideas such as these that the evidence of the case studies is presented.

The Case Studies

The case studies are presented as a synopsis of the evidence reported fully in Moon, B. (1986). It is important to stress that each must be seen in the context of considerable international activity around the modernization of mathematics teaching. In 1959 the, then, O.E.E.C. sponsored the Royaumont seminar which contained the powerful 'Euclid Must Go' appeal by Jean Dieudonne, a French Professor of the Bourbakist school. Strident pleas for change were sent to all national ministries. A compulsory one third attendance of teachers was requested. Membership of later international events, especially those organized through the regenerated International Commission for Mathematics Education (I.C.M.E.), was to become dominated by participants from Higher Education. Conferences in the early 1960s, for example at Athens and Dubrovnik, saw curriculum reform, first at secondary and then at primary levels as the main concern. As early as 1969, however, at the first I.C.M.E. conference in Lyon, France, the focus had moved towards more neutral, if equally controversial, research issues. This change in the climate of debate is reflected in the accounts of developments in each of the countries.

France

> 'Drugs, pornography and modern maths are ruining a generation of young people.'

This quote, from a speech reported in L'Express (February 6th, 1972), indicates the fervour surrounding New Maths reform in the late 1960s. It was a period of frenetic activity with textbook publishers competing vigorously to publish New Maths textbooks series. These were published in advance of any agreed national curriculum reform. Developments in the 1960s went forward regardless of the official curriculum guidelines that dated back to 1945. The primary inspectorate, largely comprised of teachers with literary rather than mathematical or scientific backgrounds, played very little part in the early period of reform. Publishing and university led initiatives created a focus of informal control outside the formal national structure. Contrary to popular opinion textbooks are not prescribed centrally, or regionally, and schools went ahead with new purchases without reference to the formal guidelines. A hotly disputed 'transitional' programme published in 1970 was one attempt to re-establish control. It was only, however, in 1980 that a full programme was agreed that contained only minimal elements of the activities advocated by the enthusiastic reforms of the earlier period. Dissemination of this programme was backed up by intense inspectorial activity, nationally and regionally. The establishment of regional mathmatics education centres in the aftermath of the debates of 1968 symbolized a freedom from central control. Towards the end of the 1970s after only a few brief years of development, they came under intense financial and political pressure. It was only the election of the socialist President Mitterand that ensured survival into the 1980s. Project development was of minimal significance, although Nicole Picard established as early as 1964 a centrally funded research programme. This led to one of the early New Maths textbook series. The role of publishers in promoting, or inhibiting reform initiatives at different periods is well represented by sales figures. It is extremely difficult to obtain this information. In France, however, figures for four 'books' in series published at different times graphically illustrate the rise (and demise) of New Maths.

Traditional 'Arithmetic Book'		Modern
No. of Copies Printed		Sales Figures
70,000	1968-69	35,078
15,000	1969-70	133,229
25,000	1970-71	316,311
12,000	1971-72	217,737
zero	1972-73	168,124
zero	1973-74	139,892

	New Maths 2nd Edition	New Publication, Direction Traditional
1977/78	5,696	2,234
1978/79	15,168	31,796
1979/80	9,966	50,951
1980/81	6,056	52,960

England and Wales

In contrast to France, the curriculum of England and Wales is categorized as decentralized. There are no mandatory national curriculum guidelines and reform is often characterized as piecemeal and pragmatic. The first new curriculum reform in mathematics, however, was highly central in character albeit outside the formal structures for control. A major national project, the Nuffield Primary Maths project, initiated by a unique linking of national inspectorate and officers of a private foundation dominated the 1960s and early 1970s. Teachers' centres were established in many parts of the countries to disseminate the ideas produced and published by the central team. As in France, textbook publishers competed vigorously and one member of the project left to write his own, very successful series of pupil textbooks for a publisher competing with publishing/consortium that produced the Nuffield materials. The early period of reform therefore, saw developers, inspectors and publishers working together to promote reform. By 1974, however, the developers had largely moved into a research role in higher education. Geoffrey Matthews, for example, the Nuffield Project Director, became the first British Professor of Mathematical Education. The national inspectorate were responding in the same period to the national backlash against the New Maths of 1960s, in part led by industrialists. Publishers, as in France, began producing alternative traditional maths textbooks that sold alongside the earlier Nuffield style publications. The mounting of a national commission of inquiry into mathematics teaching is indicative of further centralist initiatives. The second edition of the Nuffield publications, this time with pupil as well as teacher materials, was launched in 1979 solely as a publishing enterprise by a leading textbook publisher.

The Netherlands

The Dutch, like the English, have a characteristically decentralized structure for the control of education. Termed 'vervuiling' (meaning pillar and derived from the various schools of advice offered by the followers of St. Simeon Stylites, hermits who squatted out their lives at the top of pillars), it indicated the pluralism that protects Catholic, Protestant and secular interests. Reform of primary mathematics, however, was highly centralist. Early initiatives in secondary reform were carried forward by a national modernising commission. Influenced by the powerful advocacy of conferences and publications from OECD and UNESCO, leading mathematicians such as Hans Freudenthal campaigned vigorously for national intervention in primary school mathematics reform. Eventually in the early 1970s a major institute of mathematical education was to open in the University of Utrecht. From this institute a nationwide project entitled WISKOBAS was launched aimed at teacher development rather than textbook publication. Controversy, however, was to surround the development of the Institute. The rationalization of curriculum development by a new Minister of Education led to eventual closure. Some staff members moved to a department of the new national curriculum development agency at Enschede on the German border. The scale of activity was considerably reduced, and in 1980 curriculum developers were devoting a major part of their time to working alongside the authors of textbooks.

West Germany

The different German lander have almost total autonomy from federal influence in matters of education. Each has a Minister of Education and specific policies towards curriculum guidelines, approval of textbooks and even qualification recognition. New Maths provoked an intense national debate that only subsided in the late 1970s. Early advocacy by university mathematicians and by people like Zoltang Dienes (including televised primary school maths lessons) were influential in creating the climate for reform. In the late 1960s the reform cause became linked with federal intiatives from the Conference of Education Ministers in Bonn. In 1968, for example, they decreed that all lander should modernize the mathematics curriculum by 1972. Central authority in German politics was to lessen in the middle and late 1970s and the debates and quarrels over New Maths were to be lander specific in character. In lander such as Nordrheim-Westphalen, it was the conservative Christian Democrats who saw political advantage in opposing the reforms. In Baden Wurtemberg it was the left of centre Social Democrats who fought the proposals. One of the most influential projects was initiated in Hessen. Heinrich Bauersfeld, then a professor at the University of Frankfurt launched the Alef project with foundation funding. Despite local hostility, (Hessen was the only German lander other than Bavaria that would not accept the textbooks onto the approved list), Alef was disseminated nationally with the teachers guides proving particularly successful. Reforms, however, were taking place despite the existence of statutory guidelines. In Hessen the guidelines published in 1957 were not replaced until 1973. In the intervening period New Maths, through Alef and other textbook series, had a considerable take up in primary schools. In Hessen a curriculum development agency was established in 1975 that took on the responsibility for maths reform. New editions of traditionalist textbooks ('all new colour, all old maths' to quote one professor) had recaptured the market. One in particular Die Welt Der Zahl (NEU) averaged 70% take up in the schools in many of the lander. The end of the 1970s was to see some rivalry, over funding and control between the new curriculum development agency and the powerful administration within the regional Ministry of Education. By this time, Bauersfeld was leading one of the many new University Institutes of Mathematical Education in Bielefeld.

Denmark

Bent Christiansen in Denmark played a role equivalent to Freudenthal in the Netherlands or Bauersfeld in West Germany. Professor of Mathematics in the Danish Royal School of Educational Studies, he published New Maths textbooks for the secondary school in the early 1960s. Danish education is formally controlled by Act of Parliament and this includes curriculum content for all major subject areas. The Folkeskole Act of 1958 was only revised in 1975. In the years between, publication of New Maths textbooks and the advocacy of Christiansen was part of an immense amount of development work in schools. It is acknowledged that international developments, especially the Royaumont conference, were of particular significance. Translations of Swedish textbooks and the experience of teachers on exchange programmes in the USA (two of whom returned to publish New Maths textbooks) were also important to the reform process.

Opposition to reform, as in other countries, was vigorously expressed. The reassertion of central control through the 1975 Act was to see parental intervention at its most significant. Direct approaches from parents' leaders to the Minister of Education ensured that the sections dealing with mathematics were all headed (as they are to the present moment) Mathematics/Arithmetic. The third generation of textbooks, published in the late 1970s, appeared to reflect a judicious blend of 'old and new' maths very much in line with the consensus approach of the new 1979 Act.

Analysis

These accounts of the national and international activities surrounding reform of the mathematics curriculum can be reviewed with reference to the assumptions elaborated above. In the post Royaumont period pressures for reform from groups within each of the countries can be discerned. University mathematicians with close links to government were particularly prominent. Equally, the pressure of international events was also felt and the strongly worded demands from Royaumont for a 'national' response was influential even in countries where there was little tradition of central administrative involvement in curriculum affairs. The 'Bourbakist' re-assessment of the content of the secondary school mathematics led inevitably to a review of the primary sector. The publication of New Maths primary textbooks, often in translated form, fuelled this concern. Within a space of three to five years following the attempts at change in the secondary curriculum, the first significant manifestations of reform in primary schools became apparent. A markedly similar time scale for this is apparent in the events of each of the countries studied. 1964-66 is the critical period. Reform became, and was initiated through, an international rather than national debate. The response, therefore, of governments was accelerated. Government response to the modernization plea rarely respected the traditional structures established to provide a means for curriculum development and dissemination.

The most systematic example of a central, administrative response is represented by the early work of the Dutch modernizing commissions. Initiatives in mathematics, which later spread to other subjects of the school curriculum, led eventually to the founding of a centrally funded institute specifically established to promote subject based curriculum development. The needs of the primary years (the WISKOBAS programme) represented the first tasks of this institute. Despite the controversial history of the institute, the subsequent transfer of responsibility was again to a centralized curriculum development centre that stood outside the traditional pillar 'vervuiling' structure of education in the Netherlands.

In France, true to type, the Lichnerowicz commission, established by the government, set about the reform of the secondary school programme. Events, however, moved faster than government could, or would, respond. A climate was created in which the regulations became an incidental rather than central feature of the development process. Teachers in primary schools throughout France were purchasing textbooks based on principles far different from those set out in the 1945 'manual'. In Denmark and in Hessen the situation was the same. The 1957 guidelines, published coincidentally in the same year, represented a first review of those set down at the end of the second world war. By a few years they missed the wave of reform that spread across Europe. Central administrators, particularly the Inspectorate, were presented with a 'fait accompli' as teachers experimented with the implemented 'New Maths' that contrasted significantly with the ideas of 1957.

In England and Wales collaboration between national inspectorate, central administrators and a prestigious private foundation, Nuffield, created the means of providing a national response where no means for this had previously existed. In all the countries, except Denmark, projects or specialist institutions were established. The two with the most national impact and significance, Nuffield and WISKOBAS, grew in the countries with the least centralized systems for reform. Historians of the future would obtain a far from accurate picture of curriculum development in the other three countries if the formal record of curriculum guidelines and regulations were examined. Any study based solely on this evidence would be misleading to an extreme. The guidelines published in 1945 in France and in 1957 in Denmark and Hessen, in no way represented many of the primary school classrooms of the mid nineteen sixties. Throughout that period, despite the evidence of controversy and confusion, numerous observers confirm that official guidelines were largely ignored. In France most teachers, it is reported, rarely consulted the official programme, relying instead on the textbook to express the official view.

Little of this confirms the view that descriptions and categorizations of control of curriculum development are broadly related to the traditional structure of the national system of education. Neither, following this, would the evidence support the proposition that in matters of curriculum control 'over and over again we are faced with the issue of centralization versus decentralization'. Subject based development of this sort would appear, as the OECD Handbook of Curriculum Development (1975) suggests, to cross the boundary between centralisation and decentralization.

The characterization of differences between systems is unhelpful in accounting for the way events unfolded in this early period of reform in each of the countries. The notion, for example, in France of a cadre of highly trained inspectors with strong ideas about how the curriculum should develop, and clearly defined administrative techniques to carry out these ideas, would need significant qualification in any description of the curriculum reforms of the nineteen sixties. During an extended period of time, the rights of this central authority were taken over by, or subsumed within, the activities of groups external to the formal system. Equally, the assumption that the administration of curriculum development is not the responsibility of the central ministry in England and the Netherlnds is questioned by the analysis. The activites of centrally based officials were highly significant, in different ways, in both of these countries. The use of the term 'central' implies a unity of structure and purpose that masks some essential ambiguities. As Gottman (1980) points out

> .... any political and economic structure at work necessarily involves elements of centrality. How is the centre to be defined, however? (p.15)

And Lattimore (1980) in the same volume suggests that

> .... centrality may have become more nomad; it is still very potent, although in an era in which ethical and platonic ideas have regained popularity, the significance of centrality itself is changing, as it has done before, every time new ideas have emerged about the ways in which society ought to be governed. (p.223)

The concept of a nomadic centre is interesting when linked to the ideas of curriculum development as characterized by shifting amalgams of groups with particular interests to pursue. This ambiguity, however, is present in a number of accounts linking the traditional characteristics of educational systems to the process of curriculum change. The CERI Case Studies of Educational Innovation, for example, like the Handbook of Curriculum Development, express doubt about the apparent differences between centralized and decentralized systems. Reservations, however, focus on the extent to which published guidelines are followed in the classroom. This is important. Equally, however, it is interesting to speculate as to the ways in which, within the development process, the formal system can be bypassed not least by those with official positions in such a structure.

In the early years of reform, two strands of development can be observed. Firstly, in the events surrounding Royaumont central authorities had, almost through obligation, to play a role in representing national interests. In the history of curriculum reform this was a relatively new procedure. The attendance of ministerial representatives at Royaumont was in a ratio of 1:2 in relation to those from higher education. In succeeding years this was to change and the involvement of central administrators and inspectors diminished. This was most noticeable in France and Denmark, countries with a formal machinery for currriculum control and reform where a high level of such involvement could have been anticipated. Over the succeeding decade this process was to continue. In England and the Netherlands alliances between inspectorate, ministry and other groups was more characteristic of the development process. In Hessen the 'rising star' of the reformers led to bitter struggles with those holding administrative responsibility for curriculum affairs.

This brings the record up to the moment when the first group of projects became established in four of the five countries. In establishing projects, the normal channels of traditional structures were again bypassed. Of particular interest at this point is how certain apparently powerful central authorities failed, or chose not, to wield their influence in a leadership role in this first period of reform. The question arises as to the extent this represents a temporary state of affairs brought about by the international euphoria surrounding New Maths. An alternative interpretation suggests that in curriculum affairs the traditional systems had rarely operated in the structural way that many supposed. The French case study, for example, brings into question the validity of the centralist structure of French institutions for determining curriculum development.

In using 'tradition' to inform description of the curriculum change process, observers of events may fail to pay sufficient attention to the complexity of the national historical context. And so, in France, whilst the formal structure is centralist in character events may well be determined by allegiance to a second tradition of independence and freedom from central control. In the Federal Republic of Germany, although education, formally, is clearly the direct responsibility of Ministries of Education within the separate Land, the Federalist concept which developed from 1870 and Bismarck onwards is also available as a tradition to those who wish to use it. In Britain, whilst the Local Education Authorities claim responsibility for curriculum, there are many within the central ministry who wield considerable power and influence. The origins of Nuffield Maths demonstrate this. Not only, therefore, do we need to take account of alternative pasts within the nation state, we also have to look at the extent to which ties with these pasts are cut as modernization proceeds.

A tentative conclusion that begins to emerge is that in the events surrounding the early development of the primary mathematics curriculum, 'traditions' of control were not a prime determinant of how particular countries responded to the pressures for reform. 'Tradition' would appear to be only one of a collection of influences that must be accounted for in describing change. Different groups within the 'arena of change' appear to have laid claims to tradition, or a traditional role, where it served a purpose. If 'tradition' suited it was used, if it inhibited it was discarded and either an alternative stratety pursued or claims to a different tradition invoked to substantiate proposals. The concerns expressed by Broadfoot and others became more readily understood when subject based development, such as this, is examined more closely. Other related studies are appearing to provide further evidence.

Events towards the end of the 1970s provided further important evidence in this area. Inevitably, where a claim to tradition is supported by sufficient numbers of groups it is possible to argue for this as determining curriculum reform procedures. The suggestion here, however, is that in this context of subject based development, that was not the case and a reappraisal, therefore, of the significance of formal structure is necessary.

> The early period of curriculum development in mathematics was not contained within the traditional, formal structures for national curriculum control. Such structures were used if appropriate or bypassed when unnecessary. References to alternative traditions, representing different historical pasts, characterized the activities of some of the groups.

The era of 'project' development represented a new point of departure for national educational systems regardless of past histories. Earlier it was suggested that 'subject-style' curriculum development had its origins in the USA and was subsequently grafted on to different national systems. This process was seen as taking place at different times in different countries and evolving through a number of stages as development experience became more widely disseminated.

In chronological terms an R & D project approach to curriculum reform had its origins in the USA. In that country it was a period of considerable federal activity with the modernization and reform lobbies using the events surrounding 'sputnik' to gather in substantial funding. If project style R & D was a feature of the American scene, the urge to reform was international in character.

Leaders of the reform movement in the USA were keen to observe what was happening in Europe and it was very much in this spirit that American participation in Royaumont was launched. The introduction to the report talks of an interest in a 'comparative study of European education'. The initial impetus was in the direction of 'learning from' rather than 'reforming' and the membership of the conference was in sympathy with this aim. It was, after all, a European, Jean Dieudonne who presented the famous 'Euclid Must Go' entreaty.

Some accounts of curriculum history have seen the project developments as synonymous with curriculum reform. Given the interest, investment and excitement that surrounded projects, the reasons for this are apparent. Those involved in Nuffield, Alef or to a degree WISKOBAS, may have helped promote such a view. The case studies show how a vast range of influences came to bear on curriculum change. The project is a part of this but as the evidence of a number of the subject histories demonstrates, it is only one of a number of activities requiring attention.

The group of people committed to reform developed both a sense of mission and camaraderie in these early years. Ruddock (1977) uses the term the 'cognoscenti' or 'the initiated'. IOWO threatened by closure twenty years later was to have international support from members of the group in the fight for survival. By this time, however, the group had grown in size and changed in central purpose. People such as Bauersfeld and Freudenthal were to found institutes concerned with promoting mathematics education. This occurred in each of the countries and from an early small group of almost 'amateur' mathematics educators, there grew a professional class represented par excellence by the presence of this group in the 1980 Berkeley, California ICME Conference. The higher education group at Berkeley was dominated not by mathematicians or educationalists but by those, who in a variety of ways, described themselves asa mathematics educators.

In doing this, however, the focus increasingly moved away from reform. Advocacy of reform became incompatible with the opportunities, and constraints, of the new mathematics education institutions. Faced with the choice, the activists of the sixties opted for, using Kirp's (1982) phrase, 'professionalization as a policy choice'. The 1969 ICME Conference in Lyon represented something of a watershed in the movement. Up until that point reform had been the central concern, thereafter, for the mathematics educators as a group a more detached, academic approach to the politics of curriculum reform became essential. The status and credentials of this newly emerging 'field' could hardly be presented in a reform context and the second part of the period, the 1970s, saw the members of this group, effectively disassociating themselves from the evangelical fervour which had characterized the early years. The institutional basis of this development involved a readjustment in the relationship of mathematics educators to central administrators and inspectors within the educational bureaucracy. Institutionalization required funding and, in a period of increasing economic recession, there was inevitably a change in the balance of power between developers and resource providers. The mathematics education institute in the Netherlands, the regional centres in France and the curriculum development centre in Hessen all had problematic relationships with funding authorities; in the first two instances this was central government. In other words the very process of professionalization which had grown out of the reform movement of the 1960s left those with the most commitment to change in a much more circumscribed position of advocacy. In addition to dependence on government there were also links to be established with research agencies, with private foundations and with industry.

The period around 1973 has been seen as significant by a number of observers in representing a point when social conditions began to impinge significantly on educational activities. In this period there was a contraction in resources. In one sense the demise of 'the project' in part relates to these changing conditions. 'The project' was, by definition, an attempt at intervention with all the political and ideological implications that this had. It suited the conditions of the 1960s, a period of political questioning and economic expansion. It gave birth to a new professionalized group but by the early 1970s, as a style, it was inappropriate, not in tune with the times and in particular the ambitions of those who would benefit most from more limited resource input into mathematics education.

> The mathematics reforms of the 1960s developed more 'professional' roles in the 1970s supported within institutional contexts which developed out of the reform movement. The different purposes of mathematics reformer and mathematics educator were reflected in the changing styles and character of curriculum development during the period.

One of the most intriguing and fascinating groups in the New Maths debate are the commercial publishers, intriguing because obtaining data about their activities is problematic and fascinating because what little data has been obtained indicates the importance of these entrepreneurial activities in the unfolding of events. The following is suggested within the case studies. Firstly, where formal guidelines existed they did not necessarily determine publishing policy. In all the countries publishers were active, as soon as New Maths became a professional issue, in looking for commercial opportunities. Nicole Picard of France talks of being inundated with proposals from publishing companies. Secondly, there was a willingness to publish in advance of changes in formal guidelines. Related to this, publishers, through their professional contacts with mathematics educators and inspectors, did, in part, see themselves in the role of reformer. Thirdly, the sales technique used in promoting New Maths represented almost a reflection of the same linking of groups that represented the political groupings behind the reform movement. Inspectors, project developers and teachers with positions in subject associations were listed in some of the publishing programmes. As the tenor of debate surrounding New Maths changed, so did publishers allegiances and new contacts were sought out. The middle 1970s saw a period of some confusion with publishers backing different products whilst future directions were determined. The changing pattern of sales in the year 1977 and onwards shows a commitment towards an approach which reflected a reaction against the perceived excesses of the reforms.

The response of publishers to discussion of these issues illustrates the role this particular group plays. It is clear that network of contacts and influences exist which involve publishing houses. The secrecy surrounding the commercial activities of publishers make it difficult to unravel the way in which such links are established and evolve.

Summarizing, therefore, the proposition established that the interaction of different groups, and in particular the professionalized groupings around subject areas and curriculum movements, is critical to the understanding of the change process, is confirmed by these observations. New Maths is representative of the theme advanced by Ball (1982), that curriculum change is a long term, inter-personal process, based upon the establishment of subject paradigms via networks of communication and apprenticeship. The established paradigms in this study were radically challenged by a new network of influence in the period after Royaumont. The story of New Maths can be seen as the public and private operation of interdependent 'segments' of influence competing within institutional arrangements for power and for access to resources. There is, however, not necessarily a particular focus of power and influence that overrides the others. Whilst the universities clearly had a major impact on reform, this 'high status' position was used, or later abused, by groups according to their self interest and according to the group allegiances established at the time. Reference to pure Bourbakist mathematics in 1968 was significant, in 1977 another mathematics tradition, of little significance to university teaching, was brought into play. Yet again, therefore, it is necessary to turn to the view that, just as traditional structures could be used or ignored, and just as project development could be embraced or rejected, so too the high status role of the universities in determining what happened in school classrooms changed from one period to another. It was influential but only at a period in time; at other times it was ignored and other points of reference used to legitimize proposals.

> The relationships and alliances between groups, over the period the mathematics curriculum developed, were changed and modified in response to pressures internal and external to the education system. The move from broad based support for the introduction of 'Bourbakist' style, university mathematics, to the advocacy of utilitarian arithmetical 'basics' a decade

> later is a consequence of changes in the nature and interaction of interest groups.

The theoretical formulations put forward by people such as Wise reflect the preoccupations of the late 1970s. Increased federal control in the USA and marked interventionist policies by the DES under governments of different political persuasions in Britain were major issues of debate. The case studies illustrate that a different juxtaposition of influence can create situations where central authorities are bypassed in this development process. Central authorities are one of the groups competing for influence although at times the weight and authority with which politicians, administrators or inspectors enter the curriculum arena will vary markedly. To suggest that the identity and specific needs of educational bureaucracies are a major element in describing change may be true in one period, less so in another.

Increased activity, therefore, on the part of central authorities is seen as characterizing developments in primary school mathematics. In part this is a reflection of the increasing attention given to New Maths as a 'problem' with questions in parliaments, media concern and parental disquiet. Each of the case studies illustrates a growing crescendo of public concern.

Adjustments in the bureaucratic response were only part of the complex interplay of forces within the networks of interest groups.

> The evidence suggests an increase in bureaucratic and political involvement towards the end of the 1960-80 period. This is seen as relating to the contraction in resources and an increased dependence of mathematics educators on bureaucratic support for funding.

Recent work in the history of subjects suggests that the outcome of educational change reflects a much more complex interaction between interest groups than the unified concepts of control of the curriculum would imply. Change, therefore, in those terms, cannot be explained by reference solely to the internal characteristics of educational systems. The formulation by Archer goes some way towards this, in acknowledging the political influence of groups external to the educational system. Overall, however, she sees the internal attributes of the traditional structures as most critical. Whilst over time traditions and linked procedures become established within educational systems, it does not always follow that they will be adhered to. The context of curriculum change involves the integration of a range of very disparate groups which might 'loosely' be seen as institutionalized within the curriculum arena, but which have markedly different power bases which change over time according to other conditions prevailing. Whilst the strategies of such groups may be categorized, and whilst the relationship of such groups to traditional structures may be explored, there is nothing predetermined about the outcome of any particular period.

> The case studies suggest that initiatives within educational systems can be dependent upon or independent of the formal structure for control depending on the conditions in which change occurs. Interest groups develop strategies within, and outside the formal system that further the purposes they seek.

Over significant periods of time changes have occurred, working through different institutional arrangements, without necessarily feeling the constraints or controls of the systems in which the reformers moved. If this is true of primary school mathematics within a period of two decades, a number of interesting questions arise. Firstly, was the capacity to work independently of national traditions a passing phenomena? Was it a movement that, because of the right juxtaposition of people and circumstances, blossomed briefly only to disappear when the conditions changed and the people moved on? Or, secondly, does the cosmopolitan experience of curriculum reform recorded here reflect the beginning of a new period when the old national frontiers became obsolete?

A third question raises as problematic the assumptions upon which the first two are based. Is there anything distinctively different structurally, about the developments of the last two decades? Has it in fact always been the case that change must be considered more in terms of the age old forming, breaking down and recreating of alliances between different groups with an interest in any particular area of the school curriculum?

Only partial answers to these questions can be given on the basis of this specific study of the primary school mathematics curriculum. The same sorts of unity of purpose that created reform groups around the issue of 'New Maths' could well be replicated in other areas of the curriculum in this or in other periods of time. A broader base of information about other subjects, and other periods, would be necessary before judging these reforms as a passing phenomena. The declining importance of national boundaries is supported in this and other related studies.

When circumstances conspire traditional institutional controls may regain influence, but it does not follow that this will always be the case. There is much to suggest, as the third question implies, that the parts of education systems that direct and impinge upon curriculum affairs have never been as tightly integrated or responsive to each other as formal analysis might suggest.

References

Archer, M.S. (1979)
Social Origins of Educational Systems
Sage Publications, London and California.

Ball, S.J. (1982)
Competition and Conflict in the Teaching of English: A Socio-historical Analysis,
Journal of Curriculum Studies 14 : 1 pp.1-28

Beattie, N. (1977)
Public Participation in Curriculum Change: A West German Example. Compare 7 : 1 pp.17-29

Beattie, N. (1978)
Parent Participation in French Education.
British Journal of Education Studies XXVI : 1 pp.40-53

Becher, T. and Maclure, S. (1978)
The Politics of Curriculum Change
Hutchinson, London

Ben David, J. and Collins, R. (1966)
Social Factors in the Origin of a New Science, the Case of Psychology.
America Sociological Review 31 : 4 pp.451-465

Benoit, A. (1975)
A note on decision making process in the politics of education.
Comparative Education Review 19 : 1 pp.155-168

Broadfoot, P. (1980)
Rhetoric and Reality in the Context of Innovation: An English Case Study.
Compare 10 : 2 pp.117-126

Broadfoot, P. et all (Eds.) (1981)
Politics and Educational Change
Croom Helm, London

Bucher, R. and Strauss, A. (1961)
Professions in Process.
America Journal of Sociology 66 pp.325-334

Castle, F.G. and McKinlay, R.D. (1979)
Public Welfare Provision, Scandinavia, and the Sheer Futility of the Sociological Approach to Policies. British Journal of Political Science 9 pp.157-171

Christiansen, B. (1975)
National Objectives and Possibilities for Collaboration. International Journal of Mathematics Education, Science and Technology 6 : 1 pp.59-76

Christiansen, B. (1975a)
National Objectives and Possibilities for Collaboration. International Journal of Mathematics Education, Science and Technology 6 : 1 pp.59-76
Christiansen, B. (1975b)
European Mathematics Education (i) The Past and Present (ii) The Future
Unpublished papers presented to the sixth Biennial Conference of the Australia Association of Mathematics Teachers.
Perth, Western Australia, January 1976.
Colmez, F. (1979)
Mathematics Education at Pre-elementary and Primary Levels in UNESCO (1979)
Cook, T.G. (Ed.) (1974)
The History of Education in Europe
Methuen.
Cooper, B. (1985)
Renegotiating Secondary School Mathematics
Falmer, London
Cox, C.B. and Dyson, A.E. (1970)
Black Paper Two
Critical Quarterly Society.
Educational Studies in Mathematics (1969) Vol. 2.
Report of the First International Congress on Mathematics Education. August 24-31, 1969
Educational Studies in Mathematics (1976)
Five Years' IOWO. Special Edition 73.
Freudenthal, H. (1978)
Changes in Mathematics Education since the late 1950s - Ideas and Realization. The Netherlands. Educational Studies in Mathematics 9 pp.261-270
Freudenthal, H. (1979)
New Maths or New Education.
Prospects 9 : 3 pp.321-331
Golby, M. (1980)
Curriculum Research and Development in Action: A Review. Journal of Curriculum Studies 12 : 4 pp.371-373
Goodson, I.F. (1981)
Becoming an Academic Subject: Patterns of Explanation and Evolution. British Journal of Sociology of Education 2 : 2 pp.163-180
Goodson, I.F. (1983)
School Subjects and Curriculum Change
Croom Helm, London

Gottman, J. (Ed.) (1980)
Centre and Periphery : Spatial Variations in Politics. Sage

Howson, A.G. (1978)
Changes in Mathematics Education since the late 1950s. Ideas and Realization. Great Britain. Educational Studies in Mathematics 9 pp.183-223

Jones, G.S. (1976)
From Historical Sociology to Theoretical History. British Journal of Sociology 27 : 3 pp.295-305

Kogan, M. (1982)
Changes in Perspective. Times Educational Supplement. January 15th, p.6.

King, E.J. (1979)
Social origins of Eduicational Systems - A Review. Comparative Education 15:3 pp.350-352

Kirp, D.L. (1982)
Professionalization as a Policy Choice: British Special Education in Comparative Perspective. World Politics 34 : 2 pp.137-174

Lattimore, O. (1980)
The Periphery as Locus of Innovation in Gottman, J. (1980)

Layton, D. (1972)
Science as general education. Trends in Education 29 pp.11-15.

Marsden, W.E. (Ed.) (1979)
Post-war Curriculum Development: An Historical Appraisal. Mimeo History of Education Society. Proceedings of the 1978 annual Conference on the History of Education Society of Great Britain.

Moon, B. (1986)
The New Maths Curriculum Controversy Falmer, London

O.E.E.C. (1961a)
New Thinking in School Mathematics. Paris.

O.E.C.D./C.E.R.I. (1973)
Case Studies of Educational Innovation. Paris.

O.E.C.D./C.E.R.I. (1975)
Handbook of Curriculum Development. Paris.

Papadopolous, G.S. (1980)
Educational Reform Trends in the Western World: The Current Debate. Prospects 10 : 2 pp.159-168

Rowlinson, W. (1974)
German Education in a European Context in Cook (1974). See above.

Ruddock, J. et al (1976)
The Dissemination of Curriculum Development.
Council of Europe
N.F.E.R. Publishing Company.

Ruddock, J. (1977)
Dissemination as the Encounter of Cultures.
Research Intelligence 3 pp.3-5

Shafer, B.C. (1955)
Nationalism : Myth and Reality
Gollancz, London

Steiner, H.G. (1980)
Comparative Studies of Mathematics Curricula - Change and Stability 1960-1980
Proceedings of a Conference held in Osnabruck, F.R.G. January 7-11, 1980. Institut fur Didaktik der Mathematik der Universitat Bielefeld. Materidien und Studien Band 19.

Stenhouse, L. (1980)
Curriculum Research & Development in Action
Heinemann, London

Tanner, L.N. (1982)
Curriculum History as Usable Knowledge
Curriculum Inquiry 12 : 4 pp.405-411

Waring, M. (1979)
Social Pressures and Curriculum Innovation.
Methuen, London

Warwick, D. and Williams, J. (1980)
History and the Sociology of Education.
British Journal of the Sociology of Education : 3 pp.333-346

Westbury, I. (1980)
Conclusion to conference proceedings 'Reflections on Case Studies' in Steiner (1980)

Wise, A.E. (1979)
Legislated Learning: The Bureaucratization of the American Classroom
University of California Press, Berkeley.

Young, M.F.D. (Ed.) (1971)
Knowledge and Control. New Directions for the Sociology of Education.
Collier-Macmillan, London

10. JOHN DEWEY IN SWEDEN NOTES ON PROGRESSIVISM IN SWEDISH EDUCATION 1900-1945

Ulf P. Lundgren

Historical Backgrounds to Educational Change

As in most northern European nations, the law on compulsory education in Sweden was passed in the middle of the 19th century (1842). The determinants behind this law are to be found in both changes of modes of production - in Sweden mainly in rationalizations of agriculture - and in social-political movements. But this law on compulsory education has also to be seen as a codification of existing forms of education. Even if statistics on this point are rather hard to interpret, due to problems with the validity of sources, we can find that in 1839, three years before the law on compulsory education was passed, there were already little more than 1,000 schools and around 400 ambulatory school teachers in Sweden. Most of these public schools were situated in urban areas established by the community or by private donors. Thus the school law of 1842 is to be understood as a rural reform.

The law was also a continuation of earlier laws and regulations concerning the right of the church to inspect and control reading abilities. In turn these laws were consequences of the Lutheran Confession. Between 1527 and 1593 the church in Sweden was reformed into Lutherianism. In 1527 the properties of the church were, in the first step, taken over by the State. In 1593 the Confession of Augsburg (Confession Augustana) was adapted. The reformation had consequences for the demands on religious knowledge. The parents, the adults had the responsibility for the child being fostered to be a good Christian according to the Lutheran Confession. During the 16th century it was regulated that the ministers had to reach those of a certain age who still lacked the requisite religious knowledge. The teaching was aimed at mastering the "Our Father", the Ten Commandments, etc. When the child had been baptized the parents had to answer for their religious upbringing. In the Church Law of 1696 the minister was given the duty of examining the reading ability through catechism examinations. In 1726 another regulation confirmed these examinations and emphasized the duties of the parents to provide a religious upbringing for their children. And the duties for the householder in relation to his servants, in this respect, was the same. This regulation can be seen against the background of reading campaigns implemented during the first decades of the 18th century.(1)

What I want to point out is, that the law of compulsory schooling introduced a new institution, but at the same time built on tradition. I also want to point to the fact that this institution for schooling was not primarily designed to teach reading ability or arithmetic; above all the birth of schooling must be understood in relation to social changes. The compulsory law was directed towards the securing of moral order. The curriculum to be used was built on a moral curriculum code.(2)

Besides this popular education governed by the church, schools had existed in Sweden since the 13th century, (perhaps best termed as being equivalent to English grammar schools), directed towards the education of the servants of the church,(3), later also serving the needs for education of the servants of the State, and still later amalgamating needs for education from parts of the growing bourgeoisie.

Five years after the law on compulsory schooling (1847) around 4,000 of an estimated 366,000 children attended these grammar schools. The law on compulsory schooling, therefore, meant the establishment of two school systems with two different traditions; one school system (the grammar schools) preparing for higher education, developed from a specific classical text tradition, and the second school system (the public schools) stemming from the education by the church.

The development of the compulsory school was slow. It had to face severe economic problems and mistrust. For many farmers and peasants, the compulsory school meant not only extra taxation, but also a heavy burden as the children were not able to work in farming during school time. The criticism of the compulsory school was therefore heavy from time to time. The same legitimation crisis can be seen in most of the northern European countries.

With these brief notes on the history of Swedish education, I have sketched out some elements in the educational tradition that are necessary to have as a background in order to understand the changes in the conception of schooling at the beginning of this century.

Industrialization came rather late to Sweden. In 1800, 68% worked in farming and 17% in industry. By the end of the century, 55% were in farming and 28% in industry. Half a century later (1950) the percentage in farming had more than halved to 25% and the number in industry had increased to 43%. The corresponding figures for 1970 were 8% farming and 40% industry.

With the increase in industrialization and urbanization, and by the processes of democratization, the curriculum for the public school changed. The church lost much of its control over the school system. A National Board of Education was established in 1914, indicating the increase of profane control over public education. The changes in the relations between state and society that democratic political processes caused, influenced the power and control over goals and content over education. The curriulum changed in a pragmatic direction and schooling was extended. In 1919 a National Board for Vocational Education was established and the same year a new curriculum for the public education system was implemented. This curriculum emphasized the necessity to educate work habits and making the school relate to working life and the life of the citizen.

Even though we cannot use the dramatic words of Dewey and talk about a copernican revolution, we can, in the early decades of the century, see a change in conceptions about what education is and what it should strive for. A progressivist notion of education emerges in public debate and curricula. What then are the influences?

Introducing John Dewey

In 1891, a special type of open museum was built in Stockhold - Skansen. The idea was to preserve various types of building that represented the disappearing agricultural society. The museum was a concretization of national-romantic currents in the late 19th century. In 1907 the Association for Public Teachers had their convention at Skansen. The chairman, Fridtjuv Berg, gave a lecture. Berg had the year before, as Minister of Education and Church, implemented a spelling reform. Later as Minister once again, he reformed the governing of schools by establishing the National Board of Education. One of the participants of the convention writes:

> At the end of the summer course in Stockholm in 1907 we were all participants gathered at Skansen. On a hill stood Fridtjuv Berg and spoke to us. The demands on teachers in daily work increase, among other things, the new ideas of upbringing and pedagogy. One of these ideas he formulated in the following way: to learn by doing. And he mentioned the name of John Dewey. This was the first time I heard this condensed program, and it had a strong impression on me, carried out as it was by one of the enthusiastic leaders for the public school teachers of Sweden. It contained the seed for the working school and the activity pedagogy of today.(4)

The scene is symbolic and very Swedish. On a hill the leader of the new reform movement is standing, talking to representatives of the new profession. This happens at Skansen, an open museum created to remind us about a world that is disappearing. And he talks about a new role for schools. Schools of the future and not of the past. In the middle of the Swedish summer, Dewey is presented to the Swedish teachers.

But this was not the first time Dewey was introduced in Sweden. Five years before, in 1902, we find an article by Dewey in the progressive journal <u>The School</u>. This journal started that year and in its second annual issue we find a translation of the first two chapters in <u>School and</u>

Society. The purpose of this journal was to create a forum for a discussion on the planned curriculum for the grammar school. It fulfilled that purpose and was closed in 1903. The editor of the journal - Artur Bendixson - organized a school in Gothenburg between 1901 and 1904, a school that came to be central for the educational progressive movement in Sweden. In 1909, a lecture about Dewey was held at this school, a lecture that later was published.(5) The first more comprehensive work by Dewey that was published in Swedish was The Child and the Curriculum. It was published together with some articles about the experimental schools in Chicago.(6) The introduction to this book was made by Malte Jakobsson, who later became professor of Philosophy and Pedagogy at the University of Gothenburg. Gothenburg became during the first decades of the century the centre for progressive education, the college for teacher education there was of considerable importance. Returning to Skansen in 1907, we can see that this introduction of the work by Dewey was an element in an ongoing movement. That Dewey's pedagogy was read and discussed can be seen from other parts of the public debate, e.g. in the second edition of Ellen Keys' classic work The Century of Childhood. (7)

Dewey's work was also influential in the European continent at this time. The curriculum for the public school of 1919 shows how influential the work in Germany with the working school had been. The work of Kerschensteiner is especially important. Among the papers that Kerschensteiner left after his death, there is a systematic overview of the educational thinking of Dewey. In 1910, Kerschensteiner visited the USA. The same year he lectured in Stockholm. Even though Dewey was known already in Sweden, it seems that it is indirectly that his work influenced curricula and schooling. We can, therefore, see two streams of influence from American progressivism and especially from the work of Dewey; one stream that comes directly by translations of parts of his work and the awareness of his work that can be seen among influential groups, and one stream that comes more indirectly from the progressivism in Germany and that mainly comes to concentrate around the concepts of Working Schools and Activity Pedagogy. The educationalists' relation to Dewey could be likened to the modern citizen's relationship to the Bible. The opinion was that many ideas were good and ought to be brought to practice, but rather few had read the original.(8)

But during the First World War - in 1917 - the book Schools of Tomorrow, written together with his daughter Evelyn, was translated and published in two volumes.(9) That Schools of Tommorow was translated and introduced is perhaps especially interesting to reflect on. As Elenor Feinberg and Walther Feinberg have pointed out, the study presented in Schools of Tommorrow is built on experiences from the schools of Gary, Indiana, and is concentrated on the problem of how to generate a work moral that, because of a more and more elaborated division of labour, had become invisible.(10) Albeit simplified this was a central problem in creating the working school. The changes from a rural, agriculture based economy to an urban industrialized society, where wage work was to be the dominating form of work, accentuated the problem of how to create a new work moral - a new moral justification.

> "What is new", to quote Feinberg and Feinberg, "is the fact that for many the context of this justification is an abstract one, one that is not easily reinforced by the direct effect that their work has on the lives of other people .... The "community" which we serve is an abstract one, and therefore the moral justification which allows us to continue in our work is indeed best represented by a picture, by a copy of a reality that is in fact too large for us to experience".(11)

And just this moral problem was central in the transformation of the Swedish school. It is the same changes that Durkheim in his classic work on the division of labour points to, and which he means create a new type of solidarity.(12)

It is around this problem that the progressive influence in Sweden - at least initially - has to be understood. Cremin, in his book on American progressivism, claims that:

> "progressive education began as part of a vast humanitarian effort to apply the promise of American life - the ideal of government by, of, and for the people - to the puzzling new urban-industrial civili-

> zation that came into being during the latter half of the nineteenth century". (13)

The same is to some extent true in Sweden. Progressivism was a part of modernization. The urban-industrial society was formed. But compared to the USA, Sweden was much later in that transformation. However, several elements are similar. The schools followed a "degenerated" herbartian tradition. The instruction from a teachers' guide gives a sense of that:

> "Here in school one has, as thou see, many different things - Listen to what I say about the book, which I have in my hand: the book is a thing. Who of thou can say after this? Say it all together at the same time! What do I have in my hand? ...."(14)

The teacher instruction reminds us of Rice's descriptions in The Forum about American public education in the last decade of the 19th century. Even though the rate of urbanization and industrialization was not the same in Sweden as in the USA, there are similar basic problems of schooling to be faced. Progressivism was a part of modernization. (15)

Changes in Schooling and Progressivism

The difference is perhaps more important to look at. As I noted in the beginning, the changes of schooling in Sweden must be interpreted and understood in relation to existing educational traditions. The modernization of the schools triggered off a basic organizational problem, namely the relation between public schools (folkskolan) and the grammar schools (lardomsskolan/realskolan). Already in the later decades of the 19th century, voices were heard advocating a link between the two school systems. Firdtjuv Berg, who was mentioned earlier as introducing Dewey to teachers in 1907 in Stockholm, published articles already in 1897 about what was called the "basic school". The argument was, that the public schools had to be the base for further schooling. The arguments against such a construction were that it would mean a lowering of the standard for the grammar school. The advocates for the grammar school wanted either no link at all between the school system or a late differentiation. The heat of the debate on education can only be understood in relation to these two traditions and the social base for recruiting students.

At the same time, the changes of society and the expanding relationships between education and labour market forced a solution on how to reorganize the two school system. During the period from 1909 to 1927, small changes were made making individual paths from the public school to the grammar school possible. In 1927, however, a formal reorganization was made of the two school systems making the first four or six years in the public school the base for entrance to a four-year or five-year grammar school. This organization meant, thus, that the two school traditions and the two types of curricula were adjusted to each other. On top of the grammar school was an upper secondary school (gymnasium) with three or four years giving entrance to university education.

This organizational question came to dominate and overshadow the pedagogical debate. The progressive education movement was then isolated by the skirmishes between school traditions, traditions developed since the 13th century. But still progressivism was alive, and German and Austrian influences now grew in importance.

Ester Hermansson, as a member of a Swedish teacher delegation in 1931, had visited Vienna to study the Austrian school reforms. She met there Otto Glockel, one of the leaders of the Austrian reforms. In Vienna there were also teachers who had worked with the Jena plan, which was later of importance in the Swedish debate. In the German and Austrian experiments, child psychology was one scientific base for the educational work. The interest in psychology as a base for education has, of course, its roots in the herbartian tradition, but now came a new modern psychology that seemed to offer the scientific base for education, not only as science but as practice as well. The American curriculum work and American progressivism were linked to universities. In Austria, the educational development seemed more free from academic structures. The interplay between theory and practice was here more close to conditions in Sweden. Among the educationalists that Hermansson met were Elsa Kohler.

One year later, in 1932, Kohler came to

Sweden. She lectured and supervised in Activity Pedagogy. Kohler used Dewey's work. In 1936, she published the book Aktivitetspedagogik (Activity Pedagogy).(16) In the preface she explains the rationale of the book. She stresses the differences between the Nordic countries (she mentions Sweden and Norway) and the continent (especially referring to Austria and Germany). Her point is, that in Sweden educational ideas have not been so bound to political ideas. She means that pedagogy in practice must have a solid ground in psychology and biology and thereby use scientific developments. At the same time, science built on experiments and formed in laboratories cannot be used directly. The teachers have to learn to think scientifically and to observe.

> "The psychology has hitherto given pedagogy some results, that have been gained in laboratories or by freer research. These cannot, however, be directly used within education. On the other hand to make psychological discoveries in the living 'educational situation' is something different. This can offer first hand results of quite another type than what is given by older research. Here we can observe the behaviour of the child, its experiences and results in the organized context, that the school offer".(17)

She mentions Dewey as the founder of activity pedagogy in a progressive movement and gives concrete instruction for how to observe the child and build a pedagogy around the activity of the child. Psychology is the source for teacher thinking. It is from science that a more modern educational practice is to be developed. The teachers that worked together with Kohler came later to have an influence on curricula, but during the thirties it seems that her work was rather isolated as far as the daily life of schools was concerned. She returned to Austria and the contact with Sweden was lost. She disappeared during the Nazi terror. In 1947, the book Vart Arbesssatt (Our Way of Working) was published, based on the work of Kohler. This latter book came to be used extensively in teacher training.(18)

The Approach of War and Post-war Changes

What we can see is a progressive movement starting in the beginning of the century. The work of Dewey was introduced and we can see in the selection of work published how this selection was conducted in relation to the Swedish context. Even though Dewey was introduced, most of the progressive influence came from the continent. Visits to experimental schools in Austria and Germany brought the Activity Pedagogy over. We can also see how in Gothenburg experimental schools were established and how teachers were trained among others by Kohler. With time we can see a change in orientation to sources. The German orientation then goes and the interest in the American school is growing especially then for curriculum work in the USA. This change in interest mirrors the social-political situation. The growth of Fascism in Spain, Germany and Italy focused the goal for the public education and its relation to training a citizen in a democratic society. The reports from study visits in the USA show the interest in the democratic school. The Activity Pedagogy was directed towards the methods of instruction and the work of the teachers. With time, the goals of the compulsory school in a modern democratic society became focal. And behind that we can also see other political changes than the immediate ones visible in the Swedish context.

The amalgamation in the first step of the two school traditions took out of the public agenda the question of how to change the school system. The actual link between the two school system was that grammar schools still had the power over the content of the public schools, at least for the first four to six years.

In 1919, the first Social Democratic government was formed. Besides periods of coalition governments, the Social Democratic party has been in the majority up to the mid-seventies. The second prime minister, Hansson, coined the concept "welfare home". The building of the welfare society gives a background to understanding the renewal of progressivism in education. The changes that I earlier pointed at concerning the relations between education and labour market, were still more visible during the decades before the Second World War. New schools were established to meet new demands. During the forties there were, besides the seven-year compulsory school, seven other school forms, as for example, the four-year and five-year grammar school, the municipal grammar school and municipal girls' school. The upper secondary level presented a similarly divided scene. At the base were the parallel school systems after grade four to six, which made the choices regarding continued education a necessity at eleven or thirteen years of age. In its turn, this early choice of career meant, to quote the late prime minister and the first chairman of the 1946 School Commission, that:

> ".... the serious matter was that this organization division concealed a pervading characteristic. The school system functioned entirely as a class society in miniature. The various school forms recruited their students from different strata".(19)

This complicated school organization called for an administrative reform as well as for a political reform. Division in various school forms led to a series of difficult administrative and pedagogical problems. Besides that, changes in the world of work and on the labour market made necessary new strategies for curriculum change.

I will here identify four main motives for a reform of the entire school system:

1) The increase in the number of children and the demand for education. From the mid-1920s until the end of the 1940s, the number of students attending the grammar schools rose from 10% to 38% of an age cohort. Since this increase mainly concerned urban areas, a question of resource allocation also entered the picture.
2) Urbanization constitutes a further motive for reform. From the beginning of the 19th century until the beginning of the 20th century, the urban population doubled (10% to 20%). By 1943, another doubling had taken place.
3) The increased role that education seemed to play for the economy led to increased consciousness among administrators and politicians about methods and strategies for educational planning; the need for the planning of education in relation to labour market

demands; this meant both quantitative planning and qualitative planning.

4) A final motive was the political one of creating a school system accessible to everyone irrespective of social background, gender or geographical location. At the back of this political interest was not only the concern to form an egalitarian society, but also to strengthen democracy. The experiences of the political developments during the twenties and the thirties in Europe strongly fixed this question on the agenda. It is in this new discussion about the aims of schooling that a new progressivism is visible and that Dewey's work is discussed again.

Under the chairmanship of the Minister of Education, an Expert Committee was set up to investigate the grounds for a reform of the entire school system, including the upper secondary level. The work of the Committee was completed in 1947 and presented in 20 printed volumes containing almost 10,000 pages. But the Committee could not agree on the basic answer to the question of how a new, more comprehensive school was to be organized. The sides in the conflict over the comprehensive school reflected the two school traditions. The representatives from the grammar schools argued for an early differentiation and the representatives from the public school system argued for a late differentiation. Before the Committee ended its work a new parliamentary commission was established: the 1946 School Commission.

It is thus around the new school system and its objectives that the interest in progressive education is renewed. In 1942 Folke Leander, an assistant professor in philosophy in Gothenburg, published the first Swedish book about Dewey.(20) It is mainly an analysis of the ethical base of Dewey's philosophy. Leander points to two risks in the development of progressive education after Dewey. One is the "Rousseau trap", the other is "the Bacon trap". To trust a naturalistic pattern for pedagogy gives an arbitrary moral education. And to direct the studies too much towards natural sciences frames the reception of more humanistic educational patterns. So much of the progressive education had been misunderstood not because, according to Leander, of Dewey, but because we live in a secularized world lacking a firm moral base.

In the literature around the Activity Pedagogy that was published, the social context is more or less non-existent. The concentration is to didactic problems and methods of instruction. At the same time the society changed dramatically, but this was not mirrored in the progressive education. One of the legendary educators within the labour movement, Oscar Olsson, published a debate book called, literally translated, The Schools of Democracy.(21) In this book, he praises the progress of Activity Pedagogy, but wanted the school to play a more active part in creating a democratic society. He had, in the debate in the parliament of 1927, argued for a comprehensive school without success but since that date had worked patiently for it. The influence from Dewey in his educational thinking is clear. Besides Olsson, Alva Myrdal came in the forties to be one of the leading politicians who argued for a comprehensive school. Both Olsson and Myrdal had experiences from the USA. For both of them, the work of Dewey was a natural base for developing a modern comprehensive school. Together with her husband, Gunnar Myrdal, Alva Myrdal published the book Contact with America (1941).(22) In this book there is one section about education "in the centre of society". As principal of a college for pre-school teachers, she had in practice developed a progressive education. Within the 1946 School Commission, Alva Myrdal carried out influential work. To the Commission several experts were linked and many of those came with experiences from working with Activity Pedagogy. Ester Hermansson, who has been mentioned before, was one of them. By this Commission, then, the early progressive work in schools came into the planning of the comprehesive school. Progressivism and the work of Dewey was taken in the state apparatus and became a part of the new educational ideology.

What we can see then, is how experiences from the formative years were never really used in schools, except in some exceptional cases; how the traditional problem of the joining of the two school traditions dominated the pedagogical debate and pedagogical thinking. And we can see how the actual experiences that came out of the early progressive movement later was used within the work of the 1946 School Commission.

The result of the work of the Commission was a new school system with broader goals, a renewal of methods, a nine-year school system. But still the differentiation problem could not be solved. A period of experiments with various models started, ending in the 1962 decision on a nine-year comprehensive school.

I will not go into a discussion of how progressivism developed within this rather centralized school system. The discourse about schools became progressive, the administration of schools became progressive, built on the idea of a school that develops by experiments and evaluations. At the same time, it is debatable whether the inner life of the schools ever became a practice built on a living progressivism, where school traditions and conditions for teachers pushed in other directions. To examine this matter is, as the Danish writer H.C. Andersen would have said, "another story".

References

1. Johansson, E.: The History of Literacy in Sweden in Comparison with some other Countries Umea, Educational Reports, University of Umea. (1977)
2. The concept of curriculum code, see Lundgren, U.P. Between Hope and Happening. Text and Context in Curriculum. Geelong, Deakin University Press, 1983. See Lundgren, U.P. "Curriculum from a Global Perspective", in ASCD Yearbook 1985
3. See Odman, P-J.: Kontrasternas spel: Processer och forhallningssatt i svensk medeltidspedagogik. Stockholm, Institute of Education, University of Stockholm. 1983 (mimeo).
4. Sjoholm, L.G.: "Att bli undervisad. Minnen och funderingar". In Till Nils Hanningen, 27.5.1952. Stockholm, Svenska bokforlaget/ Bonniers sid. 121. Cf. Hartman, S. and Lundgren, U.P., Individ, skola och samhalle. Pedagogiska texter av John Dewey. Stockholm, Natur and Kultur, 1980 (our translation).
5. Lehman, E.: Uppfostran till arbete. Stockholm, Hugo Gebers Forlag, 1909.
6. Jakobsson, M.: Pragmatiska uppfostringsprinciper. Lund, Gleerups, 1912.
7. Lengborn, T.: En Studie i Ellen Keys Pedagogiska tankande framst med utgangspunkt fran "Barnets arhundrande". Stockholm, arsbocker i svensk undervisninghistoria, No. 140, 1977.
8. Cf. Hartman, S. and Lundgren, U.P.: Op cit. sid. 23.
9. Dewey, J. and Dewey, E.: Framtidsskolor. Lund, Pedagogiska skrifter utgivna av Sveriges allmanna folkskollararforenings litteratursallskap attioandra och attiotredje haftet, 1917-1918.
10. Feinberg, W. and Feinberg, E.: The Visible and Lost Community of Work and Education. Stockholm, reports on Education and Psychology, No. 1, Stockholm Institute of Education, 1979.
11. Op cit p.4.

12. Durkheim, E.: De la division du travail social In English translation - Durkheim, E. Selected Writings, (Ed. Giddens, A.), London, The Cambridge University Press, 1972.
13. Cremin, L.A.: The Transformation of the School. Progressivism in American Education 1876-1957. New York, Vintage Books, 1964, p.viii.
14. From Sjoholm, G.: Att bli undervisad. Minnen och funderingar. Pedagogiska skrifter, No. 231. Stockholm, Svensk larartidnings forlag, 1971, p.205 (our translation)
15. Examples are: Hermansson, E.: I amerikanska skolor (In American Schools), Stockholm, Pedagogiska skrifter 167-169. Svensk lararetidnings forlag, 1940.
Norinder, Y.: Den amerikanska fortsattnings-skolan. (The American Continuation School). Lund: Pedagogiska skrifter 127, 1929.
16. Kohler, E.: Aktivitetspedagogik. Stockholm, Bokforlaget Natur och Kultur, 1936.
17. Op cit. p.9.
18. Falk, K. et al: Vart arbetssatt. Aktivitets-pedagogik i praktisk utformning. Stockholm, Kooperativa Forbundets Bokforlag, 1947.
19. Elander, T.: 1940-1949. Stockholm, Tidens forlag, 1973 (our translation).
20. Leander, F.: John Dewey's Pedagogik och Dess etiska forutsattningar. Stockholm, Svensk lararetidnings forlag. Pedagogiska skrifter 175. 1942.
21. Olsson, O.: Demokratins skolar. Stockholm, Fritzes forlag, 1943.
22. Myrdal, A. and Myrdal, G.: Kontakt med Amerika. Stockholm, Bonniers, 1941.

11. EDUCATION FOR AN URBAN AMERICA: RALPH TYLER AND THE CURRICULUM FIELD

Barry M. Franklin

If, as some have maintained, one's prominence as a scholar often depends as much on one's longevity as on anything else (Goode, Furstenberg, and Mitchell, 1970, p.1), no individual has more of a claim to eminence within the curriculum field than does Ralph Winfred Tyler. Throughout the last quarter century, no one has played a greater role in defining the issues about which curriculum workers write and debate than has Tyler. He is often seen, it seems, as the great 'synthesizer' of the ideas of such diverse curriculum theorists as John Dewey, Franklin Bobbitt, W.W. Charters, Edward Thorndike, and the McMurry brothers (Eisner, 1985, pp.11-12; McNeil, 1981, pp.339-340; Schubert, 1980, pp.105-110; Tanner and Tanner, 1980, pp.83-88). In this vein, one contemporary educator has argued that the so-called rationale for resolving curriculum problems that Tyler spelled out in his 1950 syllabus for Education 305 at the University of Chicago, _Basic Principles of Curriculum and Instruction_, represents a 'paradigm' for the guidance of the modern curriculum worker (Tanner, 1982, p.409). If there exists a conventional wisdom among those who do curriculum work, it is, as Tyler states in his rationale (1950, pp.1-2), that in addressing curriculum problems educators should first identify their objectives, then select and organize learning experiences in light of those objectives, and finally determine whether the objectives have been realized (Beyer, 1983, p.9; Eisner, 1985, p.11; Goodlad, 1969, p.334; McClure, 1971, p.30; Saylor and Alexander, 1974, p.59).

Tyler's prominence in the curriculum field rests, it seems, primarily on his 1950 curriculum syllabus. It is this single work to the virtual exclusion of everything else he wrote that contemporary educators have relied on in assessing his contribution to the curriculum field. While certainly an innovative and important work, the volume leaves unanswered certain important questions about Tyler's thinking. First, nowhere in the syllabus does Tyler tell us how he came to the view that curriculum problems should be addressed in terms of the four questions that constitute his so-called rationale. And second, nowhere in the syllabus, despite the importance which his rationale accords to societal concerns and philosophy in resolving curriculum dilemmas, does Tyler reveal his own social philosophy.

Earlier in his career while Chairperson of the Department of Education at the University of Chicago, Tyler did, it turns out, speak to these unanswered questions. As head of one of the nation's leading institutions of graduate study and research in education, Tyler was often called on to address professional meetings of one sort or another. He was, for example, a frequent speaker at the annual conference of the Administrative Officers of Public and Private Schools. In a number of the speeches he delivered during the late 1930s and early 1940s, Tyler talked about not only the origins of his approach to resolving curriculum problems but also about his social philosophy and the role it dictated for the American public school. Although collected and housed with his other professional papers at the University of Chicago, their existence is not widely known. They have not to my knowledge been used by those who in recent years have written about Tyler and his work. The existence and availability of these speeches requires, I think, that we look again at the life and thought of this singular individual in the history of the American curriculum field.

Tyler's Career

If we are to understand Tyler, we must at the start consider his roots in the small, rural towns of Nebraska. Although born in Chicago in 1902, while his father, William Tyler, was studying for the Congregational ministry, he spent his youth and college years in Nebraska. Upon completing his seminary studies, Rev. Tyler moved his family to Nebraska, settling first in the small town of Tablerock in the southeastern part of the state and subsequently in Peru, Hastings, and Crete. It was in Crete, where the family moved in 1914, that Tyler entered Doane College, a small Congregationalist school, which he completed in 1921. He spent the next year as a high school science teacher in Pierre, South Dakota and then returned to Nebraska to the state university in Lincoln to work on a master's degree, to teach science in the university's high school, and to supervise student teachers. In 1923 he left Lincoln for the University of Chicago to study for his doctorate in education under Charles Hubbard Judd. Upon completion of his degree in 1927, Tyler taught at the University of North Carolina for two years and then, at W.W. Charter's invitation, joined the Bureau of Educational Research at the Ohio State University. In 1938, Tyler returned to the University of Chicago as Chairperson of the Department of Education. He resigned from the University in 1953 to become director of the Center for Advanced Studies in the Behavioral Sciences in Stanford, California, where he remained until his retirement in 1966 (private interview, April 1, 1985; Fohles, 1978, pp.1316-1316).

Tyler's youth and subsequent career follow a pattern similar not only to such other founding theorists of the curriculum field as Franklin Bobbitt and W.W. Charters but also to many of those intellectuals, such as John Dewey, Charles Horton Cooley, and Edward L. Thorndike, who shaped American thought during the first half of this century. Products of the nation's rural, small towns, Anglo-American in heritage, and Protestant in religion, these intellectuals saw the small town they knew from their youth with its like-mindedness and face-to-face relationships as the virtual embodiment of democracy. To their way of thinking, the rise of the city and the appearance of the corporation not only signalled the passing of the small town but also perhaps the demise of democracy itself. How, they asked, could a democratic polity, which they believed was built on harmonious and intimate social interaction, survive in a society that seemed prone to conflict and whose relationships were becoming less close and less long lasting? Despite their fears about this transformation, it was the city, whose growth depended on industrial expansion, where these thinkers came to establish their careers and to make their marks on American society.

At the outset of their careers, these intellectuals faced the dilemma of trying to reconcile their rural past with an urban future. Their solution was to try to create within an urban, industrial society the kind of co-operation which they believed to have existed in the rural town. Each in their own way, Dewey, Cooley, Thorndike, and other intellectuals of the day sought to use their knowledge to advance proposals for making American institutions more co-operative. This desire for co-operation was, I believe, a central preoccupation of those educators who established curriculum as a field of work and study. It was their desire to make the schools more co-operative that led Bobbitt and Charters to turn to the principal industrial reform of the day, the scientific management movement, for their model of curriculum making. They were, as it turns out, so impressed with the seeming ability of scientific management principles to harmonize the interaction between management and labor, that they saw the corporation with its hierarchical work relationships as a model for twentieth century American society (Franklin, 1985, chpts. 1-4).

The quarter century in age that separates Tyler from Bobbitt and Charters should not be ignored. The founders of scientific curriculum making were writing, we should remember, in an America that had given up its idealism in the wake of World War I for the indulgence offered by the mythical 'normalcy' of the 1920s. Tyler, however, was writing in a different America, a nation that had almost been levelled by the Great Depression and was in the midst of a second and larger world war. Yet despite this difference, it would be for Tyler, just as it had been for Bobbitt and Charters, the city and the factory that would set the agenda for the school and its curriculum.

Urbanization and the School Curriculum

'The urban community', Tyler noted in a speech he delivered to the Conference of Administrative Officers of Public and Private Schools in July of 1942, 'is the most significant social development of modern times' (1942a, p.1). Accompanying the shift from an economy dominated by agriculture to one dominated by industry, the city, Tyler went on to argue, was the personification of modern American life. Citing his colleague in the university's

Department of Sociology, Ernest Burgess, Tyler pointed out that the city was not simply a larger version of the rural, small town. It possessed a number of characteristics that made it a fundamentally different form of social organization.

Tyler saw the city as a place of chaos and confusion that exposed its inhabitants to noise, lights, crowds, and odors unknown in the rural town. The city appeared, according to Tyler, to have 'no pattern, no unity of meaning' (p.3). A second character of city life, Tyler stated, was mechanization. Wherever the urban resident turned, he encountered one mechanical device or another. Physical strength, which was indispensable to the resident of the countryside, was no longer needed by those who resided in the city.

A third feature of city life, Tyler pointed out, was the break down of the intimate, face-to-face relationships of the rural town. Tyler noted in this vein that in the modern workplace, 'the social distance between employer and employee has widened. The worker feels himself a cog, and a replaceable cog, in an immense economic system' (p.3).

Another characteristic of urbanization, according to Tyler, was commercialism. Where once Americans had themselves produced the basic necessities of life and devised their own entertainment, these had in the urban community become products of the marketplace. Finally, Tyler argued, as the city developed, so too did a host of organizations, including church groups, professional associations, clubs and political parties. He believed that these organizations tended to isolate individuals from each other and to emphasize their differences. As a consequence the harmony of the small town was replaced with a sense of competition and conflict (pp.4-5).

Tyler went on in his address to point out that these changes in American society were in effect defining the tasks of the nation's schools. In rural communities, he argued, there existed an informal and unplanned educational environment that naturally prepared youth for their work, citizenship, and family roles. Because of the absence of this environment in the city, the schools would have to take on these responsibilities:

> It is essential for the city school to analyze the out-of-school environment of

> its children so as to identify its deficiencies and also to note possible resources for education. It is then necessary for the city school to make some systematic plan both to compensate for deficiencies for the out-of-school environment and to use effectively the resources of the city environment (p.9).

Tyler offered a number of suggestions of how educators could address the problems of the city. They could establish after school recreation programs to provide children with an emotional 'release' from the tensions of city living. They could develop within their classrooms a 'warmly human' climate to compensate for the impersonal relationships of the city. And they could establish art and craft programs within the schools to enable city children to develop the mechanical skills no longer required in an industrial economy (pp.5-7).

Most important for us in this essay were Tyler's recommendations for the curriculum. The existing school program, he noted, should address the immediate concerns of urban, industrial life. The content of the social studies should be expanded to include an examination of the problems of city living. The natural sciences should treat the social and personal effects of technology. Within home economics classes, students should study the nature of family life in the urban environment (p.6).

In making these suggestions, Tyler was simply stating what had by the 1940s become a conventional wisdom among curriculum workers, namely that the school curriculum should include more functional content related to the social, economic, and personal needs of youth. Such a functional curriculum would enable the schools to take on those educational responsibilities that the family and the local community could no longer fulfill. It would also enable the schools to meet the immediate needs of the increasing number of students who had no desire to attend college (Tyler, 1939a, 1939b). Addressing current trends in the secondary school in an address to the 1940 annual meeting of the National Education Association in St. Louis, Tyler noted that the high schools were now directing their attention to a wider range of goals than they had in the past:

> In place of an almost exclusive emphasis upon the development of certain subject skills and the acquisition of information in the several school subjects, the schools are seeking to emphasize as well the development of effective work habits and study skills, of effective ways of thinking, of desirable social attitudes, of a wide range of significant interests, of depth of appreciations, of social sensitivity, of personal-social adjustment, and of physical health (1940a, p.1).

Education for Co-operation

Although speaking during the 1940s, Tyler expressed the same concern about the threat urbanization posed to social unity as did Bobbitt and Charters two decades earlier. In his 1942 address to the Conference of Administrative Officers of Public and Private Schools, Tyler pointed out that the complexity of city life could lead its residents to develop narrow allegiances to those groups with which they had immediate contact at the expense of 'larger loyalties' to the total community.

The schools, he noted, often abetted, albeit unintentionally, such allegiances. They promoted the formation of student groups within schools that were nothing more than elite 'cliques'. They also instilled students, again perhaps unintentionally, with a sense of 'school pride' that manifested itself in feelings of hostility toward students from other schools in other sections of the city. In place of these practices, Tyler believed that American schools should champion 'organizations which provide for the wider participation of children and youth, participation in groups which cut across class lines, geographic boundaries and economic prejudices' (p.8).

If the schools were to curb the divisiveness that seemed so much a part of modern urban life, Tyler believed that they would have to teach students to be more co-operative. In his 1941 Walgreen Lecture at the University of Chicago, he argued that the traditional school program which saw students as solitary workers in competition with each other was out of date. An appropriate curriculum for today's schools, he went on to say, was one that would teach students the skills they needed for group planning, decision making, and action. Of particular importance in this respect, he noted, was the value of compromise. If students were to work together harmoniously, they would have to be able to arbitrate their differences so as to establish common goals and common procedures for reaching them (1941c, pp.14-15).

In advocating that the schools promote co-operation, Tyler was mindful of the danger of creating an unthinking homogeneity in American society. He believed that such total like-mindedness would lead to the kind of self-satisfaction and smugness in the citizenry that would prevent needed changes from being made. He made this point most forcefully in a 1939 speech to the Conference of Aministrative Officers of Public and Private Schools:

> In some respects it may be uncomfortable to live with people who hold various views, to listen to persons who are always conceiving novel ideas, and to be continually subjected to influences which require a reconsideration of one's own pattern of values and methods of work but the potentialities for improvement of any group lie in the degree of freshness, of originality, and of the uniqueness of its members. This is not to say that groups do not need to agree upon fundamental purposes and that some degree of uniformity and standardization of action is necessary to survive, but it does mean that within wide limits individuality should be encouraged and conflicting ideas presented for examination, for reconsideration, and for tentative trial (1939c, p.6).

Tyler's understanding of co-operation was, I think, different from that of the advocates of scientific curriculum making. Bobbitt and Charters, for example, equated co-operation with the work relationships of the scientifically managed industrial plant. The standardized work procedures of such plants, they believed, offered a means whereby labor and management could join together harmoniously to increase production and reduce costs, which in turn would increase both profits and wages. The scientific management movement, however, did not hold out the same promise for Tyler. In a July, 1941 speech to the Administrative Officers of Public and Private Schools, he noted the problems that scientific management principles had created for the practice of school administration. Educational administrators, Tyler pointed out, guided in recent years by an ideology of specialization and centralized decision making, have been preoccupied with organizing the work roles within schools into a hierarchy with formal channels of communication and authority. This effort, Tyler believed, had ignored the actual functioning of complex organizations, particularly the beliefs and desires of the participants. In the end, it had sacrificed true efficiency for order and control.

Citing the now famous studies at the Western Electric Company during the mid-1920s that had set the stage for the emergence of the human relations movement in industry, Tyler argued that efficient school administration depended more on the morale and motivation of the staff than on the rigid, hierarchial control favored by the advocates of scientific management (1941a, pp.13-14). Tyler's brand of co-operation seemed, then, to allow more room for individual initiative and diversity than did that of Bobbitt and Charters.

Tyler, perhaps in response to the Depression, seemed less willing than Bobbitt and Charters to look to business for his educational ideas. In a July, 1940 address to the Conference of Administrative Officers of Public and Private Schools, he argued that curriculum objectives should be stated 'in terms of educational aims'. 'The school', he went on to say, 'is not a business institution; it is not seeking to make a profit or to distribute material goods'. Rather, it was an institution dedicated to the education of youth (1940b, p.4).

School and Society

Tyler also parted company with the advocates of scientific curriculum making when it came to defining the social role of the school. The principal task of the school for Bobbitt and Charters was to adjust youth to existing adult work and citizenship roles. Rejecting the role of the school as a vehicle for change, Bobbitt commented in the 1926 *Yearbook of the National Society for the Study of Education* that 'the school is not an agency of social reform' (Bobbitt, 1926, p.54).

Tyler, on the other hand, saw the school as an

institution of social change. In a handwritten and untitled manuscript he prepared during the 1930s while he was at Ohio State University, he stated that the task of education was to 'improve human welfare' (n.d., p.10). Tyler, however, was by no means a radical reformer. Addressing the Conference of Administrative Officers of Public and Private Schools in July of 1944, Tyler suggested that George Counts' attempt at using the schools as an instrument of social reconstruction was misguided. There was always the danger with such efforts, he argued, that the schools could become instruments, as they had in Nazi Germany, of totalitarianism. Tyler believed that it was critical that the attempt of educators to improve human welfare not be confused with 'using the schools as instruments for the attainment of a particular blueprint of social organization and economic system' (1944a, pp.1-2).

The appropriate social role for the school, according to Tyler, was best exemplified by the community school. A popular innovation of the 1930s and 1940s, the term referred to schools that either used community resources in carrying out their instructional programs or to schools that provided educational services not only to children but to all inhabitants of the locality in which they were situated (Everett, 1938, pp.v-vii, 435-462; Hanna and Naslund, 1953, pp.51-56; Seay, 1945, p.209). Community schools held a two-fold attraction for Tyler. First, children in these schools would have the opportunity not only to acquire knowledge and skills, they would also have the chance to enhance the welfare of the population. A good example, Tyler noted, was the public schools of Holtville, Alabama. There, a core curriculum had been developed that was organized around the problems of the local community. One such problem was the declining productivity of the region's farmers. From their reading and study, the students identified a number of ways of increasing yields, such as crop rotation and diversified farming, techniques they in turn communicated to local farmers. They also learned how check dams could control soil erosion, which was also causing declining productivity, and actively participated in programs for constructing them throughout the community.

Another problem included in Holtville's community school core curriculum was that of nutrition.

After studying the diet of local residents, the students suggested a number of ways that farmers could improve the community's nutrition, including the production of more diversified crops and the establishment of an area refrigeration facility so that fresh produce and meat would be readily available throughout the year.

In addition to enabling students to improve the welfare of their locality, community schools would teach co-operation. The size and compexity of community problems could only be resolved, Tyler believed, if students learned to work together to develop and implement remedies (1944a, pp.2-3).

The community school, Tyler argued, 'may not seem as dramatic as laying out the blueprint of a new social order'. Nor, he pointed out, does it 'involve vociferous support of social dogmas, political doctrines, and economic panaceas'. It was, however, an effort that required educators to be knowledgeable, resolute, and steadfast in the support of human betterment (pp.6-7).

Education and War

In advocating a more co-operative education, Tyler seemed to take what we might think of as a middle path between the efficiency thinking of Bobbitt and Charters and the social reconstructionism of George Counts. We can see his attempt to stake out the middle ground in his views on the role of the schools in World War II.

Speaking eleven months before Pearl Harbor, Tyler raised the question of the task of the schools in the context of what he saw as an emerging international crisis. Some have argued, he pointed out, that the schools should become an instrument for toughening up the population in case of war. Schools should teach patriotism and require that both students and teachers take loyalty oaths. They should also introduce a firm system of discipline and provide a rigorous curriculum that emphasized the basic subjects (1941b, p.1).

Tyler, however, thought otherwise. Americans needed, he believed, to be loyal to democratic ideals but that could not be achieved by loyalty oaths or by instruction in patriotism:

> Loyalty to democracy is not acquired through compulsory loyalty oaths or

> through special periods set aside for teaching the Constitution. Loyalty develops through an increasing clarification and experiencing of democratic values which must permeate the school within and without the classroom (p.2).

Similarly, Tyler believed that an education for democracy required more than a curriculum encompassing the 3 Rs. Democratic citizenship required more than attaining certain knowledge and skills. It required a broad understanding of American social life and the ability to think critically about existing social problems:

> The school is forced to accept increasing responsibility for such objectives as the development of democratic social attitudes, of fundamental work habits, of wide and mature interests, of clear and deeply cherished values. Unless attention is given to all of these aspects of effective citizenship, the educational program is not likely to be well rounded and effective (pp.4-5).

Tyler's moderation can also be seen in his comments about the role of the schools during the war. Speaking in November of 1942, to the Central Association of Science and Mathematics Teachers, Tyler noted that the war had created many new occupational roles that were unknown in peacetime. The military required such new specialties as gunners and bombardiers, while industry needed new workers skilled in the manufacture of munitions and aircraft. Tyler believed that the schools had to play a role in meeting these new manpower needs necessitated by the war (1942b, p.1).

He, however, was unwilling to completely subordinate educational goals to the war effort. Labor shortages could, he commented, lead to pressure to modify compulsory attendance laws so that youth could leave school to enter war related civilian work. Tyler was against such a change and argued instead for co-operative arrangements between the schools and industry that would allow students to attend school for half a day and to use the other half of the day for war related work. Such arrangements, he argued, offered 'a better correlation between instruction and work experience so as to get some educational benefit from half time spent at work'. In addition, such arrangements would be supervised by teachers who would be able to 'safeguard the working conditions of youth'. (p.6).

Tyler's Curriculum Theory

It was during the years that Tyler was addressing the role of the school in urban America that he began spelling out the ideas on curriculum planning he would express most completely in his 1950 Basic Principles of Curriculum and Instruction. In a December, 1942 talk to the parents association of the Dalton School, an independent day school in New York City that was a participant in the now famous Eight Year Study, he described what he called the 'science of curriculum building'. Curriculum building, he noted, was a systematic process for asking first, 'what are the chief ends (aims, objectives) that school must seek to attain' and second, 'what experience, what material and learning activities are most effective for attaining these ends?' Tyler, then, went on to describe three factors that must be taken into account in answering the first question, the external needs of society, the social needs of youth, and the developmental needs of youth. These three factors, he concluded, when examined in light of the 'philosophy of the school' would yield the 'major aims of the curriculum' (1942c, p.1).

If we wish to understand why Tyler took the approach to curriculum making he did in his address to the Dalton parents, we need to look at his work in the Eight Year Study. Innaugurated in 1932 by the Progressive Education Association, the Eight Year Study brought together thirty seconday schools for the purpose of experimenting with revisions of the secondary school curriculum that would enable the schools to better serve the needs of contemporary youth. In order to conduct these experiments, three hundred participating colleges agreed for a period of eight years to admit graduates of the thirty schools notwithstanding their completion of traditional college preparatory courses and credit requirements. As a means of both assessing the achievements of students within these thirty schools as well as the effectiveness of the various curriculum revisions, an evaluation staff was appointed with Tyler as director (Aiken, 1942, pp.1-24; Smith and Tyler, 1942, pp.3-5).

It was the inclinations of an evaluator, which Tyler acquired no doubt during the Eight Year Study, that led him as he did in his rationale to think of education as a process of behavior change and curriculum planning as a sequence of steps beginning with the identification of objectives (Smith and Tyler, 1942, pp.6, 19-20). Both education and evaluation, Tyler noted in an outline of one of several talks he gave in California during 1937 on the relationship of evaluation and curriculum, involved behavior change. The goal of education, Tyler argued, was to bring about changes in students. 'The changes desired are the objectives of education.' 'Evaluation', he noted on the other hand, 'is the process of obtaining evidence regarding these changes.' Tyler believed that both processes began with the identification of certain desirable changes in student behavior stated in the form of objectives and culminated with providing students the opportunity to demonstrate these desired behavioral changes (1937, p.1). Evaluation and curriculum, Tyler thought, could not be separated from each other.

The demands of evaluation only partially explain Tyler's views on curriculum. Equally important, I think, was his understanding of the role of education in an urban, industrial society. If the schools were to meet the demands of modern life, Tyler believed, as we saw earlier in this chapter, that the curriculum would have to become more functional, that is more concerned with and related to the problems which youth faced in their day-to-day lives. Addressing the Progressive Education Association on the goals of education in the post-war era in February of 1944, Tyler called on the schools to develop a 'new social orientation'. The schools would have to teach the student 'to get along with oneself and with others, happily and effectively - to take an increasingly mature role in life - to become an increasingly satisfactory member of varied social groups - family, class, work groups, and the like' (1944b, p.1).

Tyler did not think that this needed functional content could be introduced into a curriculum that was organized around traditional academic disciplines. The problems of life were not, he pointed out, easily classifiable as problems of English, arithmetic, or social science. Rather they tended to cut across traditional, subject matter boundaries. If students were to satisfactorily resolve them, they would have to bring to bear a wide range of knowledge and skills, not simply what they might learn from their study of one academic discipline (Tyler, 1939b, pp.1-2). Introducing the curriculum planning process with the identification of objectives freed Tyler from the constraints of a school program organized around distinct disciplines and allowed him to introduce the broader and more functional content he thought so important (Tyler, 1940a, pp.1-2). Similarly, thinking of the vehicle for achieving these objectives as learning experiences and not as the content of distinct disciplines allowed for the kind of participation in solving community problems as part of the curriculum that Tyler thought necessary for teaching students to be more co-operative.

Conclusions

To understand Ralph Tyler, I have argued in this essay, it is necessary to see his career and work in relationship to the other founding theorists of the curriculum field and to that of a number of other early twentieth century American intellectuals. Tyler, like these other thinkers, was a product of the rural small town who found his career in an America that was becoming increasingly urban and industrial. And like other intellectuals of his day, he sought throughout his career to find a way to preserve those qualities of small town life he thought necessary for the furtherance of democracy, its harmony and intimacy, in urban, industrial America. It was this desire, I have suggested, that led him to propose a more functional curriculum, one that was dedicated to instilling youth with the value of co-operation.

If Tyler has made a contribution to the curriculum field, it is to be found, I think, in his proposal for reorganizing the school program along more functional lines. Bobbitt and Charters, we should recall, had during the 1920s proposed how the curriculum could be made more functional. In looking, however, to the scientific management movement for their model of curriculum making, they had fashioned a school program that mirrored the hierarchical work relationships of the modern factory. It was a school program that sought to make society more co-operative by channelling youth to their appropriate place in the industrial work-force.

Although Tyler rejected the ideas of scientific management, he was not able nor did he seek to free the concept of a functionally oriented curriculum from the goal of maintaining the kind of hierarchical social relationships required by industrial capitalism. The community school he envisioned, however, did show how a functional curriculum could allow the schools to be an instrument of modest social change, an accomplishment that seemed to escape both Bobbitt and Charters.

It is, I think, unfortunate that Tyler did not in his 1950 curriculum rationale discuss his understanding of the social role which the American public school should play. Without a statement of his social philosophy, the important differences between his curriculum rationale and the efficiency ideas of Bobbitt and Charters are often overlooked. Similarly, if one does not know what Tyler's social vision is, it is easy to confuse his rationale with the technological models of curriculum planning that have been advanced in recent years by proponents of competency based education.

One might not much care for Tyler's curriculum rationale, tied as it is to a quantitative notion of evaluation that is today often viewed as being narrow and simplistic. When compared, however, to the rather crude human capital theories of schooling that currently seem to dominate our educational thinking, Tyler's work stands, perhaps if not as a shining beacon, at least as a faint light to guide those of us who continue to see the American public school as an instrument for social improvement.

A shortened version of this chapter was presented at the annual meeting of the History of Education Society, Atlanta, Georgia, November 9, 1985.

References

Aiken, W.M. (1942)
The Story of the Eight Year Study
New York, Harper and Brothers.

Beyer, L.E. (1983)
'Aesthetic Curriculum and Cultural Reproduction' in Apple, M.W. and Weis, L. (Eds.) Ideology and Practice in Schooling, Philadelphia, Temple University Press, pp.89-113.

Bobbitt, F. (1926)
'The Orientation of the Curriculum Maker' in Whipple, G.M. (Ed.) The Foundation of Curriculum Making, The Twenty-sixth Yearbook of the National Society for the Study of Education, Part II, Bloomington, Public School Publishing Company, p.54.

Eisner, E. (1985)
The Educational Imagination: On the Design and Evaluation of School Programs, 2nd Ed., New York, Macmillan.

Everett, S. (1938)
The Community School,
New York, D. Appleton-Century.

Fohles, J. (1978)
Biographical Dictionary of American Education, I, 3 vols., Westport, Ct., Greenwood Press.

Frankin, B.M. (1985)
Building the American Community: The School Curriculum and the Search for Social Control, Philadelphia, Falmer Press.

Goode, W.J. Furstenberg, F., and Mitchell, L.R. (Eds.) (1970) Willard W. Waller on the Family, Education, and War: Selected Writings Chicago, University of Chicago Press.

Goodlad, J. (1969)
'Curriculum: State of the Field', Review of Educational Research, 39 (3), pp.367-375.

Hanna, P.R. and Naslund, R.A. (1953)
'The Community School Defined' in Henry, W.B. (Ed.) The Community School, The Fifty-second Yearbook of the National Society for the Study of Education, Part II, Chicago, University of Chicago Press, pp.45-63.

McClure, R.M. (1971)
'The Reforms of the Fifties and Sixties: A Historical Look at the Near Past' in McClure, R.M. (Ed.) The Curriculum: Retrospect and Prospect, The Seventieth Yearbook of the

National Society for the Study of Education, Part I, Chicago, University of Chicago Press, pp.45-75.
McNeil, J.D. (1981)
Curriculum: A Comprehensive Introduction, 2nd Ed., Boston, Little, Brown.
Saylor, J.G. and Alexander, W.M. (1974)
Planning Curriculum for Schools, New York, Holt, Reinhart and Winston.
Schubert, W.H. (1980)
Curriculum Books: The First Eighty Years, Lanham, Md., University Press of America.
Seay, M.F. (1945)
'The Community-school Emphases in Postwar Education' in Henry, N.B. (Ed.) American Education in the Postwar Period, the Forty-fourth Yearbook of the National Society for the Study of Education, Part I, Chicago, University of Chicago, pp.209-228.
Smith, E.R. and Tyler, R.W. (1942) Appraising and Recording Student Progress, New York, Harper and Brothers.
Tanner, D. and Tanner, L.N. (1980)
Curriculum Development: Theory into Practice New York, Macmillan.
Tanner, L.N. (1982)
'Curriculum History as Usable Knowledge' Curriculum Inquiry 12 (4), pp.405-411.
Tyler, R.W. (1937)
'Relation of Evaluation to the Curriculum' The Ralph Tyler Papers, University of Chicago Library, Box 23, Folder 8.
Tyler, R.W. (1939a)
'Are the Schools Adequately Preparing our Youth for the World of Today', Abstract of a speech delivered at the Wisconsin Congress of Parents and Teachers, Madison, Wisconsin, April 18, 1939, The Tyler Papers, Box 23, Folder 9.
Tyler, R.W. (1939b)
'The Thirties in Education - the Years of Questioning', The Tyler Papers, Box 23, Folder 10.
Tyler, R.W. (1939c)
'Training Administrative Officers for Democratic Leadership', Address to the Conference of Administrative Officers of Public and Private Schools, The Tyler Papers, Box 23, Folder 11.

Tyler, R.W. (1940a)
'Abstract of Curriculum Trends in Modern Secondary Schools', Address to the National Education Association, St. Louis, Missouri, February 27, 1940, The Tyler Papers, Box 23, Folder 12.

Tyler, R.W. (1940b)
'The Place of Evaluation in Modern Education', Address to the Conference of Administrative Officers of Public and Private Schools, July 15, 1940, The Tyler Papers, Box 23, Folder 13.

Tyler, R.W. (1941a)
'Educational Adjustments Necessitated by Changing Ideological Concepts', Address to the Conference of Administrative Officers of Public and Private Schools, July 21, 1941, The Tyler Papers, Box 24, Folder 1.

Tyler, R.W. (1941b)
'Education in Defence of Democracy', The Tyler Papers, Box 24, Folder 1.

Tyler, R.W. (1941c)
'The Relation of the Curriculum to American Democratic Ideals', Walgreen Lecture, The Tyler Papers, Box 24, Folder 2.

Tyler, R.W. (1942a)
'Relations of the Urban Community and the Modern School', Address to the Conference of Administrative Officers of Public and Private Schools, July 20, 1942, The Tyler Papers, Box 24, Folder 5.

Tyler, R.W. (1942b)
'The Role of Education in our Present Emergency', Address to the Central Association of Science and Mathematics Teachers, November 27, 1942, The Tyler Papers, Box 24, Folder 5.

Tyler, R.W. (1942c)
'The Science of Curriculum Building', Address to the Dalton School Parents Association, December 6, 1942, Box 24, Folder 16.

Tyler, R.W. (1944a)
'The Responsibility of the School for the Improvement of American Life', Address to the Conference of Administrative Officers of Public and Private Schools, July 17, 1944, The Tyler Papers, Box 24, Folder 14.

Tyler, R.W. (1944b)
'Role of the Schools in Post War Plans for Soldiers and Youth', Address to the

Progressive Education Association, February 24, 1944, The Tyler Papers, Box 24, Folder 16.

Tyler, R.W. (n.d.)
'The Function of the University in Effecting Major Cultural Transitions', The Tyler Papers Box 23, Folder 3.

Tyler, R.W. (1950)
Basic Principles of Curriculum and Instruction: Syllabus for Education 305, Chicago, University of Chicago Press.

Tyler, R.W. (1985)
Private interview with Ralph Tyler, given in Chicago, Illinois, April 1, 1985.

12. CURRICULUM HISTORY IN ENGLAND AND NEW ZEALAND

Gary McCulloch

According to Foster Watson, writing in 1909, 'It will be generally admitted that it is high time that the historical facts with regard to the beginning of the teaching of modern subjects in England were known, and known in connexion with the history of the social forces which brought them into the educational curriculum.'(1) Even so, it was not until the late 1970s that serious attention began to be given to curriculum history of the kind Watson had described. This development was encouraged in the English context by a variety of educational, social, and political influences which also dictated the aspects upon which curriculum historians tended to concentrate. By contrast, in New Zealand curriculum history has not yet developed as a field of enquiry. A comparison between the situation in England and that in New Zealand offers lessons of potential benefit for curriculum history in both countries. For New Zealand, it highlights the value of historical approaches to the curriculum. For England, it may point the way towards a wider focus of enquiry in curriculum history.

I Curriculum History in England

While hopeful that history could make an important contribution to the study of the curriculum, the historian Kenneth Charlton was acutely aware in 1968 that this contribution was but little appreciated by those concerned with 'the new star in the heavens which is called curriculum theory and development'.(2) Ten years later, W.E. Marsden could still note that the role of history remained potential rather than actual: 'It would be difficult to dispute the fact that the continuing curriculum debate of the last twenty years has been but little illumined by historical appraisal.'(3) Just as curriculum specialists neglected history, social historians tended to overlook the wider significance of curriculum change. It was observed as late as 1978 that 'Most historical work bearing upon the development of curricula has appeared as M.Ed. theses dealing with secondary education.'(4) Over the last decade this situation has changed rapidly in one sense while remaining stable in another. New interest in 'curriculum history' has been shown among historians, sociologists and curriculum specialists with diverse backgrounds and perspectives, and this development has been reflected in an upsurge of published research. On the other hand, curriculum history has continued to focus principally upon the curriculum of secondary schools. Indeed the rise of curriculum history in the past few years might be regarded as the latest manifestation of concern relating essentially to the secondary school curriculum, concern which had begun to be expressed in the late 1950s.

In the post-war years, education was widely acknowledged to be a vital asset that would bring important benefits to individuals, society and the nation as a whole. In particular, the promise of 'secondary education for all', held out by the Education Act of 1944, was accepted universally not as a burden or luxury but as a national investment. As a right shared by all boys and girls up to the age of fifteen, the new secondary education was an integral part of the 'welfare state'. At the same time it offered, at least to some, a pathway to the 'affluent society'. It was noted in 1958 that a recent 'most encouraging growth of public interest in education' seemed to have been brought about 'first, by the widespread realization that our national future is closely bound up with the rate of progress in our schools; and secondly, by the concern of individual parents that their children should enjoy the best possible start in life'.(5) The Crowther report _15 to 18_, published in 1959, called for 'the progressive development of English education' on the grounds that it was both a 'social service' and an 'investment in national efficiency'.(6) Considerable resources were used to maintain, expand and modernize educational facilities.

It was soon found, though, that the adjustment of the secondary school curriculum in line with contemporary demands and opportunities raised problems different in nature from the building of new schools and classrooms. The curriculum involved traditions, values and subject-matter that had been transmitted to a privileged minority of young people through secondary education in the decades before 1944, for different purposes and in quite different circumstances from those in which the schools now operated. The Yearbook of Education in 1958, devoted to 'The Secondary School Curriculum', suggested that tradition was a fundamental aspect of the curriculum. It was remarked that education tended to be a conservative element in society, whether through explicit ideology or the inertia of institutions, yet that 'of all educational institutions the curriculum is the most conservative and resilient to change'.(7) The Minister for Science, Lord Hailsham, complained that 'all the lumber of past technologies and past science' was stored in the school curriculum, making it difficult to introduce new content and ideas.(8) These tendencies in the curriculum formed a barrier to change and modernization. By the same token, it was thought that if a way could be found to reform and revise the curriculum it would provide the best means for equipping future citizens with knowledge, values and attitudes more appropriate to the late twentieth century.

Control of the curriculum was another issue that presented peculiar difficulties. In the 1950s, with no single agency responsible for curriculum change, a 'vacuum' of authority created confusion and inaction. The Crowther report's findings on sixth forms finally prompted direct involvement in the 'secret garden of the curriculum' by the Minister of Education, Sir David Eccles, who signalled his desire to extend the Ministry's active role:

> I regret that so many of our education debates have had to be devoted almost entirely to bricks and mortar and to the organisation of the system. We hardly ever discuss what is taught to the 7 million boys and girls in the maintained schools... Of course, Parliament would never attempt to dictate the curriculum, but, from time to time, we could with advantage express views on what is taught in schools and in training colleges...

> I shall, therefore, try in the future to make the Ministry's own voice heard rather more often, more positively, and, no doubt, sometimes, more controversially.(9)

The 'Curriculum Study Group' established within the Ministry in 1962 engendered protests from teachers and local education authorities, and gave way in 1964 to a more 'representative' body,(10) less accountable to the Ministry. This was the Schools Council for the Curriculum and Examinations, intended to 'assist, co-ordinate and stimulate work to be carried out by as many appropriate agencies as can be induced to join in a great co-operative effort'.(11) The Schools Council soon became an important sponsor and resource for curriculum development as well as a forum of debate.

In the early 1960s the problem of curriculum change was seen by and large as a technical or organizational one, requiring good management and planning. New ideas competently produced and thoroughly implemented would, it was assumed, succeed in overhauling school curricula very quickly. According to _The Times Educational Supplement_ in October 1965, 'for all the ink and vitriol spilt over the organisation of education, this decade is more likely to be remembered for the quiet revolution in the field of the school curriculum'.(12) As late as 1967, Professor J.F. Kerr remained confident that 'At the practical and organisational levels, the new curricula promise to revolutionise English education.'(13) It soon became clear, however, that in most cases the 'new curricula' were for some reason not being taken up by schools, or were being interpreted by teachers in ways contrary to the intentions of the reformers. The Schools Science and Technology Committee, established in 1968 to co-ordinate various projects in this area, quickly became aware of 'the restricting circle of examination papers, syllabuses, books, teacher training and experience'.(14) The co-ordinators of Schools Council curriculum projects, despite the extensive resources at their disposal, often became frustrated by the persistent opposition of various interest groups.(15) Within a few years confident plans had given way to disenchantment, especially with declining financial resources in the 1970s. As Macdonald and Walker reported in 1976:

> The optimism of the pioneer innovators is now muted, in part because planned change has turned out to be a more formidable problem than was initially assumed... The enduring problem that has plagued the sponsors and planners of curriculum innovation is not the problem of creation, but the problem of impact, the failure to achieve anything like the mass conversion to new aims, new content, and new approaches that they aspire to. The schools have not, it seems, been transformed by all the organised, systematised, specialised efforts of the professional innovators.(16)

In this changed context, curriculum studies came to stress not so much the exciting prospects of reform as the inertia of the system.

This darkening vision led in turn to the adoption of various new approaches to the study of the curriculum, including an increased emphasis on its social and historical aspects. Marsden pointed out that 'Recent experience has inevitably demonstrated that sophisticated theoretical frameworks are not enough, and has shifted the emphasis to the constraints imposed by economic and political factors, the conflict of personality and group interest, ... by the level of teaching skills available, and by the sheer complexity of the exercise.'(17) Philip Taylor, himself formerly closely involved in the work of the Schools Council, conceded in 1979 that the 'procedural, managerial paradigm' in curriculum studies should give way to fresh perspective, concluding: 'The trend in research would seem to be away from the _scientific_ toward the _practical and the human_; a trend which suggests that future curriculum research may lean more toward the research models of literature, drama, history and art for its informing stance.'(18) In more 'radical' vein, Lawn and Barton stressed the need for a 'critical appraisal' of curriculum studies, arguing that they should be related in a systematic way to contemporary realities and extra-curricular factors. In particular, they suggested, 'we need to delineate the historical, stuctural and contextual factors involved as well as the interpretations and strategies that teachers use to cope with the realities of their job and how each of these inter-relate in a dynamic process'.(19) A similar shift in emphasis took place during the 1970s within the Department of Curriculum Studies in the Institute of Education at the University of London. In his inaugural lecture as Professor of Education at the Institute in 1978, Denis Lawton recalled that one of the reasons for establishing the Department at its inception in 1972 was that 'it was felt that curriculum, perhaps even more than other educational issues, needed to be studied simultaneously from the viewpoints of several educational disciplines'. However, according to Lawton, 'as the department has developed, historical aspects of the curriculum, or studies of the curriculum in its historical context, have loomed larger'. In fact, he concluded, 'In so far as I can speak for all my colleagues in the department, I think it would be true to say that we find it difficult, if not impossible, to discuss curriculum in a meaningful way unless we look at specific curricular issues set in a social, cultural and historical context.'(20) It seems clear that new awareness of the complexity, contexts and constraints of curriculum change, the product of bitter experience, had encouraged novel interest in historical accounts of the processes involved.

Curriculum history was also closely associated with and drew strength from other insights relating to the social and political character of the school curriculum. One such source was the sociology of knowledge. In 1961, Raymond Williams pointed out that 'academic' knowledge has been historically related to the social and political elite, while future 'hewers of wood' have traditionally been confined to 'utilitarian' curricula.(21). This theme, stressing a close correlation between the school curriculum and social inequalities, was elaborated upon during the 1970s by advocates of the 'new' sociology of education. Michael Young complained that 'We have had virtually no theoretical perspectives or research to suggest explanations of how curricula, which are no less social inventions than political parties or new towns, arise, persist and change, and what the social interests and values involved might be.'(22) The notion of examining curricula as one might 'political parties' or 'new towns' offered opportunities for historians as well as sociologists. Young also suggested that teachers might have vested interests in the stratification of knowledge which took place through the school curriculum: 'for teachers, high status (and rewards) will be associated with areas of the curriculum that are (i) formally assessed, (ii) taught to the "ablest" children, (iii) taught in homogeneous ability groups of children who show themselves most successful within such curricula'.(23) Thus teachers were seen not as concerned, disinterested and humane but as paid agents of an unjust social order. The curriculum itself was interpreted as an instrument of power for the purposes of social control and the reproduction of social class patterns. So far as Frank Musgrove was concerned, 'In the 1970s we have rediscovered the working class and Gramsci's prison notebooks, and interpretation of the school curriculum has lost its innocence. Class, ideology and above all hegemony have become key concepts in curriculum studies.'(24) The stratification of knowledge in the school curriculum was viewed as the key to understanding relationships and conflicts in the wider society.

Socio-historical treatments of the school curriculum were further encouraged by the new interest among historians of education in the relationships between education and society. The history of education had traditionally been concerned principally with the expansion of schooling and the rise of a teaching profession, often examined in isolation from wider social and political changes. The historian Brian Simon complained in 1966 that 'It is the present tendency to review the past development of the English educational system, and of particular institutions within it, as if this took place by its own momentum rather than in relation to changing social pressures and needs.'(25) Simon's view that historical study should in fact be 'primarily concerned' with 'the study of education as a social function'(26) became orthodox opinion by the 1970s. As Harold Silver has recently demonstrated, educational history has 'increasingly become complicated by the recognition of relationships with other social phenomena'.(27) The school curriculum, in its new guise as a social process conditioned by competing ideologies and vested interests, was suitable territory for a 'revisionist' history devoted to critical analysis of 'education as a social function'. Efforts to broaden the focus of educational history to embrace educational activities in all phases of life and society were also made but tended to be limited in their impact. Indeed, the new historians' interest in curriculm might be seen as a manifestation of the traditional emphasis upon aspects of schooling as well as a product of more recent insights into the curriculum as a 'social invention'.

The relationship between education and politics in the 1970s also influenced the trend towards awareness of the historical character of the curriculum. The roles of party politics and of national government in education were underlined by the debate over comprehensive schooling. Tensions between competing policies and ideologies on the character of secondary education fostered awareness of distinct political traditions in this area. Increasing intervention in the education system by governments of both major parties, Labour and Conservative, made it clearer than ever that educational changes were related to wider factors, criteria and objectives than were active within the educational system itself. It also provided an object lesson in the limits of educational change. The 'Great Debate' launched by the Labour Prime Minister James Callaghan in the autumn of 1976, signalled an admission that the hopeful initiatives and planning of the 1960s had failed. It was prompted by a desire to relate education to the needs of society and industry, and efforts towards this end increased over the following decade as the economic and industrial difficulties of the nation increased. Different state departments began to show active interest in the difficulties of education. The Department of Education and Science (DES), set up in 1964, was now faced with competing activities and priorities emanating from bodies such as the Manpower Services Commission (MSC), which was accountable to the Department of Employment. These national political pressures strained the relationship between dispersed educational interests and national government. The school curriculum was a central locus of this dispute. Robert Cooke, General Secretary of the National Association of Head Teachers, was hostile to the active role of government in the 'Great Debate': 'I was teaching in Nazi Germany in the thirties and saw what happened where the curriculum was nationally controlled.'(28) The Technical and Vocational Education Initiative, launched by the MSC in November 1982, was resisted partly on the grounds that it might create 'a divided curriculum perpetuating Victorian views of knowledge and social class'.(29) Hostility to state control thus gave added point to the view of the school curriculum as an instrument of power. The political characteristics of the curriculum itself also became clearer. Becher and Maclure, for example, observed that the many different groups involved in education each had their own interests and traditions regarding the curriculum: 'How the various groups interact in respect of curriculum development reflects its public character and the dynamic relationship between education and society.'(30) Lawton identified five distinct levels at which the politics of the curriculum took place - national, local, school, department and classroom. In stressing the complexity of the interplay of processes among and within these levels, he was going a long way towards explaining the difficulties of curriculum change.(31)

These various factors combined not only to create the 'curriculum history' of the 1980s but also to fashion its dominant approaches and perceptions. First, appreciation of the social and political relationships of the curriculum has clearly been an important feature of curriculum history. A general account of curriculum change in the nineteenth and twentieth centuries by Peter Gordon and Denis Lawton was based on their view that 'curriculum change is the result of complex patterns of interaction between influential individuals and general processes of social, political and economic change'.(32) Such relationships have been paramount in the work of David Layton, who in one of the earliest 'modern' accounts of the history of the curriculum showed that administrative decisions in the late 1850s, made for a variety of social and political reasons, 'set the seal on earlier events, and proved a crucial determinant of the place of science in the school curriculum'.(33) In his subsequent work, Layton has continued to stress the social and cultural context of curriculum change, going so far as to 'assert the over-riding importance of cultural contexts and the relative unimportance of classroom factors in determining the outcome of attempts at curriculum innovation'.(34) Scrutiny of the evolution of other 'subject' areas has highlighted their political character as well as their cultural contexts. Ivor Goodson, analysing the emergence of geography from low-status pedagogical and utilitarian origins to become a prestigious academic subject, has pointed to the preferential treatment given to academic subjects in terms of resources, staffing ratios, salaries and career prospects: 'The link between academic status and resource allocation provides the major explanatory framework for understanding the aspirational imperative to become an academic subject.'(35) According to Goodson, school subjects 'represent substantial interest groups', each fighting for greater resources and academic status. For this reason, he concludes, much curriculum debate might be interpreted 'in terms of conflict bwtween subjects over status, resources and territory'.(36) Conflicts and tensions within school subjects have also been examined, further indicating their nature as broad coalitions involving an often uneasy combination of different traditions, interests and constituencies. Barry Cooper has found from his study of school mathematics that a 'subject' may be understood as 'a set of segments, or social movements, with distinctive missions, or perspectives, and material interests'.(37) Stephen Ball suggests that long-term curriculum change in English has been 'based upon the establishment of subject paradigms via networks of communication and apprenticeship'.(38) Michael Young has located the history of school science within his general perspective of state schooling as a form of social control.(39) Tensions between 'practical' and 'liberal' conceptions of education have also begun to be placed in their historical, social and political contexts.(40)

A common emphasis upon complexity, constraints and the disappointments of curriculum reform has been a second feature of recent curriculum history. Layton, analysing the failure of initiatives of the 1850s to introduce science into the elementary school curriculum, concludes: 'that plans so carefully laid and apparently well supported should fail to achieve their purpose is a striking indication of the manifold determinants of curriculum change.'(41) Michael Young emphasizes the failures of curriculum innovation in school science in the 1960s as an aspect of 'problems which have their origins and their resolution in a particular kind of society and its transformation'.(42) For Young, then, intractable problems of curriculum change will continue so long as capitalist society exists. Others have suggested a close link between the belated introduction of science into the school curriculum and its pure, academic character once there established, and Britain's relative economic decline of the past century. The argument of such historians as Martin Wiener that a 'cultural cordon sanitaire' has encircled 'the forces of economic development', with disastrous effects for British industry and the economy,(43) has been echoed by several recent curriculum historians. According to Gordon and Lawton, for example,

> ... the public school classics-based curriculum transformed many of the potential technologists and industrial leaders into "gentlemen" who looked with disdain on the practical knowledge of science and engineering, and it may not be too far-fetched to link this attitude to some of the contemporary economic problems in the United Kingdom.(44)

Goodson, similarly, argues that 'The very price of success in achieving high status in an academic discipline is to renounce practical connections and relevance to the personal and to the industrial and commercial world... As a formula for economic decline such a pattern of curriculum negotiation and investment could hardly be perfected.'(45) Curriculum history, in analysing the constraints and disappointments of curriculum change, seems often to have offered an explanation, or at least an allegory, of 'national decline'.

A third element in curriculum history has been its general preoccupation with the curriculum of secondary schools. A major exception to this rule was Layton's Science for the People, which was concerned with elementary schools of the nineteenth century. By and large, however, the emphasis has been upon explaining curriculum change, and lack of change, in the secondary schools, usually in the context of 'secondary education for all' since the Education Act of 1944. This limited focus may be explained in terms of the traditional parameters of curriculum studies, which historians and sociologists have so far failed effectively to challenge. Also, curriculum historians have usually been either former secondary school teachers, or addressing themselves to students preparing to become secondary school teachers.

A recent collection of articles in curriculum history edited by Ivor Goodson, Social Histories of the Secondary Curriculum: Subjects for Study, demonstrates all of these characteristics. A sharp sense of social, cultural and political contexts is displayed by the various contributors. They generally emphasize the 'complexity of curriculum change',(46) and usually also the conservatism of curriculum traditions. The focus throughout is upon the 'secondary curriculum'; indeed Goodson concedes that 'clearly in future work studies must be undertaken at all levels of the educational system and must deal with the relationship between these levels'.(47) If we have here a 'paradigm' of curriculum history, it is one that includes these particular traits. Above all, curriculum history in England bears clear marks of the educational, social and political environment in which it has arisen.

II History and the Curriculum in New Zealand

Although New Zealand is situated 12,000 miles away from England, the influence of the English has always been particularly potent in this country. The Treaty of Waitangi in 1840 formally established New Zealand as a British colony, and in the twentieth century bonds remained strong. A.E. Campbell, later Director of Education, declared in 1941 that 'The education system of New Zealand as it stands today is incomprehensible unless one bears ever in mind that it originated and developed in a British colony in the nineteenth century.'(48) The same was true of the school curriculum. A leading authority on the curriculum in New Zealand, J.L. Ewing, pointed out that trends in educational thought in the mother country had 'naturally enough' given the main leads to curriculum change in New Zealand: 'Sometimes it has taken a decade or more before new ideas and their implications for the classroom have filtered into the New Zealand system and become generally accepted; sometimes our response has been immediate.'(49) The Cross report of 1888, the Hadow reports of 1926 and 1931, the Newsom report of 1963, the Plowden report of 1967 and the Schools Council were just a few of the English 'landmarks' which had guided curriculum change in New Zealand. Moreover, as Ewing also noted, 'Since the 1950s the flow of books and articles on curriculum topics into New Zealand from overseas has increased considerably, and exchanges of teachers and the visits of curriculum specialists from other countries have also introduced new ideas.'(50) Curriculum history is so far at an early stage of development in New Zealand. There are then two issues to consider in the present situation: first, whether curriculum history should be encouraged to develop further in New Zealand, and second, if it should do so how far its approaches and preoccupations should imitate those in England.

Although several useful historical accounts of the curriculum have been written in New Zealand, these have not generally been informed by the recent insights in the politics, sociology and history of education which have helped to stimulate the field in England. So far as 'curriculum history' has existed at all it has been within the ambit of a tradition of educational history low in the esteem of most academic educators and historians, and remote from the concerns of most curriculum specialists. The dominant tone of New Zealand educational history was set by A.G. Butchers in the interwar years. The style of this history was intended to give the impression of 'an independent, disinterested study of the facts',(51) but underlying this were liberal assumptions about the nature and effects of education. The 1877 Education Act, and the system of free, compulsory and secular schooling which it helped to create, were taken as symbols of liberal progress and civilization. A similar view was maintained in the 1950s and 1960s, as Ian Cumming, most notably, followed in the same general tradition as that of Butchers. (52) A leading recent historian of education, David McKenzie, has recognized that 'The conventional wisdom in New Zealand educational history still owes much to the ideology laid down in the pioneering works of A.G. Butchers.'(53) This has clearly been true with respect to the curriculum.

The main historical study of the curriculum in New Zealand is J.L. Ewing's two-volume work on the primary school curriculum since 1840.(54) This is a detailed and scholarly account. However, Ewing does little to show the relationship between curriculum change and the wider society, and generally expressed traditional liberal assumptions on the nature and role of education in new Zealand. In particular, George Hogben, Inspector-General of Schools and Secretary to the Department of Education, is seen as a 'progressive' influence on the curriculum, as are Peter Fraser, Minister of Education in the Labour government in the late 1930s, and the Thomas Committee which reported on the post-primary school curriculum in 1944. Ewing's work offers a largely inspirational view of the past, a story of difficulties overcome and reactionaries defeated. J.J. Lee, District Senior Inspector at the Auckland Education Board, was in no doubt over the appropriate lesson to be learned from Ewing: 'Ewing's book shows clearly how our New Zealand curriculum was liberalized ..., until today we have a well-balanced and integrated curriculum including both basic and cultural subjects.'(55) Such a tale of progress is not conducive to recognition of vested interests and ideology in relation to the curriculum. This might then be regarded as a good example of work in the history of the curriculum in the classic mould, uninfluenced by recent developments in the field.

This tradition of educational history has tended to play a comparatively minor part within educational research as it has developed in New Zealand. Here the academic study of education was established in the interwar years. Chairs in education were created in the university colleges in the 1920s, and the New Zealand Council for Educational Research (NZCER) was set up in 1934. Contemporary developments in psychology and the 'New Education' made an important impression on educational research in these formative years. The 'New Education' inspired faith in liberal reform in education, while the dominant role of psychology encouraged a 'scientific' view of education. Sir Thomas Hunter, the first President of the NZCER, later recalled that modern psychology had 'produced little short of a revolution' so far as New Zealand educational study was concerned, 'for whereas in earlier years the point of interest was the subject taught, now it is the child and his development.'(56) Raymond Adams, Professor of Education at Massey University, has recently argued that the dominance of psychology has had important consequences for educational research in general:

> Critical self-analysis has not yet become an acceptable tradition in education - partly because psychology, not noticeably self-critical, has been dominant and partly because the necessary self-confidence is lacking... Accordingly, what is defined as research tends to be in the positivist tradition, quantitative, technocratic and reportedly "value-free".(57)

Educational history has thus been subordinated to a 'strongly psychological' emphasis (58) at the same time that it has sought to conform to the dominant traditions of educational research in New Zealand - uncritical, liberal and positivist. For these reasons writings on the history of the curriculum have served to bolster liberal-progressive assumptions about education in New Zealand rather than subjecting such assumptions to critical scrutiny.

The history of the curriculum as it has usually been conceived has generally been remote from the concerns of curriculum specialists. As in England, academic interest in the curriculum grew during the 1960s. A Curriculum Development Unit was established within the central Department of Education, following the recommendations of the Currie Commission on Education in 1962. Curriculum development was seen in terms of disseminating plans drawn up by teams of experts, but, again rather like England, often led to disappointing results. There has so far been little evidence of increasing interest in the cultural context of the curriculum, nor in historical or long-term analyses of curriculum change, of the kind that has developed latterly in England. In a collection of articles on 'Curriculum issues in New Zealand' published in 1980, the role of history is seen in terms of 'setting the scene', sketching the familiar Acts and personalities responsible for the shaping of the public curriculum in New Zealand.(59) Having established the historical 'background', the subsequent essays in the collection concentrate on the contemporary scene. Curriculum projects have also neglected the possible contribution of historical appraisal. The Learning in Science Project based at the University of Waikato, for example, in stressing the need to understand children's ideas on science, has depended on empirical analysis of such ideas in a classroom setting, with little or no reference to wider considerations.(60) A certain lack of historical awareness is also evident in a core curriculum review published by the Department of Education in March 1984, which, as the education policy study group at Massey University has recently pointed out, seems to assume 'that the content of school subjects is static and their relative status self-evident'.(61)

Little assistance in encouraging historical approaches to the curriculum has come from social historians or sociologists. Research in educational history has been largely confined to university education departments. This has meant that the dominance in the field of such as Butchers and Cumming was relatively unchallenged, and also that social historians in other fields have made little contribution to redirecting attention towards education as a social phenomenon. At the same time there was scant critical social analysis current in New Zealand at least until the 1960s, whether at an academic level or in society at large. Sir Thomas Hunter noted in June 1940 that 'In this democratic country it is surely a reflection upon us that not one of the constituent colleges has made adequate provision for the study of sociology and its allied subjects.'(62) The first Chair in sociology was not established until 1966, and the subsequent career of this academic discipline has remained as D.W.G. Timms described it in 1971: 'erratic and even contentious'.(63) Thus for different reasons the role of social history and sociology, and especially critical social analysis, in curriculum studies and educational history has been strictly limited.

It is clear, then, that there have been several constraints in New Zealand which have hindered the growth of anything that might be recognized as 'curriculum history'. Even so, there have been some signs of change in the last few years. 'Revisionist' educational history seems at last to be superseding the approach of Butchers and Cumming, raising the possibility of more critical treatment of curriculum issues in their social, cultural and historical relationships.(64) The sociology of education has also begun to follow recent overseas developments. Richard Bates maintained in the late 1970s that 'New Zealand can hardly claim to have emerged into the era of traditional, let alone come to grips with the new, sociology of education',(65) but this judgement might now appear a little harsh. A wide-ranging collection of essays on current perspectives in this area has recently been published.(66) Meanwhile, the emergence of policy conflicts over education as national political issues seems to have encouraged a growth of interest in the politics of education in New Zealand.(67) It might be concluded that several of the preconditions of curriculum history in England have been met in New Zealand.

Indeed existing literature in this field,

athough scanty and little appreciated, already shows some awareness of the social, political and historical characteristics of the curriculum. J.J. Lee's optimistic, liberal-progressive view of educational history obviates the need for critical analysis, but his recognition that the historical dimension is vital in 'defining the curriculum' in any country goes some way towards a sense of the potential role of curriculum history.(68) David McKenzie, in a recent article on 'Politics and School Curriculum', still tends to stress the 1877 Education Act, George Hogben and the Thomas Committee, but discusses the social and political aspects of curriculum change in an interesting and valuable way. He points out that in the 1877 Education Act, designed by Charles Bowen, the curriculum was viewed as a form of control: 'Bowen's clear distinction between primary and secondary schooling signified the link between curricula and class structure which the New Zealand settlers had brought with them from Britain.'(69) John Codd too relates curriculum change to social and political interests, arguing that if 'legitimated sources of power' such as curriculum 'experts' are to be better understood, 'there is clearly a need for sociological research into the structure and dynamics of school curricula, particularly into what counts as knowledge and how it is organized'.(70) Codd goes on to argue that 'social determinants of the school curriculum' have been particularly strong in New Zealand:

> Historically they provided the very basis upon which our public education system was built. For it was the social demand of industrial and technological expansion in the nineteenth century, with its resultant needs for specialised skills and a well-trained work-force, which gave impetus to the whole political movement towards universal compulsory education.(71)

The 'new' sociology of education also provided the starting point for Richard Bates to question the meaning of 'the array of new curricula introduced into New Zealand schools during the past decade'. In particular, he suggests, 'What is needed is a research which treats as problematic what counts as knowledge in, say, Social Studies, by making explicit the content, form, stucture and framing of what counts as knowledge in classrooms where social studies is being done.'(72) A useful doctoral thesis on the history of a secondary school subject, history, has also been produced, tracing that subject's decline in popularity at the secondary school level in relation to wider educational and social changes and the pervasive influence of the English.(73) It seems then that despite various constraints curriculum history may already have begun to develop as a field of academic activity in New Zealand.

III Curriculum History in England and New Zealand

If curriculum history is to continue to develop in New Zealand, and to draw further strength from overseas research such as that in England, it seems useful at this stage to try to distinguish between the necessary attributes of curriculum history and characteristics which are contingent upon the English experience. Even if this can be accomplished the peculiar features of English curriculum history may develop in New Zealand also, if only because of the important role that English attitudes have traditionally assumed in New Zealand education. It would however be possible to confront such issues without regarding them as inextricably linked with the theory and practice of curriculum history itself. Curriculum history might even prove to be a means of analysing the processes of cultural imperialism, rather than merely its latest manifestation.

In general, then, we may say that curriculum historians interpret the curriculum as a social and political construct, and curriculum processes as inherently historical. This implies that in order to understand and promote curriculum change the curriculum should be seen in its wider social, cultural, political and historical contexts; also that the curriculum is an appropriate topic for historical inquiry. For historians it promises a new route of entry into the sphere of education, as well as a fresh kind of source shedding light on social and political attitudes and practices. For both historians and educators it is a vivid reminder of the social and historical character of education as a process. It should also be no less valuable for curriculum specialists not only in helping to define the nature of the curriculum, but also for reaching a greater understanding of curriculum change which might in turn bring greater success in its reform. As Goodson remarks, curriculum history involves transforming as well as extending accounts of the curriculum, posing new questions and pointing towards fresh agendas for study.(74) It renders problematic cherished assumptions about aspects and areas of curriculum. According to William Reid, for instance, 'Much as teachers might like to believe that the categorical significance of a subject relates to its intrinsic character, curriculum history demonstrates that this is not the case.'(75) Historical study of the curriculum can also help to distinguish between 'change' and 'progress',(76) and thus 'inform and influence policy and practice'.(77) Curriculum history is concerned with critical analysis of the curriculum and the society of which it is part, adopting historical methods as the best means towards these ends.

Characteristics of curriculum history in England which are not integral to such a general notion of curriculum history would include the emphasis on secondary education and the tendency to stress complexity, failure and disappointment. These features explain much about past and present social attitudes and curriculum change in England. On the other hand, they need not be taken by curriculum historians in New Zealand or elsewhere, or indeed in England, as being inherent qualities of curriculum history. By contrast, prominent features of English curriculum history such as its penchant for critical analysis and clear appreciation of social and political factors might well be regarded as vital elements in curriculum history whether in England, New Zealand or anywhere else. This view seems to imply that further development of curriculum history in England depends largely on the ability of curriculum historians to capitalize upon the critical perspectives displayed in much recent literature, while extending their range beyond secondary schooling. In this way, English curriculum history may transcend its origins as a new phase in curriculum studies to demonstate its full significance as an integral aspect of social and political history.

One relatively straightforward way of widening the focus of interest in curriculum history in England might be to develop critical perspectives on the history of the primary school curriculum. Carolyn Steadman, for instance, has recently suggested that despite the official ideology of progressivism as expessed in the Plowden report, primary school history 'has gone on quietly demonstrating the heroic virtues of the rich and powerful behind all the noise of methodological change in secondary school history, and in the way it always has'.(78) Including the primary school curriculum in historical studies might shed new light on the way in which school subjects are and have been 'negotiated', while also giving rise to fresh interest in the history of children's play and other activities in the school setting.

Another possible approach to curriculum history in England would be to analyse the changing fortunes of a particular curriculum topic across the various levels of the expanding education system. The history of technical education, for example, should highlight competing claims on its value at the levels of secondary, further and higher education, in their shifting social and political context. Not only the relationship between 'the liberal and the vocational', but also that between secondary and further education would be understood more fully through an analysis of long-term changes in the status and content of technical education.(79) Engineering education could also be explored historically in the various senses of the term used by the Finniston report on the engineering profession in 1980. In one way, Finniston argued, engineering education may be seen as an appropriate component of the curriculum of all school pupils: 'Instilling an appreciation and understanding of industry and technology is a highly desirable, if not essential, requirement of school education both for potential engineers and also for all the others who will live and work in a technology-dominated world.'(80) In another way it is seen as a preparation for the 'formation' of careers in engineering, developing 'technical and personal capabilities' to this end: 'This process starts while he or she is still at school and is taken much further during his or her time in higher education, but it can only be properly brought to fruition in the working environment in which he or she will practice as an engineer.'(81) Finniston's third definition of engineering education, by contrast, involves the education of the public and of those in positions of influence about the nature and importance of engineering.(82) Historical analysis of engineering education would need to take account of these different dimensions and what they imply in terms of teaching and learning skills, methods of communication, and the relationships between education, society and industry.

It may indeed be possible to extend the scope of curriculum history beyond the bounds of schooling and formal educational institutions, into the many phenomena involving 'informal' education in all areas of society. The editors of the 1958 Yearbook of Education were confident that 'instruction needs schools to become curriculum'.(83) Curriculum historians should be well equipped to question this assumption. Even in England, mass schooling has existed for little more than a century, and 'secondary education for all' is an even more recent concept and practice. Also, even as formal education has expanded over the last hundred years, a number of informal sources of education have developed at the same time. Especially with successive extensions in political democracy and the growth of the mass media, it has become both possible and necessary to educate and inform the public on a variety of issues. Health education on the importance of personal hygiene and the dangers of smoking, alcohol and other health risks has taken place through a variety of means for the public at large as well as in schools. As law has expanded to become part of the daily life of all citizens, for consumer protection, travel, divorce, business and recognition of legitimate personal and group freedoms, it has become necessary to explain the effects as well as the purpose of such changes. Political issues such as defence and economic policy have become contested sites in which popular support legitimates alternative courses of action. Newspapers, advertising, adult education, the Open University, book clubs and radio are all important sources of education. From traditional units like the church and family to the new information technology, education has been used outside the school setting to encourage both stability and change. The question remains whether the critical perspectives involved in curriculum history may be adopted to explain the content, values and significance of these informal agencies in their social, political and historical contexts.(84)

Such themes may also be relevant and useful in the New Zealand context. Here, though, it seems important first to consolidate on the early signs of activity in this field, and to debate how, if at all, curriculum history in New Zealand will differ from the English variety. Appropriate areas for discussion might include the strong role assumed by central government in curriculum change since the Education Act of 1877. The treatment of the primary school curriculum offered by J.L. Ewing, as well as the psychological and empirical approaches to the primary school curriculum which have been customary, could also be subjected to rigorous historical scrutiny. The influence of the English on the curriculum in New Zealand also seems a suitable focus of attention. That is to say, just as curriculum history allows critical analysis of curriculum and social change to supersede the usual liberal assumptions, it provides a useful means of interpreting the pervasive English influence rather than ignoring it or taking it for granted.

According to Denis Lawton, the curriculum is a 'selection from a culture'.(85) If this is true, curriculum history should be a portrait of a culture, rich in texture and depth. In both England and New Zealand there are grounds for believing that further progress may be made towards this end over the next decade. Curriculum historians in other countries too may find clues in the related experiences of England and New Zealand. It might be concluded also that curriculum history is most likely to remain established as an area of academic interest in those places where it makes efforts to be accepted not only as an approach to the study of the curriculum, but also as an integral part of social history.

Notes

1. Foster Watson, The Beginning of the Teaching of Modern Subjects in England (1909; reprinted 1971), viii.

2. Kenneth Charlton, 'The Contribution of History to the Study of the Curriculum', in John F. Kerr (Ed.), Changing the Curriculum (London: University of London Press Ltd., 1968), 63

3. W.E. Marsden, 'Historical Approaches to Curriculum Study', in W.E. Marsden (Ed.) Post-War Curriculum Development: An Historical Appraisal (Leicester: History of Education Society, 1979), 77.

4. Roy MacLeod, Russell Moseley, 'Breadth, Depth and Excellence: Sources and Problems in the History of University Science Education in England, 1850-1914', in Studies in Science Education, 5 (1978), 105.

5. Ministry of Education, Secondary Education for All: A New Drive (London: HMSO, Cmnd. 604, 1958), 4.

6. Ministry of Education, 15 to 18 (London: HMSO, Vol. I, 1959), 59-60.

7. The Yearbook of Education, 1958: The Secondary School Curriculum, (London: Evans Brothers Ltd., 1958), 34.

8. Times Educational Supplement, 7 October 1960, report; 'Scientific Lumber: Curricula Outdated'.

9. Hansard, House of Commons debates, 21 March 1960, cols. 51-2.

10. Sir William Alexander to Derek Morrell, 11 March 1963 (Association of Education Committees, file A31(a); University of Leeds Special Collections).

11. Ministry of Education, memorandum, 'Proposed Schools Council for the Curriculum and Exami-

nations', 24 May 1963 (AEC papers, file A31(a)).

12. TES, 8 October 1965; 'Comment'.

13. J.F. Kerr, Changing the Curriculum (1968), 15.

14. SSTC, meeting, 28 April 1969, minute 3(iii) (c/o Standing Conference for Schools' Science and Technology).

15. e.g. Lawrence Stenhouse, 'The Humanities Curriculum Project', in his Authority, Education and Emancipation (1983), 73-89; and Geoffrey Harrison, 'The Role of Technology in Science Education', in C.P. McFadden (Ed.), World Trends in Science Education (Halifax, Nova Scotia: Atlantic Institute of Education, 1980), 18-26.

16. Barry MacDonald, Rob Walker, Changing the Curriculum (London: Open Books, 1976), 2, 4-5.

17. W.E. Marsden, 'Historical Approaches to Curriculum Study', in W.E. Marsden (Ed.), Post-War Curriculum Development: An Historical Appraisal (1979), 94-5.

18. Philip Taylor (Ed.), New Directions in Curriculum Studies (Lewes: Falmer Press, 1979), xi, 117.

19. Martin Lawn, Len Barton (Eds.), Rethinking Curriculum Studies: A Radical Approach (London: Croom Helm, 1981), 14.

20. Denis Lawton, 'The End of the Secret Garden? A Study in the Politics of the Curriculum', in Peter Gordon (Ed.), The Study of Education (London: Woburn Press, Vol. 2, 1980), 306.

21 Raymond Williams, The Long Revolution (London: Chatto and Windus, 1961), esp. Section 2, Chapter 1, 'Education and British Society'.

22. Michael Young, 'An Approach to the Study of Curricula as Socially Organized Knowledge', in Michael Young (Ed.), Knowledge and Control: New Directions for the Sociology of Education (London: Collier-Macmillan, 1971), 24.

23. *Ibid*., 36.

24. Frank Musgrove, 'Curriculum, Culture and Ideology', in Philip Taylor (Ed.), *New Directions in Curriculum Studies* (1979), 57. See also e.g. Michael Young, Geoff Whitty (Eds.), *Explorations in the Politics of School Knowledge* (Driffield: Nafferton Books, 1976).

25. Brian Simon, 'The History of Education', in J.W. Tibble (Ed.), *The Study of Education* (London: RKP, 1966), 91.

26. *Ibid*, 93.

27. Harold Silver, *Education as History: Interpreting Nineteenth- and Twentieth-Century Education* (London: Methuen, 1983), 7.

28. *TES*, 15 October 1976, report, 'DES report to Prime Minister sparks off angry protests'.

29. Maurice Holt, 'The Great Education Robbery', *TES*, 3 December 1982.

30. Tony Becher, Stuart Maclure, *The Politics of Curriculum Change* (London: Hutchinson, 1978) 166.

31. Denis Lawton, *The Politics of the School Curriculum* (London: RKP, 1980).

32. Peter Gordon, Denis Lawton, *Curriculum Change in the Nineteenth and Twentieth Centuries* (London: Hodder and Stoughton, 1978), 2.

33. David Layton, *Science for the People: The Origins of the School Science Curriculum in England* (London: George Allen and Unwin, 1973), 160.

34. David Layton, 'Cultural Contexts and Science Curriculum Changes in England and Wales', in Philip Adey (Ed.), *Innovation in Science Education* (London: Proceedings of UK-Japan Seminar, 1980), 106. N.B. also David Layton, 'Science or Education?', in *University of Leeds Review*, Vol. 18 (1975), 81-105, and David Layton, *Interpreters of Science: A History of the Association for Science Education*

(London: John Murray and ASE, 1984).

35. Ivor Goodson, 'Becoming an Academic Subject: Patterns of Explanation and Evolution', in Br. Jnl. of Sociology of Education 2/2 (1981), 117.

36. Ivor Goodson, School Subjects and Curriculum Change (London and Canberra: Croom Helm, 1982), 3-4.

37. Barry Cooper, 'On Explaining Change in School Subjects', in Ivor Goodson, Stephen Ball (Eds.), Defining the Curriculum: Histories and Ethnographies (London and Philadelphia: Falmer Press, 1984), 60.

38. Stephen Ball, 'Competition and Conflict in the Teaching of English: A Socio-historical Analysis', in Jnl. of Curriculum Studies 14/1 (1982), 25.

39. Michael Young, 'The Schooling of Science', in Geoff Whitty, Michael Young (Eds.), Explorations in the Politics of School Knowledge (1976), 47-61.

40. See especially Roy Lowe, 'The Divided Curriculum: Sadler, Morant and the English Secondary School', in Jnl. of Curriculum Studies, 8/2 (1976), 139-48; Harold Silver, 'The Liberal and the Vocational', in his Education as History: Interpreting Nineteenth- and Twentieth-Century Education (1983), 153-72; Nanette Whitbread 'The Early Twentieth-Century Secondary Curriculum Debate in England', in History of Education, 13/3 (1984) 221-33; and Gary McCulloch, 'Pioneers of an "Alternative Road"? The Association of Heads of Secondary Technical Schools, 1951-64', in Ivor Goodson (Ed.), Social Histories of the Secondary Curriculum: Subjects for Study (London and Philadelphia: Falmer Press, 1985), 313-42.

41. Layton, Science for the People, 118.

42. Young, 'The Schooling of Science', 47.

43. Martin Wiener, English Culture and the

Decline of the Industrial Spirit, 1850-1980 (Cambridge: CUP, 1981), ix.

44. Peter Gordon, Denis Lawton, *Curriculum Change in the Nineteenth and Twentieth Centuries* (1978), 3.

45. Goodson, *School Subjects and Curriculum Change*, 202-3.

46. Ivor Goodson, 'Subjects for Study: Case Studies in Curriculum History', in Ivor Goodson (Ed.), *Social Histories of the Secondary Curriculum: Subjects for Study* (1985), 10.

47. *Ibid*., 12.

48. A.E. Campbell, *Educating New Zealand* (Wellington: Dept. of Internal Affairs, 1941), 1.

49. J.L. Ewing, 'Curriculum Development in New Zealand: An Introductory Survey', in *Education*, 17/3 (1968), 10.

50. *Ibid*., 11.

51. A.G. Butchers, *Education in New Zealand* (Dunedin: Coulls Somerville Wilkie, 1930), ix.

52. See especially Ian Cumming, *Glorious Enterprise: The History of the Auckland Education Board, 1857-1957* (Christchurch: Whitcombe and Tombs, 1959), and Ian and Alan Cumming, *A History of State Education in New Zealand, 1840-1975* (Wellington: Pitman, 1978).

53. David McKenzie, 'Ideology and History of Education in New Zealand', in *New Zealand Journal of Educational Studies*, 19/1 (1984), 2.

54. J.L. Ewing, *Origins of the New Zealand Primary School Curriculum, 1840-1877* (Wellington: NZCER, 1960), and *Development of the New Zealand Primary School Curriculum, 1877-1970* (Wellington, NZCER, 1970).

55. Auckland Education Board, District Senior Inspector's Report, December 1970.

56. Sir Thomas Hunter, 'The Development of Psychology in New Zealand' (1952), in Ross St. George (Ed.), The Beginnings of Psychology in New Zealand: A Collection of Historical Documents and Recollections (Palmerston North: Delta monograph 2, 1979), 35-44.

57. Raymond Adams, 'Educational Research in New Zealand', in John Nisbet (Ed.), World Yearbook of Education 1985: Research, Policy and Practice (London and New York: Kegan Paul and Nichols Publishing, 1985), 153.

58. L.S. Hearnshaw, 'Psychology in New Zealand - A Report', in Ross St. George, op. cit., 55.

59. Ian Mclaren, 'Curriculum Making in New Zealand, 1877-1962', in Peter Ramsay (Ed.), Curriculum Issues in New Zealand (New Zealand Educational Institute Yearbook of Education No. 8, 1980), 19-31.

60. See e.g. Roger Osborne, Peter Freyberg, Ross Tasker, Towards Changing Children's Ideas (Hamilton: University of Waikaco Learning in Science Project, 1982).

61. New Zealand Department of Education, Review of the Core Curriculum for Schools (Wellington, 1984); Massey University Education Policy Study Group, 'A Critique of the Core Curriculum Review', in Delta, 34 (July 1984), 13.

62. Sir Thomas Hunter, The Place of the University in the First Hundred Years (centennial lecture, Auckland University College, 1940), 36.

63. D.W.G. Timms, 'The Teaching of Sociology within New Zealand', in Jerry Zubrzycki (Ed.), The Teaching of Sociology in Australia and New Zealand (Sociological Association of Australia and New Zealand, 1971), 33.

64. See e.g. David McKenzie, Education and Social Structure: Essays in the History of New Zealand Education (Dunedin: New Zealand College of Education, 1982); Roy Shuker, Educating the Workers? A History of the

Workers' Educational Association in New Zealand (1984); and Gary McCulloch, 'Educating Historians', in New Zealand Journal of Educational Studies, 20/1 (1985) 100-104.

65. Richard Bates, 'The New Sociology of Education: Directions for Theory and Research', in NZJES, 13/1 (1978), 17.

66. Peter Ramsay (Ed.), Family, School and Community (Auckland: George Allen and Unwin, 1984).

67. See especially Margaret Clark (Ed.), The Politics of Education in New Zealand (Wellington: NZCER, 1981); and John Codd, Richard Harker, Roy Nash (Eds.), Political Issues in New Zealand Education (Palmerston North: Dunmore Press, 1985).

68. J.J. Lee, 'Defining the Curriculum', in G.H. Robinson, B.T. O'Rourke (Eds.), Schools in New Zealand Society - A Book of Readings (Auckland: George Allen and Unwin, 1980), 92-100.

69. David McKenzie, 'Politics and School Curricula', in W.J.D. Minogue (Ed.), Adventures in Curriculum (Auckland: George Allen and Unwin, 1983), 23.

70. John Codd, 'Democratic Principles and the Politics of Curriculum Change in New Zealand', in Margaret Clark (Ed.), The Politics of Education in New Zealand (1981), 52.

71. Ibid., 56.

72. Richard Bates, 'The New Sociology of Education: Directions for Theory and Research', in NZJES, 13/1 (1978), 17-18.

73. Roy Shuker, 'History in the New Zealand Secondary School: A Study in Aspects of Curriculum Development' (unpublished Ph.D. thesis, Victoria University of Wellington, 1978).

74. Ivor Goodson, 'Subjects for Study: Towards a Social History of the Curriculum', in Ivor

Goodson, Stephen Ball (Eds.), Defining the Curriculum: Histories and Ethnographies (1984), 42.

75. William Reid, 'Curricular Topics as Institutional Categories: Implications for Theory and Research in the History and Sociology of School Subjects', in Ivor Goodson, Stephen Ball (Eds.), Defining the Curriculum: Histories and Ethnographies (1984), 71.

76. Daniel Tanner, 'Curriculum History', in Encyclopedia of Educational Research (New York: Macmillan and Free Press, 5th Edn., 1982), 419.

77. Ivor Goodson, 'Towards Curriculum History', in Ivor Goodson (Ed.), Social Histories of the Secondary Curriculum: Subjects for Study (1985), 7.

78. Carolyn Steadman, 'Battlegrounds: History in Primary Schools', in History Workshop Journal, 17 (spring 1984), 103.

79. Harold Silver, 'The Liberal and the Vocational', in his Education as History (1983), 153-72, makes a useful contribution to developing such an approach. See also A.J. Peters, 'The Changing Idea of Technical Education', in British Journal of Educational Studies 11/2 (May 1963), 142-66, and P.W. Musgrave, 'The Definition of Technical Education, 1860-1910', in P.W. Musgrave (Ed.), Sociology, History and Education (London: Methuen, 1970), 65-71.

80. Engineering Our Future: Report of the Committee of Inquiry into the Engineering Profession (Finniston report, Cmnd. 7794, 1980), 79.

81. Ibid., 77.

82. Ibid., 34-4.

83. G. Bereday, Brian Holmes, Joseph Lauwerys, 'Editors' Introduction: The Content of Education', in The Yearbook of Education, 1958: The Secondary School Curriculum (1958), 3.

84. e.g. David Layton, 'Cultural Contexts and Science Curriculum Changes in England and Wales', in Philip Adey (Ed.), Innovation in Science Education (1980), 105-15, and Brian Simon, 'The History of Education', in Paul Hirst (Ed.), Educational Theory and Its Foundation Disciplines (London: RKP, 1983), 62-83, have recently sought to encourage interest in historical approaches to the content and values of informal agencies of education.

85. See especially Denis Lawton, Social Change, Educational Theory and Curriculum Planning (London: Hodder and Stoughton, 1973), The Politics of the School Curriculum (1980), and Curriculum Studies and Educational Planning (London: Hodder and Stoughton, 1983).

NOTES ON CONTRIBUTORS

Stephen J. Ball is lecturer in the sociology of education, and Course Tutor for the MA in Urban Education, at the Centre for Educational Studies, King's College, London. He is author of **Beachside Comprehensive: A Case Study of Secondary Schooling**, editor of **Comprehensive Schooling: A Reader**, and co-editor (with Ivor Goodson) of **Defining the Curriculum**, and **Teachers' Lives and Careers**. He has written several previous papers on English teaching and is the English correspondent of the International Mother-Tongue Education Network.

Barry M. Franklin is an Assistant Professor Curriculum and Instruction and Learning Disabilities Specialist at Kennesaw College in Marietta, Georgia, USA. His research and writing is concerned with the history of the school curriculum and the history of special education. He has recently written a history of the American school curriculum entitled **Building the American Community: The School Curriculum and the Search for Social Control** (Falmer Press), and he is presently preparing an edited volume entitled **Learning Disability: Dissenting Essays** (Falmer Press).

Jim Gaskell is an Associate Professor in the Department of Mathematics and Science Education in the Faculty of Education at the University of British Columbia in Vancouver, British Columbia, Canada. He has an undergraduate degree in Physics, trained as a teacher at Oxford University, taught at the United Nations International School in New York and completed his doctorate in Science Education at Harvard University. He is currently involved in a research project on the social construction of the physics curriculum in British Columbia.

Ivor Goodson is Professor of Education at the University of Western Ontario. He previously taught in comprehensive schools before moving to the University of Sussex in 1975 as a research fellow. He subsequently became Director of the Schools Unit before moving to Ontario in 1986. He is author of **School Subjects and Curriculum Change** and **The Making of Curriculum**, co-author of **European Dimensions and the Secondary School Curriculum**, editor of **Social Histories of the Secondary Curriculum** and **International Perspectives in Curriculum History**, co-editor of **Defining the Curriculum: Histories and Ethnographies** and **Teachers Lives and Careers**. He is the founding editor of the **Journal of Education Policy** and the editor of the Falmer Series **Studies in Curriculum History**.

Bjørg Brandtzaeg Gundem is Associate Professor in education at the Institute for Educational Research, Oslo University. She has been senior lecturer at Oslo Post-Graduate Institute of Teacher Training, educational adviser to the Nordic Council, Inspector of English, and she has taught in schools. Her research and publications are especially in the field of curriculum theory and higher education.

Derek Hodson completed a first degree and a Ph.D. in chemistry at the University of Manchester. Following a PGCE course at the University of Exeter, he spent ten years teaching science and mathematics in a number of secondary schools, including several years as a Head of Chemistry. After a year at UCNW (Bangor) teaching curriculum studies, he moved to the University of Manchester, in 1978, as Lecturer in Science Education. At present, he is Senior Lecturer in Education at the University of Auckland, New Zealand. His research interests include (1) philosophy of science and its implications for the science curriculum, (2) history of the science curriculum, (3) problems of assessment and evaluation, and (4) computers in education.

Ulf Lundgren is a Professor in the Department of Educational Research at the Stockholm Institute of Education. He is the author of a range of books on curriculum notably **Frame Factors and Teaching Process: A Contribution to Curriculum and Theory of Teaching** (1972) and **Model Analysis of Pedagogical Processes** (1981).

Dr Gary McCulloch is Lecturer in Education at the University of Auckland, New Zealand. He read history at Christ's College, Cambridge and completed his doctorate there on the British Left in the 1930s and 1940s. He is author (with Edgar Jenkins and David Layton) of **Technological Revolution?** (Falmer Press, 1985).

Colin Marsh is an Associate Professor of Education at Murdoch University, Perth, Western Australia. His research interests are in the areas of curriculum history, diffusion and implementation. Currently he is editor of the Australian Journal, **Curriculum Perspectives.**

Dr Robert Moon taught in an Inner London comprehensive school before moving to Stantonbury Campus, Milton Keynes, where he became Head of the first new school, Bridgewater Hall. He is currently Head of the Peers School, Oxford. Close involvement with the curriculum development movement has included consultancy roles on Open University curriculum courses and Deputy Editorship of the journal **Curriculum.** He has edited **Changing Schools: Changing Curriculum** with Maurice Galton for Harper and Row and **Comprehensive Schools, Challenge and Change** for NFER/Nelson. In 1986 Falmer Press publish 'The New Maths Curriculum Controversy' a full account of the research published here.

Patricia Rowell is currently Research Associate in the Department of Mathematics and Science Education at the University of British Columbia. She studied biochemistry at London and Oxford, and did research in Boston and Eugene, Oregon. She taught secondary school biology in Edmonton, Alberta where she completed her doctoral work in secondary education.

Louis M. Smith: AB, Oberlin College, 1950; Ph.D., University of Minnesota, 1955; Psychology School Psychologist, St. Paul, Minnesota, Public Schools 1953-55; Professor of Education, Washington University, 1955-present. Major activities include teaching: educational psychology, anthropology of education, field methods of research; advising Ph.D. candidates; and research on schooling. Research and writing: **Educational Psychology** (with Bryce Hudgins), 1964, **The Complexities of an Urban Classroom** (with Pat Keith), 1971, and **Educational Innovators: Then and Now** (with Kleine, Prunty and Dwyer), in press.

George Stanic is an Assistant Professor in the College of Education at the University of Georgia. He received his Ph.D. in curriculum and instruction from the University of Wisconsin-Madison and his A.M. in curriculum from Stanford University. His primary research interests are in curriculum history and mathematics education.

INDEX